RISE OF THE LONE STAR

A Story of Texas
Told by Its Pioneers

CABEZA DE VACA FINDS HIS LOST COMPANIONS

RISE *of the* LONE STAR

A Story of Texas Told by Its Pioneers

By HOWARD R. DRIGGS, PH.D.
Professor of English Education, New York University
Author of "The Pony Express Goes Through"

and SARAH S. KING
Principal of Bowie School, San Antonio, Texas

Illustrated in color and black-and-white by
EDWIN W. DEMING

FREDERICK A. STOKES COMPANY

NEW YORK   MCMXXXVI

Printed in the United States of America

CONTENTS

PART I

TEXAS IN THE MAKING

PART II

PIONEERS BRING BACK HEROIC DAYS

[v]

14267

CONTENTS

ILLUSTRATIONS

FOREWORD

TEXAS—Land of the Lone Star—roots deeply into an all-American history. No other part of our country has drawn into itself more of the varied and picturesque elements of America's making than has this great borderland state. Woven into its stirring tale are the mystery of prehistoric peoples, the life and lore of our Indians, the valor and endurance of Spanish and French adventurers, memories of old missions, the courage and hardihood of our home-building pioneers, and the challenging heroism of our frontiersmen battling to the death for the principles of American liberty.

The age-old lure of gold was the indirect cause of bringing the first white men into the land of Tejas. Way back in the beginnings of the Sixteenth Century, Spaniards, baffled in their quest for treasure they hoped to find in the realms of the north, came into the edges of old Texas. All they brought out of it was a sketchy knowledge of its shorelines, its woodlands, and its far-stretching plains over which roamed countless buffalo and wild tribes of Redmen. Yet on these enforced explorations Spain based her claim to this frontier

[ix]

land, which in the after years she made into a kind
of buffer province to hold back rival nations then
crowding down out of the Northlands.

Forces of France, lured by the wealth of furs,
and fired with ambition to extend their domain in
America, followed the first Spaniards into Texas.
The stay of the French in this borderland was brief
and tragic; but its results loom large. Rivalry between these two nations for dominion in the Southwest not only helped to shape the destinies of the
land of the Lone Star, but also laid the larger foundations on which our nation was later to build.
Challenged by the advent of rivals in her territory,
Spain began immediately to send her soldiers of the
cross to build missions and make more secure her
claim to the regions north of the Rio Grande.
Meanwhile, France, though tragically unsuccessful
in her effort to plant a colony in this domain, still
carried forward the empire-building dream of La
Salle by planting New Orleans and other posts to
bring the vast valley of the Mississippi under the
French flag.

The somewhat uncertain eastern boundaries of
Texas became for about three-quarters of a century
the borderline between France and Spain in
America. Then the French and Indian War
brought swift changes in this international scene.
Defeated France, to keep the English out of Louisi-

ana, transferred that territory to her less bitter
rival, Spain; and with the treaty of peace which
closed the conflict, she ceded to England all her
other possessions in America up to the Father of
Waters. These acts set the Spaniard and the
Anglo-Saxon face to face along that Western frontier. Twenty years later the new born American
nation came into possession of practically all the
realm between the Atlantic and the Mississippi.

Free land was now the lure that brought thousands of Americans across the Alleghanies. The
valleys along the southwestward-flowing stream began to fill with hardy settlers whose sires had fought
through the Revolutionary War. The fertile clearings were soon showing the fruits of husbandry—
rich crops to be harvested, and sleek animals multiplying. Much more than was needed for home use
was being produced. Where could a market be
found for the increasing surplus? There was just
one opening—and that down the rivers to the Gulf
of Mexico. But the Spaniards held Louisiana and
New Orleans; and they demanded tribute for the
use of the Mississippi. Whereupon the free Americans began to demand freedom of the streams.
Out of that demand came the purchase of Louisiana, which territory, again through French politics,
had been shifted back into possession of France.
Napoleon had revived the dream of La Salle; but

the financial pressure of his wars caused him to give up this dream and sell his vast holdings in the new World to young America.

Then followed another rush for the free lands beyond the Mississippi. Americans from all the old Thirteen Colonies and from the newer settlements on the western slopes of the Alleghanies kept on the heels of the pathfinding hunters and trappers. New territories—Louisiana, Arkansas, Missouri—were carved out of the new domain. Log cabins gradually took the place of wigwams and tepees; pioneer villages displaced the old trading posts. Canoes gave way to flatboats, while Indian trails were widened to roads for the covered wagons. Young America was expanding farther and farther westward.

Boundary lines were just uncertain enough to be a constant source of trouble. It took the War of 1812 to settle some questions between England and America on the Northeastern frontier. That conflict, bringing the mountaineers under Andrew Jackson into a clash with the British forces at New Orleans, left the American frontiersmen flush with victory, and a bit eager for new fights that were then brewing in Southwestern borderlands. The question of the exact boundaries of Louisiana was yet to be settled.

Meantime the rich lands of Texas were luring

Americans to them. Thoughts of colonization of this vast, fertile region began to fill the mind of Moses Austin, a far-seeing son of old Connecticut. This enterprising leader had already left his native state to try his fortunes first in Virginia, where his son Stephen was born, and then in Missouri—the portal state to the farther West. While living there he was seized with the desire to plant a colony on the virgin soil of Texas, and journeyed southward to open up negotiations with officials of the Mexican government for a grant of land and permission to carry through his plan. It was a difficult quest, but the dauntless man finally succeeded in acquiring a choice section of this great territory, with authority to colonize and develop it. The hand of death ended the enterprise so far as Moses Austin was concerned; but his stalwart son Stephen stepped into his father's place and carried on. American home-builders were soon establishing themselves in this frontier realm.

They came just at the time when Mexico was fighting to throw off the yoke of Spain. With patriotic zeal they gave their strength and wisdom to a cause close to their American hearts. The shackles of old Spanish tyranny were broken and Mexico came forth, as her sister nation on the north had done, a free country. The constitution adopted was basically like our own. Naturally there was great rejoicing among the Texas pioneers in the promise for the future of the new-born republic to which they had come.

No constitution, however, can assure to any people liberty unless it is sustained by the hearts of its people and by their chosen leaders. This truth was soon to be taught in tragic terms to the liberty-loving folk who had made Texas their home. Spanish tyrants had been driven out of the leadership of Mexico; but Spanish tyranny still ruled in the heart of Santa Anna, the newly elected President of liberated Mexico.

The new constitution was violated. Liberties that had been granted to the people were trampled on, and the clash came. Naturally it was the Texans who first challenged the actions of the dictator. Not only the American-born settlers there, but also the liberty-loving Spaniards who years before had come into the land, rebelled at Santa Anna's usurpation of power. He had broken a solemn covenant. There was just one way to bring back the liberties that had been guaranteed, and that was to fight anew the battle for freedom.

History-making events followed in swift succession. Austin, who had gone to the Mexican capital to plead the cause of liberty, was thrown into prison. A band of Americans, after defeating the Mexicans on the outskirts of San Antonio, charged

on into the heart of that city and forced General
Cos, the brother-in-law of Santa Anna, to surrender. The enraged Presidente, to crush down the
rebellion, led his Mexican armies into Texas, and
flung his forces against a small band of heroic
Texans entrenched in the Alamo. While they battled to the death against the Mexican horde, another
group of Texans drafted a declaration of independence. The fall of the Alamo and the brutal massacre of Texans at the Goliad fed the fires of
patriotism. Then Sam Houston and his forces
crashed on to victory at San Jacinto. Santa Anna,
captured and dragged before the wounded Houston, was forced to grant Texas her freedom. The
domain over which had flown the banner of Castile,
the Fleur de lis, and the flag of Mexico, became the
Land of the Lone Star.

Such are the salient facts of the beginnings of
Texas. But mere facts are only the warp of history. The rich woof of this stirring epic must be
found in the lives of the men and women who lived
through the thrilling drama. It is from their own
lips or pens that the story in all the warm and
blended colors can come. The central purpose of
this book is to bring together the warp and the
woof of this stirring tale—to make the dramatic
story of the rise of Texas live again. The historical
romance of reality presented here is woven out of

the story stuff left by the pathfinders, the mission-building fathers, and the pioneers who builded the Lone Star State.

Happily for our purpose, the pioneer stories that make up the major part of this volume have been collected directly from the pioneers themselves. Sarah S. King, a true daughter of old Texas, for years has been performing a devoted service in gathering from first-hand sources this priceless heritage. Her own father, Charles F. King, a son of old New Hampshire, was one of the Boys of '36 who helped Texas win and hold her freedom. Her mother, Emily Brackett, born in old Syracuse, New York, played the part of a pioneer girl first in Indiana, then went on with her parents in 1845 to San Antonio, where later she played the heroic mother rôle in the pioneering of a new state. Born of such fine American parentage, and reared in such historic surroundings, Sarah King could hardly do other than catch the spirit and absorb the story of her homeland. She did more: As a teacher she radiated the story of young America. For years, the Bowie School, over which she now presides as principal, has been a center of historical influence in Texas. We deem it good fortune for others that now, through this book, some of the throbbing all-American story thus preserved for us can be radiated to young and old all over our country.

FOREWORD

We are fortunate, too, in securing as our illustrator a famed American artist who has an intimate and an appreciative knowledge of the Land of the Lone Star. Edwin W. Deming portrays the life that has been woven into the making of Texas with an understanding heart and an artistic touch. His effort with ours has been to bring forth a great story with vibrancy and with fidelity to truth.

HOWARD R. DRIGGS

PART ONE

Texas in the Making

CHAPTER I

IN THE DAYS OF THE CONQUISTADORES

THE Lone Star rose out of the flames of conflict on our Spanish frontier. How the Spaniards came into that frontier and what led to the clash that gave rise to this radiant emblem and the great state of Texas it represents is a historical epic that reaches almost to the discovery of America. It opens with the pageantry of the Conquistadores who followed in the wake of Columbus. The stirring drama rises in climax through three centuries to days when sons and daughters of our Revolution, who had made their homes in these borderlands, fought to heroic victory a new fight for American freedom.

In its beginnings the tale is a series of magnificent misadventures. The very first story we have of the land of Tejas—so far as records by white men go—is one of shipwrecked Spaniards. Narvaez, in 1527, with high hopes of conquest and treasure had set forth from Spain for Florida. Barely a year later, with his forces decimated by desertions, disease and Indian attacks, he tried desperately to get the remainder of his army back to Mexico in boats made of the skins of his horses. A gulf storm drove the frail craft on to the shores of Texas. Narvaez with others went down in the waves; while the few that were cast up by the sea found themselves at the mercy of savages. The story of their rescue by these redmen, their after enslavement and adventures—was written for us by one of the officers of the ill-fated expedition, Cabeza de Vaca. He gave us our first glimpses of this region and its red inhabitants.

Tribes of differing caste and habits peopled somewhat sparsely the land of Tejas when these Spaniards came. Along the coast was a lower type of Indians who eked out an existence by digging edible roots and gathering such shell and fish food as the shores afforded. Another group of Indians lived among the woods farther inland. These built villages, fished and hunted, and also enriched their substance by raising corn, melons and other foods in the clearings. From the largest of these timberland tribes—the Tejas—came the name Texas. Over the plains to the westward, the Comanches, Lipans and other nomadic tribes held sway; while still farther West among the mountain ranges were the fierce Apaches.

Cabeza de Vaca and his companions were thrown first among the poor, root-digging Indians of the coast. Later, Vaca, forced by his captors to play the rôle of a white medicine man, was brought into close contact with other tribes. Then, having learned several of the Indian dialects, he became an itinerant trader among the redmen, carrying on for them a bartering of shells, skins and other primitive commodities. In this capacity he traveled rather widely and, being an intelligent observer, gathered much valuable information about the topography of the land, the manners and customs of the Indians, and of the flora and fauna of the region. To Vaca we are indebted for the first description by a white man of the bison, or buffalo, which has played so important a part in America's making.

He describes these animals as having "small horns like the cows of Morocco"; and hair "very long and flocky like the merinos. Some are tawny; others black." He thought the flesh of the buffalo "finer and fatter" than that of the Spanish cattle. He tells also how the Indians used the skins of the younger buffalo for robes; and those of the older ones for moccasins and belts. These animals, he adds, range as far south as the coastal plain, where many of them are killed for food and for their useful skins, which are scattered through trading far and wide among the tribes.

During the seven long years of his wanderings among the Indians, Vaca was almost entirely without the companionship of white men. Of the eighty that had been cast with him on what he named Malhado (Misfortune) Island, only fifteen survived the exposure and starvation of the first winter. When summer came, all but three of these —Vaca, Oviedo and Alaniz, who were too ill for the hazardous venture—attempted under the guidance of an Indian they had bribed, to make their way along the mainland to Mexico. Alaniz soon died and Oviedo resigned himself to his miserable lot. Despite all efforts of his faithful friend Vaca, who returned repeatedly from his wanderings to plead that they try together to win their way back home, the disheartened man was stolid. Only once, when Vaca brought word that he had heard of other Spaniards not far away, did Oviedo yield— and then but temporarily. The two made their way from the island of misfortune to the mainland; but shortly afterwards, when danger of new capture threatened, Oviedo weakened and turned back. He was never heard of more.

Stout-hearted Cabeza de Vaca kept on in spite of difficulties and dangers. This son of a noble line of old Spain—made over by gruelling hardships into a naked, sun-bronzed, wandering trader and miracle man among the Indians—never lost his high character. Heroic, loyal, inured to every hardship, and schooled in infinite patience, he never lost hope that he would regain his homeland, his leadership under the banners of Castile.

Somewhere in the wilds of Tejas, Vaca finally found the Spaniards of whom he had heard. Four of them—three of Spanish blood and a Christianized Moor who had followed Narvaez—were all that were left of the twelve that had made their escape from Malhado Island a few years before. Vaca came upon these four survivors among Indians who were gathering their winter's supply of pecans. It was a joyous meeting in captivity. The reunion renewed in all of them the hope of freedom and home. Their greeting and exchange of news over, the men began secretly to plan their escape. Life among the wily redmen had taught them the value of taking their time and being cautious; so a full year elapsed before they made the attempt together to win their liberty.

When opportunity came, they fled westward first to a tribe called the Avavares, with whom Vaca had made contact in his previous wanderings. One of these Indians lay ill, and a demand was made upon the white medicine man to cure the native. The mystic rites performed by Vaca brought success—and food. From this time forward, the fame of the miracle man spread. As he and his companions were passed on from tribe to tribe into the southwest, the Indians brought their sick to be healed, and supplied Vaca and his companions with the choicest of game and other foods they could gather. Their trail to freedom led them across the plains of Texas and the Rio Grande, and over the rugged Sierra Madre Mountains. Towards its end, the journey became something of a triumphal procession, with red heralds going before to announce the coming of the miracle man, and hundreds of feathered Indians following in his train.

When the strange pageant finally came down the Yaqui River to the shores of the Gulf of California, it was met by a band of slave-hunting Spaniards. What were the feelings of these men to come upon this skin-clad, weather-beaten remnant of the army of Narvaez on this wild coast is difficult to imagine. The joy of the Miracle Man and his companions to stand face to face with men of their own land of Spain was poured out in praise to God. Yet the rejoicing was somewhat tempered in Cabeza de Vaca's heart when he came to the realization that the trustful Indians who had followed him for blessings were suddenly brought into grave danger of suffering at the hands of the slave-catchers the same hard fate that had befallen him and his com-

[8]

panions. He strove to avert this tragedy, but though the leaders of the band of dealers in human misery gave evasive promises not to lay hold on the Indians, they did seize and carry many of the poor redmen off into captivity. It was just another instance of treacherous dealing with the natives that characterized the earlier days of Spanish conquest of the New World.

Vaca and his companions were taken at once to the Governor of New Galicia, who received them with all kindness. It was some time, however, before these men, who had lived eight years in nakedness and slept on the bare earth, could get comfort again out of soft beds and the clothing of whitemen.

All Spain was soon ringing with the stories told by the restored followers of Narvaez. Vaca, after a brief visit to Mexico City, went on to Santo Domingo, and then he sailed for his homeland, where his tale stirred the whole nation. Something of a challange was in the disaster of Narvaez. Cabeza de Vaca, himself, had hopes of being appointed *adelentado* or governor of Florida to carry forward the work of conquering this land of the fabled "Fountain of Youth"; but this position had already been given to Hernando de Soto.

The rest of the life of the heroic, human-hearted Vaca was filled for the most part with disappointment. It is true that following his return to Spain he was made *adelentado* of the Rio de la Plata region in South America; but because of his too considerate treatment of the natives there, others under him stirred up trouble for their leader. Vaca was arrested and returned to Spain, like Columbus, in chains. After six years of imprisonment, he was stripped of his doubtful honors and exiled into Africa. Meantime he had become a center of controversy among the clerics as to whether he had had any right as a layman to play the rôle of a miracle man among the Indians. What finally happened to this splendid Spaniard is not certain. It is believed and hoped that he was permitted to spend the closing days of his life at home in peace. At all events, we do know that Cabeza de Vaca has left for us a heritage of history and for himself a lasting memorial in the story he wrote of his man-testing adventures in the land of Tejas.

The next white men to come into this untamed region were baffled followers of the haughty Hernando de Soto. In April 1538, this Conquistador, as Governor of Cuba and *adelentado* of Florida, sailed from Spain under waving banners, and mid the blare of trumpets and roaring cannon to set himself up as overlord of the land where Ponce de Leon had failed and Narvaez had met disaster. About two months later, De Soto landed confidently with his forces on the shores of this region near Tampa Bay.

His first reception was a flight of arrows from hidden Indians. These redmen, who had felt the cruelty of Spaniards before, were ready to resist to the death the new intruders. A charge by the mail-clad soldiers resulted in the killing of two Indians; but the others escaped into the everglades where the encumbered horsemen could not follow. That night signal-fires were flashing warnings to all the tribes. It was an ill-omen.

De Soto drove some distance inland. Coming upon a deserted Indian village he pitched camp, had his men clear away the trees all round to a distance far enough to assure safety from Indian arrows, and then dispatched bands of soldiers to reconnoiter and drive back the lurking natives. One of these detachments returned with six men wounded— one fatally. Other Spanish scouts returned with a white man they had found among the Indians. He proved to be Ortiz, a lost follower of Narvaez. For eleven years, Ortiz, a man of noble lineage, had lived, like Vaca, a life of wandering captivity among the tribes of Florida. His knowledge of the various dialects and of the region roundabout made him invaluable as an interpreter and guide for the Spaniards.

Was there gold in the new domain? was the first

question. Ortiz in all his travels had found none; but the Indians had told him of Appalachen—a realm of great riches not far inland. This word was a call to action for De Soto. Leaving fifty of his force to hold the fortified camp he had set up as a base, the bold leader struck out at the head of his other five hundred and fifty well-armed horsemen to make conquest of this region of treasure.

Three years later the proud Conquistador lay dying near the banks of the Mississippi, which he had discovered. Baffled in his efforts to find the fabulous realm of wealth to conquer; his forces cut down to about half their number by battles with the angered Indians, and by disease; and facing the bewilderment of no certain knowledge of a way out of the untamed regions, the broken-spirited De Soto, himself, fell prey to the ravages of fever. Before he passed away, he gathered his officers about him and asked them to select their own commander; but they requested that he make the choice. This done, De Soto died. He was buried at first near the fort they had erected. Later, however, to keep the Indians from learning that the "Child of the Sun," as he had proudly styled himself, was no more, the Spaniards stole out by night and sank the weighted body of the fallen Conquistador in the Father of Waters.

One thought possessed the minds of his followers: How to get back home. It was decided first to try to reach Mexico by traveling overland. The attempt was futile. Floods of the Red River held them for a time from crossing the Texas border; red tribes of that region, forewarned of the treachery and bloodshed they might get from these Spaniards, fought them at every step; the storms of on-coming winter threatened further delay and disaster. In the face of these waxing difficulties, the invaders retreated out of the land of Tejas.

Some of these baffled followers of De Soto, in boats they had built on the Mississippi, afterwards made their way down that stream and along the coast to the mouth of the Panuco River, not far from the present Tampico. Met here by Indians in Spanish clothing, they learned of a town some miles inland; and thither they went—not as haughty horsemen in armor; but as a broken band of refugees, scantily clad in blackened buckskin, humbly giving thanks to God for deliverance; yet dragging with them a few miserable Indian captives—the only trophies of their tragic misadventure.

During the long drawn days that De Soto was pursuing his vain quest for a realm of riches in Appalachen, another proud Conquistador was carrying on a like fruitless search for fabled wealth in our Painted Deserts farther west. Indian legends of the seven cities of Cibola in this mysterious northland—cities whose gates were studded with gems and within which were heaps of gold—stirred Mendoza, the viceroy of New Spain, to action. The return of Vaca and his companions spurred up the excitement.

Coronado, newly appointed governor of Galicia, was to carry forward the conquest of the fabled realm. The moor, Estevanico, who had come out of these regions with Vaca, was retained as guide and interpreter. As a preliminary to the expedition, he and Fray Marcos were sent northward to "spy out the realm" and cultivate friendship with the Indians. Estevanico, pressing on with a band of friendly redmen, met his death at the hands of hostiles. Fray Marcos went far enough to get a view of what he supposed was one of the mythical cities—possibly some Pueblo magnified in his eyes by a mirage common to that desert region. Planting a cross on the eminence from which he had his view, and claiming all the region for Spain, the well-meaning friar hastened back with an embellished report of his discovery of one of the cities of Cibola. The word of the finding of a New Mexico spread like wildfire. Mendoza, the viceroy, immediately began enlisting men—mostly of knightly blood—for an expedition under Coronado.

In February 1540—less than a year after the departure of De Soto from Spain—Coronado with his

CORONADO LEADS HIS GOLD-SEEKERS INTO TEXAS

forces set forth for the conquest of the realm of the Northern Mystery. The Conquistador was clad in golden armor, while that of his followers shone like polished silver. With horsemen, foot soldiers, priests and a retinue of Indians decked with feathers and daubed with paint, the cavalcade looked invincible. Mendoza, himself, had journeyed to New Galicia, to send Coronado and his army away with pomp and ceremony.

Again the net result of it all was to be disappointment and disaster. The trail of Coronado, like that of De Soto, was one of weary wanderings, blood stains, and blasted hopes. The only lasting result to come out of both these ill-starred ventures was that of charting of unknown regions. These bold men did map the ways for those who came after them.

Across what is now Arizona, and all through the regions of our New Mexico, Coronado led his men. Towards the end of his vain search, he stumbled down the eastern slopes of the Sierra Madre on to the great plains of Texas. Here in the land of the bison, somewhere perhaps on the Brazos River, the baffled commander divided his army and ordered the larger part of it to return to Mexico. The men pleaded with the Conquistador not to leave them to perish in the wilderness; but he had his way. With thirty chosen men, he went on with his vain quest until finally, after months more of wandering, he gave up and turned back home. Another magnificent adventure had come to an inglorious end.

Looking back through the vista of the years, it would seem that some higher power had decreed that the iron heel of Spanish tyranny should never be planted in the soil of Tejas. Narvaez, De Soto, Coronado, touched the borders of this region only to be driven back mainly by elements beyond man's control. The land of the Lone Star, with its vast treasures of hidden wealth, was to be held in reserve for those who would come in the spirit of constructive conquest when the days of the Conquistadores had long passed away.

CHAPTER II

AFTER Coronado, nearly a century and a half
went by before white men came again in
force to the land of Tejas. Then it was not Spain,
but her rival, France, that attempted to gain foot-
hold in this region. The venture was born of a
mistake and soon ended in disaster; but it brought
a sequence of events that have woven most colorful
strands of international history into the epic of
Texas.

The backgrounds of this story of the linking of
France with the land of the Lone Star are to be
found in the conquest of the northlands, and particularly in the heroic life-work of La Salle. During the years that followed the retreat of the
Conquistadores back into the Spanish domains of
the farther south, the French were carrying on
their quest for furs into the heart of North

America. The discovery of the St. Lawrence by Cartier in 1524, the founding of Acadia and Quebec by Champlain, and the devoted work of the Jesuit missionaries carrying the cross to the red tribes of the north all opened the way for the final extension of the French dominions right up to the Spanish frontier.

This building of a New France in the New World went on apace during the reign of the lordly Louis XIV and succeeding kings of the Bourbon line. The latter half of the seventeenth and the first half of the eighteenth centuries found French adventurers most active in the borderlands of America. Voyageurs threaded the streams to their sources; coureurs-de-bois roved the woods and prairies in search of furs; black-robed priests, bearing the message of good will to the redmen, played also the rôle of heroic pathfinders. Other bold leaders, winning the alliance of the Indian tribes, planted fortified posts at strategic points to promote the fur trade and to bring the whole vast realm under the banners of France.

Outstanding among all these adventurous spirits was the courageous dreamer, Robert Cavelier, Sieur de la Salle. It was this loyal leader who gave to the French king the vision of an empire overseas; and it was through the sacrificial efforts of La Salle that the visioned empire was extended over the valley of

the Mississippi down to the Gulf of Mexico. Even
the land of Tejas was brought for a brief time
within the vast domain outlined for his country by
this splendid son of France; for in 1685 he planted
the first white settlement ever built in this region
and set the flag of his nation flying over it.

This bold leader was born in Normandy. Perhaps it was the Viking blood in his veins that set
him as a youth in the path of adventure. The story
of Champlain, which he read as a schoolboy, doubtless turned his thoughts toward helping to carry on
for his country in the New World. Young La Salle
had entered the Jesuit order and was being trained
for service in the church, but this longing for adventurous leadership made him resolve to change his
course and enter upon a career in America. At the
age of twenty-three, he made the first step towards
carrying out this resolution by securing an honorable release from whatever vows he had taken with
the Jesuits. Then, selling for about three thousand
dollars the life annuity his merchant father had bestowed upon him, the youthful La Salle set forth to
try for fame and fortune on the frontier.

His first venture there was the founding of a
small colony at a strategic point on the trail of the
Iroquois a few miles to the west of Montreal.
Probably it was through the influence of an elder
brother, then one of the priests of Saint Sulpice in

Montreal, that La Salle was helped to secure a tract of land for his pioneer community. It was a dangerous outpost, but in the danger was a good chance for the young leader to show his mettle. Seizing the opportunity, he set to work with such vigor and intelligence that he soon had one of the best protected and best organized colonies in New France.

The name given by La Salle to his new settlement is of historical significance. Because he believed it was planted on the direct route to China, he called the place La Chine. The lure of the riches of the Orient and the hope of finding a westward way to them had persisted with the explorers of America since the days of Columbus. It was a common belief with the French, that China lay on the western edge of North America. So confident was the pathfinder, Nicollet, of this, that on first crossing the divide between the Great Lakes and the Mississippi, he actually donned a Chinese costume in anticipation of meeting the mandarins of that oriental realm. What he did meet was only more American Indians; yet some thirty years later we find La Salle imbued with the idea that China was just beyond the borders of New France.

His hope of discovering some shorter, easier way to the riches of the Orient was soon to be given new impetus by tales brought to him by the Indians. A band of Senecas, who camped for a time near his post, told the ambitious young French leader of a beautiful river, the Oyo, which flowed southwestward on to the great sea. La Salle's imagination was kindled. Perhaps this stream found its way into the Gulf of California. His eagerness to explore the river from source to mouth grew. The vision of bringing the Oyo and all the lands it drained under the French flag, of planting trading posts along the river, and of winning thus a feasible, shorter route to the treasures of China and India stirred him to action.

Not many months had passed before he had gained the permission of the governor of New France, and taken on himself the role of explorer. La Chine was sold to raise funds. With this money he procured four canoes, necessary arms and supplies, and employed fourteen hardy men to ply the paddles and otherwise help him carry forward his purposes. The priests of Saint Sulpice, intent on promoting their work among the Indians, added seven more men with three more canoes to the exploring expedition.

The plunge into the western wilds was taken in July 1669. Two years later, the dauntless La Salle returned to Montreal alone. What had happened during those two eventful years is still shrouded to some extent in mystery. The exploring party we do know was baffled in its attempts to reach the

Ohio across the territory of the Senecas, and took the northern way over Lake Ontario past the mouth of the Niagara River. The roar of the great falls they could hear in the distance. Somewhere near the head of the lake, La Salle found a Shawnee Indian prisoner who could guide him to the river he sought. He bought the freedom of this redman. Then came the meeting with Joliet. The priests, listening to this pathfinder, decided to leave La Salle, and carry on their missionary work among the Pottawatomies and other tribes round the Great Lakes. La Salle, bent on his quest, followed the Shawnee guide southward until his canoes glided out into the waters of the Ohio. While he was exploring the river, La Salle's men, worn down by the hardships, and fearful perhaps of the fierce Iroquois, stole away to the Dutch and English settlement to the east leaving their brave leader to make his perilous way alone back to Canada.

The intrepid young explorer has left no record of the details of that hazardous journey through a thousand miles of Indian-infested regions. His personal hardships were never of moment to him. It was the thought of extending the dominion of his country in the New World that was ever uppermost. What signified these personal sufferings and dangers in the face of the fact that he had discovered "La Belle Rivière"? That act gave to

LA SALLE RAISES THE FRENCH FLAG OVER TEXAS

France a solid claim for possession of the rich valley drained by the beautiful Ohio.

This signal service for his country was not left unrewarded. On his return to France after his trip of exploration, La Salle was raised to the rank of nobility by his king. Besides this, Frontenac, the powerful new governor of Canada, gave to La Salle staunch support for further adventures in the great West. With such honor and such influence back of him, La Salle had little trouble in gathering means for carrying forward his expanding enterprises in America.

It is not to the central purpose of our story to detail the events that crowded the next few years of this leader's adventurous life. His activities at Fort Frontenac; his building of the ship Griffon to ply the waters of the Great Lakes; his explorations of the Illinois region with his faithful Italian lieutenant Tonty and Father Hennepin; his masterful diplomacy in bringing the Miamis and other tribes into a coalition against the powerful Iroquois, all mark him as a great leader. His unfailing courage in the face of the sinking of his ship, the disloyalty of trusted followers, and mounting financial loss reveals his strength of character and his tenacity of purpose. The vision and hope of making France the major power in the New World sustained him

through every difficulty to the close of his empire-
building career.

One event that spurred La Salle to a master
stroke towards the realization of his dreams for
France was the re-discovery of the Mississippi by
Father Marquette and Joliet. The report that these
pathfinders had found this river and followed it
from the Wisconsin for nearly a thousand miles
southward stirred in La Salle the determination to
explore the great stream to its mouth, and lay claim
for his country and king to all the vast valley
drained by the "Father of Waters." There was to
be no further quest for a route to the Orient. La
Salle was certain now that the Ohio was a branch
of this larger stream, and that the Mississippi emptied not into the Pacific, but into the Gulf of
Mexico. To possess this vast region would bring
the French possessions in America right up to the
Spanish border, and perhaps open the way for
France to win a goodly share of the gold and silver
that was then pouring into the coffers of a rival
monarchy.

In 1677 La Salle sailed again for France to present his report to King Louis, and to petition this
monarch for a commission to carry through his far-
reaching plans. It was just such a magnificent
proposition as would challenge the active interest
of "The Grand Monarch." For a few months the

bold adventurer was kept waiting in luxurious France and then his petition was most generously granted. On May 12, 1678, La Salle was called to the royal court to receive letters-patent bearing the seal and signature of his king. The stately paper began:

"Louis, by Grace of God King of France and of Navarre, to Our dear and well beloved Robert Cavelier, Sieur de La Salle, Greeting:

"We have received with favor the very humble petition which has been presented to Us in your name, to permit you to endeavor to discover the western part of New France; and We have consented to this proposal the more willingly, because there is nothing We have more at heart than the discovery of this country, through which it is probable a road may be found to penetrate to Mexico."

This royal commission bestowed upon La Salle authority not only to explore the western frontier, but to build such forts as he deemed necessary to secure this realm for France. It further granted him a monopoly in buffalo hides to help defray the expenses. As to trade in beaver and other furs, that was somewhat restricted; and further, a time limit of five years was placed on the ambitious enterprise. Frontenac and other officials in New France were ordered to add their signatures to the document.

The way was now open for La Salle to carry on with confidence towards the realization of his plans. Not even the whole-hearted approval of his king, however, could make the way that lay ahead a path of roses. Every day was to bring new problems and added difficulties; yet the dauntless Norman, meeting each challenge with determined and constructive action, pressed forward for his country and his church.

His early training kept him close to those who were promoting the cause of religion in the New World. Accompanying him on all his important ventures were courageous priests who ministered to the spiritual needs of La Salle and his men, and carried on what missionary work they could among the Indians with whom they came in contact. These trained couriers of the Christian faith performed also another invaluable kind of service in keeping written records of this adventuring in the western wilds.

La Salle seemed to make very few staunch and intimate friends. He did win one, however, whose loyalty rooted ever more deeply through all the heroic days they worked together on the frontier. This was young Henry de Tonty, an Italian by birth, who had been reared from babyhood in France, and had adopted the French nation as his own. His devotion to the Norman leader whose life work he had chosen to share, shines like a beacon down the years. Tonty was the chief reliance of La Salle in every difficult adventure. He always more than justified the trust reposed in him. Like his commander, he was fearless, yet diplomatic in the handling of Indians. He dealt with them in kindness, yet when occasion required he could use an iron hand. This statement may be taken both literally and figuratively; for Tonty, having lost one of his hands in some battle for the French, had replaced it with another made of iron, which he usually kept covered with a glove. There is record of his having used this hand effectively on the heads of refractory Indians. It was "bad medicine" for them not to obey Tonty.

Another loyal friend of La Salle was his constant Indian companion, White Beaver. Playing the role of guide, guard, and hunter, this redman clung to the French leader like a kindly shadow. There is some uncertainty whether White Beaver was the Indian, known by the name of Nika, who followed La Salle on his last trip to France and afterwards sailed with him to Texas; yet the same unfailing devotion was there; and the likelihood is that Nika was just another name given to this earlier devotee of the White Chieftain.

The thrilling adventure of exploring the Father of Waters came during 1682. Early January of that year found La Salle, Tonty, Father Membre, and Sieur Dautray, whose father had been a high official in New France, making their way from the shore of Lake Michigan southwestward to the Mississippi. Accompanying these French leaders were voyageurs, frontiersmen, and a band of friendly Indians. Dragging sleds laden with canoes and supplies, the party made its way first along a frozen stream, called Chicago by the redmen, to the Illinois. The water of this river being more open, sleds were discarded, and the adventurers took to their canoes. On February 6 they first reached the great river they sought.

After a few days waiting for dangerous floating ice to pass by, the eager explorers pushed out in their canoes and plied them with rhythmic paddles on towards the realm of never-ending summer. Every day brought new sights and thrilling experiences. Indians of unknown tribes gazed from the shores at the little fleet. At times the white men paused briefly to smoke a pipe of peace and exchange tokens of friendship with the curious redmen. Frequently time had to be taken out to replenish the food supply with game and fish. But most of the days were spent going on and on down the great river.

Enthusiasm waxed as the panorama of rich woodlands and fertile valleys, teeming with bird and animal life, glided by. Tonty wrote delightedly of the country as being "very beautiful, having an abundance of peach, plum and apple trees." "Buffaloes, deer, bear, turkeys," he continued, "are very numerous. Little snow falls there during the winter, and the ice is no thicker than a dollar." Father Membre likewise made record of the rich variety of fruit and nut trees, and of the palms and laurels and blossoming vines along the banks of the stream farther south. To these men inured to the cold northland these products and pictures of the southland were most alluring.

The explorers were nearing the end of their journey. Early April found them at the parting of the waters—the head of the delta where the Mississippi divides into several streams. Here La Salle divided his band into three groups, with Dautray at the head of one, Tonty leading another, and himself the third, and down the different branches of the river the explorers went to a place where the outspread Father of Waters meets the tides of the Gulf of Mexico. The great quest had come to a successful close.

The French commander reassembled his little force of pathfinders on the shore. There they raised a cross, and a shaft bearing the arms of their country, and this inscription:

RISE OF THE LONE STAR

Louis Le Grand
ROI DE FRANCE ET DE NAVARRE, REGNE
LE NEUVIEMME AVRIL, 1682

Father Membre led the group in singing sacred songs of the church. A salute of musketry was fired, and all joined with lusty voices in "Vive le Roi." Then La Salle, holding aloft his royal commission, proclaimed impressively that all the lands drained by the Mississippi, the Ohio and their tributaries henceforth belonged to France. The new realm was named Louisiana in honor of the monarch of the French Empire.

It was one thing to lay claim to such a far-flung region; another actually to bring it under the dominion of France. A first step towards this control must be the planting of a strong French post at the head of the delta of the Mississippi. To assure growing power and permanency for such an outpost, colonization was essential. La Salle hurried back up the great river, both to report the results of his explorations and to carry through his plans for establishing such a settlement in lower Louisiana.

Unfortunately for the immediate carrying forward of his purpose the splendid commander was taken seriously ill. Not far from the place where De Soto, discoverer of the Mississippi, had been

stricken more than a century before, the explorer
of the great river was now likewise seized with a
raging fever, that all but cost him his life. For
some months La Salle, attended by the faithful Father Membre and White Beaver remained at Fort
Prudhomme, a post the exploring party had paused
to build on their downstream journey.

Meantime loyal and efficient Tonty had pressed
on. At La Salle's direction he had led the main
band northward, and sent forward to Frontenac an
official report of the historic adventure. Then,
with vigor and initiative he turned attention to the
upbuilding of French power in the Illinois country.
Chiefs of the tribes La Salle had brought into alliance for protection against the Iroquois, and for the
furthering of the purposes of the French, were
brought into council. It was planned to restore
and enlarge the old Indian village the fierce Iroquois
had destroyed two years before near the Rock of
St. Louis.* On this mighty buttress overlooking
the Illinois river and valley as a center of trade and
a citadel against the red raiders from the far East,
Tonty began the building of the fortress previously
projected by La Salle.

In September of 1682, the commander, still weak
from his illness, rejoined Tonty at this fortified post
in the heart of the prairie lands. The satisfaction

* Known now as Starved Rock.

that must have come to La Salle at finding his empire of the West thus being developed under the loyal leadership of his lieutenant must have been medicine to his body and soul. If he could have had more of such unfailing support, complete success would doubtless have crowned his efforts. Few friends he had, however, who remained true. Financial reverses, envy stirred by his successes, and Bourbon politics multiplied his enemies.

When La Salle did finally return to Canada, he found conditions that would have daunted any man of less heroic mold. Sneering creditors hounded his steps. Jealous rivals plotted to lessen the power and authority he had been granted by the king. Finally his staunch supporter, Frontenac, was recalled, and the governorship of New France was given to La Barre, who seemed bent on destroying all that La Salle had built.

One hope remained for the courageous adventurer. He would carry his cause again to his king. If he could but gain the ear of the grand monarch, he felt sure he could thwart his enemies in their attempts to wreck the empire-building he had carried forward with such promise. So confident was he that he could win the king's further support of his plan to build a French outpost near the outlet of the Mississippi, that he arranged with Tonty to meet him there the following year to help carry through the enterprise. Then he sailed straight to France.

La Salle was not to be disappointed in his quest for renewed confidence and support. His modest yet stirring story of the exploring of the Mississippi and of the claiming of its vast valley for France won the heart of the French monarch. The great realm of Louisiana must certainly be brought more securely under his dominion. The king met La Salle's request for two ships laden with soldiers, settlers and supplies, by granting him four such laden vessels. Thus generously reinforced the Norman leader was soon on the high seas intent to carry out his plan of planting his colony near the outlet of the Father of Waters.

The following excerpt from a letter written by La Salle to his mother just before he sailed on what was to be his last adventure, is most revealing:

Rochelle, 18 July, 1684
Madame, My Most Honored Mother,
At last, having waited for a long time for a favorable wind, and having had a great many difficulties to overcome, we are setting sail with four vessels, and nearly four hundred men on board. Everybody is well, including little Colin and my nephew. We all have good hope of happy success. We are not going by way of Canada, but by the Gulf of Mexico. I passionately wish, and so do we all, that the success of this voyage may contribute to your repose and comfort. Assuredly

we shall spare no effort that it may; and I beg of you, on your part, to preserve yourself for the love of all of us.

From your most humble and obedient servant and son,

DE LA SALLE

My brother, my nephews, and all the others greet you, and take leave of you.

It would be pleasant to record that the high hopes expressed in this last letter from a devoted son to a fond mother were realized, but the fates did not will it so. Divided authority over the expedition led to dissension, disappointment and disaster. La Salle was not assigned full command by the minister of marine, but he had to share the responsibility with Beaujeu, a bluff sea captain, who was given charge of the little fleet. This unfortunate arrangement was the prime cause of the tragic troubles that followed.

Misfortune was piled on misfortune. First, through the stubbornness of Beaujeu, in refusing to follow La Salle's directions, one of the French ships was captured by the Spanish. Then, through some mischarting of the course the fleet missed the mouth of the Mississippi, and sailed on southwestward for some hundreds of miles into what was probably Matagorda Bay on the shores of Texas. An insubordinate captain of another of the ships here drove his vessel, deliberately it would seem, upon a reef at the mouth of the bay and wrecked it. Following

this disaster, Beaujeu sailed back to France with his
flagship laden with soldiers and precious supplies,
leaving La Salle with just one ship and about one-
third of the force with which he had set forth on
this expedition.

The resolute leader would not be baffled by these
tragic losses and desertions. He set his followers
immediately at work building out of the timbers of
the wrecked ship a fortress for their shelter and
protection. While the construction was in progress, he led a small party to the southwest in a vain
search for the mouth of the Mississippi. During
this exploring trip he discovered a river which he
called La Vaca from the buffalo cows he found near
it. At any rate, the place looked more favorable
for his venture in colonization, so he had his followers move to a new site he had selected on this
stream, and built there a second and larger outpost.
It was named Fort St. Louis in honor of the king.

A rather strange group of French folk were those
who founded this pioneer settlement in the land of
Tejas. Many of them were soldiers recruited from
the slums of Paris. There were a few young
women, but of a generally inefficient sort. Me-
chanics and strong-bodied workmen were scarce,
most of these having returned to the home country
with Beaujeu. The leadership was reduced to La
Salle himself, Joutel, Father Membre, and several

priests, among whom was Jean Cavelier, a brother of the commander. Besides there were two nephews of La Salle, his French servant, Saget, and his loyal Indian guide and hunter, Nika.

"The difficulty," Joutel afterwards wrote, "was our great number of men and the few of them fit for anything but eating. The company was not unlike Noah's Ark, which contained animals of all kinds."

More hindrance than real help was to be expected from such a motley band. Despite all the human handicaps, however, the brave leader pressed forward with the work of placing the colony on a self-sustaining basis. Happily there was no lack of food. Game there was in abundance; and besides, the settlers kept within the fort cows, pigs and chickens. They were soon raising grains and vegetables. Their fort gave them protection from the Indians. With his people thus cared for, La Salle appointed Joutel to take command at the settlement, while he again sought the outlet of the Mississippi.

The captain of the *Belle,* his sole remaining ship, was ordered to join in the quest by sailing cautiously along the shores of the Gulf. La Salle meanwhile with a group of trusted men went southward on the same eager search. When the little party of explorers after five months returned from their fruitless quest, the colonists were almost in a panic. No tidings had come from the *Belle;* but they were soon to learn from some survivors of the wrecking of the ship at sea. It was the breaking of the last link that might draw the wanderers back home. Yet La Salle rose above this disaster.

One hope was left. He might find his faithful Tonty. Again he struck out, but as before, he went in the wrong direction. During this trip he came upon Indians who knew of the Spaniards. They had coins, clothing, utensils and horses which had been obtained from these white men farther to the south. It was only a few "sleeps" to the land of these people. To the priest the Indians reported that the Spanish were teaching them religion but treating them cruelly. La Salle endeavored to impress them with the kindness of the French. He bartered with them for several of their horses; and with the help of these animals returned more easily to Fort St. Louis.

Convinced now that Canada and the Mississippi lay to the northeast, the undaunted leader laid his plans to make another effort to reach that stream and his friend Tonty. Two long years had elapsed since the French fleet had sailed by mistake into the Matagorda Bay. Distressful, uncertain years they had been; but now with renewed determination to find a way out, the great leader laid careful preparations. The Christmas of 1686 was celebrated with some touch of the old fervor, and the New Year dawned.

Some time in early January La Salle left Fort St. Louis for the last time. Among the men selected to accompany him on this important journey were Joutel, the priests, Jean Cavelier and Douay, his two nephews, Morganet and Cavelier, the servant, Saget, and the Indian, Nika.

Before leaving the Fort, La Salle had gathered his followers and addressed them. His eloquence moved most of them to tears. All he could do he had done for their protection and sustenance. Now he was going on a hazardous journey to bring help to those whom he was forced to leave behind. He gave them sound advice as to their keeping united and being cautious in their dealings with the Indians. After his address, public prayers were offered, and the little band of men left the pioneer fortress forever.

About two months later, somewhere in the land of Tejas a black tragedy occurred that ended the career of this great frontiersman of France. Four murderous men in his band—Duhaut, Liotot, Heins, and L'Archevêque—turned assassins, and killed La Salle's nephew, Morganet, his servant Saget, and the faithful Nika, while they slept. Then they ambushed and shot La Salle to death.

This brutal slaying occurred, it is thought, some-where on the Trinity River, though the exact spot will never be known.

The murderers meted out a swift penalty upon themselves for their dastardly crime. Heins and another cutthroat killed Duhaut and Liotot. Heins was killed later by the man who had helped him to murder these men, while L'Archevêque fled to the Indians never to be heard of again.

The rest of the party after this terrible tragedy took up the trail under the leadership of Joutel to-wards the north. After terrible hardships the men finally reached the Rock of St. Louis on the Illinois River where Tonty was carrying forward the work of La Salle. These refugees for a time kept the news of his commander's tragic death from the faithful lieutenant. Tonty, fearing for the safety of the expedition, had once made a trip down the Mississippi to its mouth, but not finding his leader, had again set up the shaft and the cross, and re-turned to Illinois. On learning of the dangerous situation of the French settlers in Texas, he set out on an expedition to rescue them, but after almost losing his life in the attempt, he returned.

The ill-fated colony was to end in dire tragedy. Lacking the constructive leadership La Salle and Joutel had given it, the settlement went from bad to worse. Disease thinned the ranks; and finally

the Indians, luring the colonists out of the fortress
to trade, fell upon and massacred most of the survivors.   A few were carried away into captivity.
The flag of France ceased to fly over the land of
Tejas.   There was to be no Bourbon king claiming
"divine right" ruling over this realm of freedom.

CHAPTER III

MEMORIES OF OLD MISSIONS

SCATTERED over the Lone Star State are a few
old missions that link the throbbing present
with the long ago. Inwoven with the memories
that cling to these time-worn structures, is a great
part of the story of Texas. Their crumbling walls,
broken arches, and half-effaced ornamentation recall nearly two centuries of history, filled with devoted service, romance, and high heroism. The
dreamer, lingering round these old piles, still hears
the echoes of mission bells, voices of priests and
Indians at work and at worship, lowing of cattle
and bleating of flocks. Crashing through these
sounds of peace come too the cries of battle, rifle
and cannon shots, and moans of wounded and

dying men who made some of these old missions
their fortresses during the fight for liberty.

Rivalry between France and Spain first brought
the mission-building fathers into the land of Tejas.
The advent of the French in this region at the close
of the seventeenth century spurred civil and religious leaders in Mexico to join forces to hold that
domain Spanish. When the hardy Captain Alonzo
de Leon with his little army crossed the Rio Grande
to find and drive out the invaders, he was accompanied by Father Massanet and other Franciscan
friars intent on bringing the red children of that
realm into the fold of the Master.

For nearly four years the Spaniards sought vainly
for the outpost La Salle had planted in these wilds.
Finally in 1689, coming upon a French captive
among the Indians, they impressed the hapless man
into service as their guide. What they found when
this prisoner led them to Fort St. Louis on the Vaca
River, was a scene of death and desolation. No
enemy was there to oppose them. The fort had
fallen into the hands of the Indians a short time before their arrival, and every one of the ill-fated
colonists had been killed or dragged off into captivity. The remains of such dead as they discovered
were given Christian burial by the priests. A few
half-burned books and other articles strewn about
were collected and carried back to Mexico as mute

evidence of the attempt of the French to gain foot-
hold in this borderland claimed by the Spanish.

The need to make this claim more secure was
plain. Although disaster had befallen the rival outpost, there was no assurance that the aggressive
French would not follow with others. Missions reinforced by presidios at strategic spots in that frontier region would both protect the Spanish interests
and promote religious work among the Indians.
The authorities in Mexico gave active support to
this suggestion. It was not long before Father
Massanet was leading a small band of friars into
Texas; and with him went Captain Alonzo de Leon
with one hundred soldiers armed with long guns
and carrying plenty of ammunition.

The eager interest of Father Massanet in this mission was inspired by Mary Coronel de Agreda.
And here our story links with one of the most interesting legends of the land of Tejas—that of "The
Woman in Blue." Mary Coronel, born in Agreda,
Spain, and surrounded with every comfort, became
as a little girl intensely interested in the stories of
the Indians in far-off America. As the beautiful,
kindly-hearted Mary grew to womanhood, she devoted herself to saintly service, ministering to the
ill and needy and oppressed. She founded a society
to help her radiate her good work.

All the while she had a longing to carry the light

and help of the gospel to the redmen overseas. Continually she prayed for them and for the devoted men who were working for their welfare. At last, so the legend goes, the way was opened for her to visit these children. In vision she found herself in the New World among certain tribes that seemed superior to the common Indians. They lived in villages, built round houses of straw or rushes, and had some sort of government. They carried on a kind of fire-worship; and were generally kind and hospitable. Legend has it that this saintly woman made various visits to this tribe of Indians, teaching them the gospel, and ministering to their needs. They grew to love and reverence her, and made promise that they would welcome the white brothers that she would send to teach and help them.

Whatever may account for this spiritual experience, we do know that its effects were those of reality. The good woman kept the vision in her heart, and strove unceasingly for her red children in the land of Tejas. She wrote letters, describing with vividness the tribes she had visited in spirit, and pleading for missionaries to be sent to them. Finally she exacted a promise from the Custos (Guardian) of New Mexico, whom she met in Spain, that he would do all he could to carry out her desires. Then came Father Massanet. Inspired by one of her letters, this courageous friar went to the northern border of Mexico eager to pioneer the missionary work in the region northeast of the Rio Grande.

His opportunity came when the Captain de Leon led his soldiers across that river to search out the French. It was spurred on when during that expedition the good father met the chief of the Tejas Indians. The warmth of welcome given by the red leader to the earnest friar and his fellow missionaries, and the urgent invitation of the Indian chieftain that they come into his realm to teach his people the way of light, was an expression of the devotion of these Indians to their memory of "the woman in blue."

Some time afterwards, when the mother of this chief died, he asked Father Massanet for some cloth of blue for a burial shroud. The priest asked the reason for the color, and was told that a beautiful woman, who had often come to visit his tribe, was always dressed in blue. They wanted to be clothed like her when they went into the spirit world. The Indians of many snows had remembered her, and had kept in their hearts the promise she had made that white men in dark robes would one day come as teachers to show them a better way of life. It is not improbable that the story of Mary Coronel had in some way been carried to these Indians and become a legend with them. There is small wonder, however, that Father Massanet, finding such faith among them, was ready to dare the dangers and endure the hardships attendant on opening the missionary work in the land of Tejas.

In late March of 1690, this courageous father, leading his band of friars and accompanied by the Captain de Leon with his soldiers, set forth to begin the establishing of missions in Tejas land. They paused at the desolate Fort St. Louis long enough to consign it to flames, Father Massanet himself applying the torch. This was done to remove temptation from the French to reoccupy the ill-fated outpost. Later, in reconnoitering the country round about for other traces of the rival nation, the captain found two French boys among the Indians and freed them from captivity.

The pioneering priests and soldiers pushed on northeastward, dispatching messengers to tell the chief of the Tejas tribe of their coming. Some days before they reached the village, they were met by this friendly leader and fifteen of his tribesmen. Extending welcome to Father Massanet, the Captain and their followers, the chief led them on to his people. Arriving at the Indian village on the Neuces River, the Spaniards went in procession, through it. "The priests on foot," wrote Father Massanet, "bore their staffs and a crucifix and sang the Litany of Our Lady while one of the lay members bore an improvised banner of the Blessed Virgin."

On reaching the home of the chief, the friars were invited by him to make it their home while they remained there. Father Massanet expressed through an interpreter the appreciation all felt for this kindly hospitality; but since they must needs have a place to worship, it would be better that they build a home for themselves near it. This explanation was accepted by the chief, and they were given his permission to select a site for their mission home and also to use what materials they needed for building it.

"The next morning," records the good father, "I went out with Captain Alonzo de Leon a little way, and found a delightful spot close to the brook, fine woods, with plum trees like those in Spain." On the same day the work of building the first of the missions in Texas was begun. Trees were felled and carted; and within three days they had a roomy dwelling and a church wherein to say mass. In front of the church was set a high cross of carved wood.

"The Indians watched with wondering eyes these strange activities. On the day when the formal dedication occurred, they came in great numbers. Again there was a procession, and following it an impressive mass. The royal standard of Spain, bearing a picture of the crucified Christ, was raised. After this the royal salute was fired by the soldiers. Then came the singing of Te Deum Laudamus."

The final touch to the founding of this pioneer mission in Tejas land occurred later. Among these Indians was a medicine man, or Indian priest, to whom the tribe looked for religious guidance. He was conducted to the newly built mission, and treated with respect befitting his high place in the tribe. After observing the strangers and being invited to dine with them, this leader, instead of pronouncing a blessing, made with some food he took out of the dish a sign suggestive of a cross, pointing with it north, south, east and west. Then to his people he said that he was no longer needed by them —that these dark-robed priests with white faces who had come among them were the true priests of "Ayimat Caddi"—the "Great Captain."

The mission San Francisco de la Tejas, begun thus auspiciously, was not to continue long in good fortune. Shortly after establishing it, Father Massanet returned with the Captain de Leon to Mexico. A rather sharp controversy occurred between these two leaders on their going as to the number of soldiers that should be left behind. The Captain wanted a garrison of fifty; and the Father insisted that three soldiers were sufficient guard for the three priests who were to be put in charge of the mission. The Father had his way. Promise was given by the chief of the Tejas tribe that these white brothers would receive his protection. Then with the chief's brother, his nephew, and two other relatives accompanying them to visit the Mexican authorities and receive gifts to bring back to those that remained at home, the return trip was begun.

No attacks on the mission San Francisco de la Tejas came from the Indians, but difficulties enough of other kinds beset the faithful friars left there. During a dreadful pestilence that swept the tribe, one of the fathers died. Then came a drouth that added the peril of starvation. Some of the medicine men interpreted these calamities as coming from the white man's religion. The lives of the handful of priests and soldiers were in danger. Finally orders came for them to abandon their missionary work on that far frontier. Accepting the decree, the friars buried their heavy mission bell at night; and despite the entreaties of the few Indians they had gathered into their fold, departed for Mexico.

A quarter of a century passed before further efforts were made to establish missions in the land of Tejas. Then it was again the presence of the French in that region that stirred the Spanish to action. This rival nation, after building New Orleans, began to push out for trade over Louisiana.

One enterprising French leader, St. Denis, having established himself on the Red River in a post called Natchitoches, began to look with longing eyes for trade in the Spanish realm. Finally the lure of gold and silver he knew the Spaniards possessed made him dare to lead a small trading party with pack mules laden with goods, across the boundary line. He and his men found the deserted mission on the Neuces, and round it hundreds of sheep and cattle that had descended from those the fathers had brought with them.

No Spaniards were there to trade with them so on they went to the Rio Grande. There near the present site of Eagle Pass they came upon a Spanish outpost under command of one Captain Ramon. St. Denis and his men were immediately arrested and their goods taken. The French leader assured them he came only with peaceful intent to trade with a neighboring nation. Captain Ramon was undecided what must be done. While he kept the adventurous Frenchman a prisoner, something of moment was happening; the Spanish Captain's beautiful daughter, Marie, and the handsome St. Denis were falling desperately in love with each other.

Legend has it that St. Denis was thrown into a dungeon only to be released through the pleadings of his sweetheart. What truth is in this part of the story is uncertain. Something, however, of a better understanding between the French and the Spanish in these borderlands was to result from this romance. St. Denis did not care who governed Texas. He wanted to trade goods for Spanish silver and gold; and his heart was set on winning the hand of the beautiful señorita. In both these quests he was finally successful. The confiscated goods were restored, and Marie became his bride.

Then to reassure the Spanish officials that his purpose in coming into Texas was only to promote friendship and trade, he proffered to act as guide to such forces as they would send into that region. The proposition was accepted. It was not long before a band of mission-building fathers with some home-building settlers and an escort of soldiers under Captain Ramon were crossing the Rio Grande under the guidance of the French adventurer. The Spanish were determined this time to establish their rule over Tejas land. With St. Denis went his Spanish bride to make her home at his outpost, Natchitoches. The trail followed by this international expedition was later to become the famous old Spanish Trail of history and romance.

Mission building along this historical highway now began in earnest. The pioneer mission, San Francisco de la Tejas, was restored and other missions were established in the same region. The friars record a joyful welcome from the Indians there. Because of his close friendship with the redmen, St. Denis was also able to help keep this spirit of good will toward the efforts of the Spanish fathers. His marriage alliance doubtless had much to do with the promoting of peace and coöperation for a time on this frontier.

While the mission-building was in progress near the Louisiana border, other missions were being established at strategic points on the old Spanish Trail. In making their journey to Natchitoches, St. Denis and Captain Ramon had camped at some beautiful springs near what is now San Antonio. The conditions there were so favorable for missionary work that the fathers made this one of the most important centers for their activities. Stone being available, more enduring buildings could be constructed.

The historic missions that still stand in various stages of preservation in southwestern Texas were erected during those days. From 1715, when St. Denis guided the Spaniards across that region, until nearly the close of that century, the mission-building fathers kept on with their work. Through these years not only were the pine log missions in eastern Texas established, but the old Alamo (known first as Mission San Antonio de Valera), the Mission Concepcion, the beautiful San Jose, with other missions, were founded, and their buildings made of more lasting material. Those that still remain are monuments to the zeal and energy of the humble friars whose patient efforts brought them into being.

The inspirational leadership for this second movement to found missions in Texas was given by Father Anthony Margil. This good Padre, born of humble parents in Spain, became as a youth a follower of St. Francis. On taking his vows he volunteered to devote his life to the Indian missions in America. For years before he led his soldiers of the cross into Tejas land, he had labored unceasingly throughout Mexico—always walking barefoot, fasting and praying continually for the souls of the red children. It is said that he baptized more than 80,000 of them during his life of devotion to the cause of the Master. His only weapon in the face of danger was his crucifix; and with it he never failed to bring even savages bent on killing him to laying down their weapons and listening to his message of love and peace.

Following St. Denis to the Louisiana border, he set to work, with his friars and Indian followers he gathered there, rebuilding the old San Francisco mission and establishing others. In 1719 when trouble with the French occurred on that frontier, these missions were abandoned, and Father Margil turned his zeal and energy to the founding of missions in and around San Antonio and at other favorable places in the southwest. Under his inspirational leadership nearly a score of these outposts of Christian civilization were established.

The purpose of the frontier missions was to effect practical Christianity among the Indians. To this end they became more than mere places of worship; they were also homes and schools and centers of industry. When the friars came, they brought with them not only the cross, the Bible and other essentials for the conducting of their ritual, but also seeds and vines and trees for planting; cattle, sheep, and other domestic animals needed for the material support of the missions. Farming and fruit-growing and ranching were promoted among the red tribes that received the missionaries. Some of the Indians who gathered round the missions were trained in the rudiments of carpentry, masonry and blacksmithing. Sewing, cooking and weaving were taught to the girls. Art and music, too, were cultivated.

Teaching religion was of course not forgotten. Prayer and hymns of praise, mass, and simple lessons were among the daily spiritual activities. The Indians at first came in goodly numbers to watch the mysterious proceedings. The lighted candles,

A SPANISH ARTIST ADORNS THE MISSION NEAR SAN ANTONIO

the attractive altar and the ceremonies excited their wonderment. How much of the gospel teaching they really caught is a question. The story of the Christ Child and his Mother, of his work among the poor and sick and downtrodden was more readily understood, especially when it was made concrete in dramatic plays and by the kindly deeds of the fathers. A few of the Indians who listened with something of understanding hearts, were brought to baptism and followed in the footsteps of the friars. Some of them assisted materially in the building of the missions and labored through the years to help maintain them.

Much of the labor of love was poured into all this work. This is clearly revealed in the artistry still shown in some of the old structures. Nothing save the touch of affection could have created the statuary, the ornamentation and particularly the rose window that adorns the stately Mission San Jose de Aguayo near San Antonio.

Legend has surrounded the reputed sculptor, Huicar, with romance. One story is that this artist of common birth dared to make love to a lady of royal lineage. For this, despite his talents, he was exiled to Tejas. In memory of his sweetheart, Señorita Rosina, he created the now famous rose window; while she, the story goes, died for love of him in a Spanish convent. Another tale is that the

[55]

twining roses round the window gave it the name. Be this as it may, one can well believe that love was in the heart of the artist who made these dreams in stone come true. Huicar lived on in the land of his exile, and later married a girl in whose veins flowed Spanish and Indian blood. His name still lives in Tejas land.

Other Spanish names of high respect that link with the old mission building days may also be found there. When the fathers came in those long ago times, a number of fine families from the Canary Islands accompanied them. The government of Spain, sensing the vital need of establishing home-makers along with mission builders, had given substantial encouragement to these settlers. Unlike the soldiers, who too often undid with reckless acts the good work of the friars, these Spanish fathers and mothers and their children exercised a beneficent and steadying influence. The plan was right. Unfortunately the cost of this pioneering was felt too great; and the government did not lend support to the plan beyond the beginning. Those families that did come, however, became a power for good, radiating the best in Spanish culture and education, and sustaining the fathers in their good work through the years.

They sorely needed all the help and encouragement they could get. The mission service in Texas tested their faith and endurance to the utmost. Only a comparatively few Indians were brought even during the palmiest days within the influence of the missions. The attempt to extend the work to the wilder tribes of the plains and mountainous country resulted in tragic failure. The mission planted at San Saba was repeatedly attacked, priests and their followers were massacred, and the buildings were finally set in flames. Stark pestilence often visited these outposts of Christianity, making sad inroads on the Indians who had accepted the faith. Yet, despite all such heartrending difficulties, the courageous friars carried on until their work was brought to a close in 1794.

With the transferring of their duties then to the regular parish priests, the record of the good Franciscan Friars in that realm was officially ended. Their mission buildings fell into disuse and began to crumble away. Yet round the ruins still cling, like tendriled ivy, a million memories that keep verdant these shrines of history, legend and romance and give color and life to the story of the old mission days.

CHAPTER IV

AMERICAN ADVENTURERS ON THE FRONTIER

A SWIFT stroke of diplomacy just before the close of the French and Indian War brought the English and Spanish face to face along the American frontier. France, realizing that defeat for her was imminent, kept her hated rival from the full fruits of victory by suddenly trading to Spain for a small island in the Mediterranean all of Louisiana. The great Ohio Valley however was lost to the conquering nation, and the Mississippi River became a new international boundary line in the New World.

The passing of this trans-Alleghany region into the sure possession of England, opened an inviting opportunity for her American colonists. Daring ones among them began to search out the mountain passes and to explore the westward-flowing streams and rich valleys they drained. Pioneers with their wives and children followed cautiously the lead of pathfinders like Daniel Boone to build their log cabins and stockades for protection, and to till the fertile soil in the clearings. Free land, free air and sunshine, freedom to work out their own economic and social problems, freedom to worship God, gave to these frontier folk all the reward they wanted to make them dare and endure.

The American Revolution found these hardy folk trained and ready to fight for that freedom. Out of these backwoods people came Patrick Henry to sound the keynote, Thomas Jefferson to pen the Declaration of Independence, and George Rogers Clark to carry the conquest right up to the Mississippi. George Washington knew and appreciated the spirit and the fighting qualities of these frontiersmen, for he had been given as a youth much of his practical training on the frontier. With buckskin-clad boys from the backwoods he had forced surrender of the French at Great Meadows, and had later kept the British troops under Braddock from being completely wiped out. What these frontierbred boys would and could do was shown again by Morgan's sharpshooters at Saratoga, and by the long riflemen at King's Mountain. Let any trample on the natural rights of man, and those native sons of liberty were ready to fight to the death. To understand this background is to get closer to the inner spirit of Davy Crockett, James Bowie, and Sam Houston, who with many of the other heroes that fought for the freedom of Texas came from this same frontier stock.

The winning of the Revolutionary War flung the portals of the West wide open for the new nation. Like the lure of gold for the Spaniards, the lure of furs for the French, came the lure of free lands for Americans. By the thousands they began to follow the pathways of the pioneer vanguard across the Alleghanies. Beyond the Blue Ridge and the Big Smokies lay smiling valleys and rolling prairies waiting to be turned into fertile farms, and offering rich ranges for cattle, while wide streams draining these vast lands provided arteries for transportation and commerce.

Youthful America struck with confidence into its conquest of these western wilds. Woodlands on the sunset slopes of the mountains rang with multiplying axes; homes increased in the clearings; old trading posts grew into villages and towns; Indian trails were changed to covered wagon roads; cultivated fields spread farther and wider over valleys and rolling hills. The map of the nation was constantly being reshaped as new states, new counties and new cities were being created over the great domain.

With this westward onthrust of America, new and vital problems came. Our first President had to cope with the "Whisky Rebellion"—an expression of protest from the backwoods folk, who insisted that they had a right to carry their "corn liquor" to market unvexed by revenue officers who demanded a tax. Washington dealt firmly with these refractory spirits and won. Indian troubles persisted on the frontiers. It took all the fighting genius of "Mad Anthony" Wayne to settle those in the Northwest Territory. The backwoodsmen in Kentucky and Tennessee took care of the troublesome tribes in their region, whipping Creeks and Cherokees in true frontier spirit and style, and training themselves the while for more fighting to come.

When Jefferson became president other problems arose. By this time it was Young America that faced Spain along the Mississippi and the Florida boundary lines. At first there was little serious clashing in these borderlands. The Spaniards up the river were especially friendly to Americans who came their way. When Daniel Boone in 1795 packed up his belongings and trailed out of overcrowded Kentucky for the wilds of Missouri, where one of his stalwart sons had settled, he was given a

royal welcome by the Spanish officials in frontier
St. Louis. One thousand arpents of land were
granted to the famous hunter and scout provided
he would bring one hundred other American families into Missouri. Daniel accepted the generous
gift, chose a site for his new cabin by a clear spring
where deer and elk came to drink and wild turkeys
roosted in the near-by trees. And there he stayed
while gradually his friends from Kentucky and
Tennessee came to settle near their old leader.
There was a friendly intermingling of folk of various nations at this time in these untamed regions.

Trouble farther down the Mississippi, however,
brought America close to a clash with Spain. The
trans-Alleghany folk needed that stream for their
trade. The Spaniards holding New Orleans began
to play the part of the robber barons of the Rhine,
demanding tribute for use of the Father of Waters.
Flatboats laden with produce intended for the New
Orleans and the Gulf markets would be held up and
exorbitant duties exacted. The angered frontier
folk were ready to fight it out with these river dons,
when diplomats succeeded in arranging a treaty
which granted the Americans freedom of the big
river and the right of using New Orleans for reasonable fees as a place of deposit. While this agreement, made only for three years, was in force, all
went well; but when at its expiration an intendant

of Spain in charge at New Orleans abruptly tried to restore the old robber baron régime, the demand for freedom of the streams rang across our land. Politicians and diplomats went into a conclave to get the difficulty straightened out once more.

Something had been happening meantime that settled the problem with finality and set up an entirely different situation in America. Napoleon had dreams like those of La Salle of making France a power in the New World. To that end, by secret treaty, he reclaimed Louisiana for his Empire. Then came a pressing need for more money to carry on his wars, and the French Emperor made a swift bargain with the American diplomats Jefferson had sent to France to buy New Orleans. They had offered ten million dollars for that strategic post on the Mississippi. For fifteen million he would sell them the whole of Louisiana. The proposition was accepted forthwith. That purchase ended all problems as to freedom of the Father of Waters for America; but it left another disturbing question as to the exact boundary line of the Spanish-American frontier. A good many years passed and much precious blood was shed before that question was settled.

There was temporizing over the problem at the outset. Our Country claimed that the Sabine River was the southwestern boundary line of its

newly acquired domain. Some even insisted that
Louisiana, by reason of La Salle's occupation, extended to the Rio Grande. The Spanish maintained
that the boundary was the Arroyo Honde, consid-
erably to the east of the Sabine. When General
Wilkinson, then in command of the American
forces at New Orleans, led his troops into the strip
between those two streams, he found Spanish soldiers in that disputed territory. Herrera, their
commander, refused to obey Wilkinson's order that
they withdraw beyond the Sabine. There was
threat of an open clash, but the two generals put
their heads together and thought through a scheme
that kept peace for the time. The strip in question
was declared neutral ground.

This "no-man's land" became really a resort for
the lawless, and for adventurous spirits. It har-
bored a motley population made up largely of Indians, Mexicans, Spanish, French, Americans; and
added a peppering of picturesque characters from
other climes. Out of such an explosive human
mixture there was certain to come some history
making of a stirring and romantic cast.

One of the first episodes to stir up strife was
the activities in Texas land of an American named
Philip Nolan. Gaining permission from the
Spanish Governor of Louisiana to gather wild
horses from that region, Nolan in 1797 took a small

band of men and made a successful quest for the mustangs. While on the trip he took time to do a little trading with the Indians and made some sketch maps of the country. In 1800 Nolan decided to repeat his horse-hunting, but this second venture ended disastrously.

The Spaniards had become suspicious of this map-making American adventurer in Texas. Nolan and his twenty men had succeeded in rounding up about a hundred mustangs on the Waco when they suddenly found their camp surrounded by a hundred Spanish soldiers. A fight ensued in which Nolan was killed. Peter Ellis Bean carried on in place of the fallen leader until the ammunition of the Americans was exhausted and they had to surrender.

For seven years these Americans were kept in a Spanish prison. Then a royal order was sent from Spain directing that every one in five of the prisoners be hanged, and the rest be given ten years of hard labor. By the time this cruel decree came, only nine of the original band had survived the hardships of the Spanish dungeon. The officer in charge made these kneel while he read the decree; then, with a touch of mercy, he decided that only one of the nine need suffer death. The courageous fellows by throwing dice, settled the question among themselves as to which this one should be.

Ephraim Blackburn, the oldest one of the group, made the fatal throw and accepted the decree of fate with heroic cheer.

Stories of this type of torture and tragedy practiced on those who fell into the clutches of the Spaniards fed the fires of hatred. Something of the same type of treatment was meted out to Captain Zebulon Pike when he happened to cross the boundaries of New Mexico while exploring Southwest Louisiana at the time Lewis and Clark were searching out the Northwest. The explorer and his men were made prisoners and thrown for a time into filthy dungeons. In contrast to this treatment, Pike records a delightful time and a cultural environment in Texas. Legend has it that Lafitte, the French privateer who operated for years against the Spanish in the Gulf of Mexico, was stirred to his piratical activities because of cruel treatment his sweetheart had suffered at the hands of the Spaniards. Whatever the truth here, it is certain that there was a growing enmity all through this border realm against the Spanish. The cause was not one-sided of course, for outlawry was rampant on the frontier; but tyrannical treatment on the part of officials of Spain acting under orders from royalty overseas surely inspired more hatred.

The waxing ill-will against the Spaniards was not confined to Americans and others outside the dominions of Spain. Within Mexico and Texas there were many who resented bitterly the tyranny of their official overlords. Indeed, these lovers of liberty in Mexico broke out in revolt during 1810 against tyrants who were misruling their country. This uprising was led by Father Hidalgo, who could no longer bear seeing his people suffer at the hands of the hated Gachupins, as the Spanish ruling classes had come to be called. This courageous soldier-priest fell fighting for freedom, and his followers were killed or driven into hiding. One of his lieutenants, Bernardo Gutierrez, escaping, carried the cause to Washington and pleaded for support from our Country. His plea denied, the patriot returned to New Orleans steeled to open some other way to carry on.

There Gutierrez met a young American, Augustus Magee, who was fired with a kindred purpose. Magee a short time before had been sent as a Lieutenant of the United States Army to help hold outlawry in check in the Neutral Strip. The influx of all sorts of desperate characters into that "no-man's land" had brought intolerable conditions. The young lieutenant and his troops succeeded in capturing and punishing a good many of the marauders who were preying on travelers across the ungoverned territory; but despite all their efforts the plundering and killing continued.

[67]

A challenging idea came to the young army officer, and out of it a bold plan. In his closer contacts with these men that were making trouble, he had found that many of them were of a Robin Hood type, in exile because of Spanish tyranny. They all hated the Gachupins like poison. Why not gather those with a righteous grievance, and organize them as a filibustering band to fight and free Texas from misrule? His zeal for the plan grew until finally, to absolve his own country from all part in it, Magee went to New Orleans, and resigned his commission in the army, that he might fling himself into the cause.

Gutierrez and this ardent American were soon working like blood brothers to achieve their common purpose. The Neutral Strip was just the place to recruit their forces; so there they went, set up headquarters in the old town of Nacogdoches, and began to organize what became known as "The Republican Army of the North." There was no secrecy as to their intentions; indeed through numerous manifestos printed and scattered by their spies through a good part of Texas, the patriot-leaders called openly upon all who prized liberty to join in the fight to crush the Gachupins.

Adventurous Americans, Texans, Mexicans, and Indians, together with some liberty-loving Spaniards and a sprinkling of those from other lands, rallied to the call. Arms, ammunition, with clothing and supplies, were obtained through friends at New Orleans. Not many months had passed before the determined little army had crossed the Sabine and was marching southwestward along the old Spanish Trail to strike the first blows for the independence of Texas.

For some months the fight for freedom was waged with heartening success. Slipping round an army Governor Salcedo had led out from Goliad to drive them back, the republican soldiers seized and held the town. The outwitted Spaniards, beaten with serious loss in trying to dislodge their adroit enemies, and failing to starve them out through a siege, finally withdrew to San Antonio. Meantime the courageous Magee fell a victim of consumption and died; but the spirit of this liberty-loving American lived. His men selected Major Samuel Kemper as colonel and pressed forward under his efficient leadership.

San Antonio became the next objective. It took some fierce fighting to whip the forces intrenched there under the command of Salcedo and General Herrera, but the little army of freedom won. The town was finally taken; and the Spanish leaders, on promise of safety, surrendered with all their men. The Mexican leaders in the republican army wanted to execute the Governor, Herrera, and others in high command forthwith; but Kemper would not consent. Then Gutierrez insisted that these prisoners of rank be sent to New Orleans to be held until cessation of hostilities. To this Kemper agreed; and unsuspectingly he accepted the suggestion that they be placed under escort of Captain Delgado and his men. The Captain seized this opportunity to wreak vengeance on Salcedo and the others for the murder of his father. A few miles out of San Antonio he had them bound and put to a brutal death.

This breaking of a pledge of honor came nearly breaking up the forces that had banded together for freedom. Colonel Kemper and many of the other Americans left the army in disgust; and Gutierrez was deposed as leader. Enough of the republican army forces held together, however, to win another victory shortly afterward over General Elizondo, who had led another force into Texas to crush the rebellion.

Flushed with this added triumph the filibusters grew incautious. They selected as commander a Spaniard named Toledo, which displeased the natives. Finally they fell into a trap laid for them by another army under General Arrendondo. This shrewd Spanish leader, ordering his vanguard to feign retreat in face of a fierce attack on the Medina River, by the republican forces, lured his enemy into ambush. The entrapped fighters battled on until their ammunition gave out; and then came the slaughter of the heroic band by the soldiers of the relentless Arrendondo. Not more than ninety of the little army of patriots escaped to tell the tale.

This tragic defeat closed only the opening chapter in the struggle that was on to free Texas. Even though it might hold it down for a time, hard-handed tyranny could not crush the spirit of liberty. The cruelties meted to those who had sympathized with the rebellion served just to keep the embers of freedom quietly burning on. Some hundreds of Texas families fled into the Neutral Strip to escape the wrath of Arrendondo. Others less fortunate were captured by him and crammed into a dungeon at San Antonio—since called "The Black Hole" because eighteen of these prisoners suffocated there the first night. It was barbarities like this revealed the ugly face of tyranny; but the patriots had to bide their time.

Americans during this period had their hands full with the War of 1812. That conflict was brought so close to the borders of Texas that it became a potent influence in shaping later events in the Lone Star Land. A host of frontiersmen followed "Old Hickory" into the battle of New Orleans. Naturally when these men with the help

of other fighters from the borderland of Louisiana
and Texas won a signal victory over the "Redcoats"
who had overthrown Napoleon, they found themselves more deeply interested in these southwest regions. Not a few of them stayed on to settle and
help develop Louisiana, while a good many others
learning of the rich, broad lands of Texas began to
cast eyes toward that realm of opportunity.

The prospects for settlement and development of
Texas at the time were far from inviting. It was
still under the iron heel of Spain. The outlook for
winning freedom for Mexico or Texas was gloomy;
but some of the patriotic group still kept up hope.
A number of the zealous ones, in defiance of the
Spanish government, set up on Galveston Island a
republic of their own. From this vantage point,
they sent out privateers to prey upon Spanish commerce; and for a time they were remarkably successful in capturing vessels laden with gold and
supplies. They soon had wealth in abundance, but
their ill-won riches were one source of their undo-
ing. The leaders began to fight among themselves.
The privateers grew reckless about attacking ships,
and extended their nefarious activities to vessels of
other nations, and to traffic in slaves. Roused by
their rampant outlawry, our Country was getting
ready to root out this menace when the offenders

decided to fire their own buildings and seek a more congenial clime somewhere in Central America.

Galveston Island, however, was not left lonely for long. In 1817, Jean Lafitte, reputed an adept in privateering, and bearing an undying hatred for Spaniards, chose the island for his headquarters. This bold leader had refused a British bribe to fight the Americans. He had given substantial help in way of ammunition and some good fighters to help General Jackson give the English army under Packenham a crushing defeat—this unfortunately came as heaped up measure after the War of 1812 was officially closed. For a time after this Lafitte had a rather free hand in the Gulf of Mexico. But when some of Lafitte's men overlooked the fact that vessels they wanted to loot were flying the Stars and Stripes, Uncle Sam called a sharp halt, and drove Lafitte and his followers from the realm he had fitted up in lordly style.

The United States was beginning to take hold with a firmer hand in and around these southern waters. Some troublesome questions were faced squarely with Spain, and a few misunderstandings were cleared away by a new treaty. In 1819 the Spaniards agreed to sell Florida to our Country, provided we would give up all claims to Texas. Under the same treaty, the Neutral Strip was relinquished to us as a part of Louisiana.

That arrangement seemed generally satisfactory except to some folk in the southwest. These were angered about the deal, maintaining stoutly that the United States had no constitutional right to cede away our rights to the land of Tejas. A group of people in Natchez, Mississippi, took this matter so seriously that they not only protested, but raised an expedition to invade Texas and establish an independent republic there. Dr. James Long was chosen to head the enterprise.

The same year that Florida was purchased this intrepid leader set out with his wife and child for Texas. He left Natchez with a force of eighty men. On his way the Mexican patriot, Bernardo Guiterrez, joined the expedition. The force was increased to about three hundred by the time Nacogdoches was reached.

At this historic town the little army paused and made formal declaration that Texas was a free republic. Long, elected president, proceeded with all earnestness to administer the duties of his high office. Lands were offered for sale; and certain favorable places on the Trinity and Brazos Rivers were designated for trading posts. The new president then sought out Lafitte to enlist his active support; but the practiced privateer refused to join in the doubtful enterprise. To make it successful, he felt, would take a strong army of dependable men. He was loath to lend himself to any losing game.

While he was on his way to meet Lafitte, Long heard of a royalist army on its march to destroy the force he had gathered. A messenger was dispatched to tell his wife to flee to Louisiana with their child until he could send her further word. Bad tidings kept coming all the way back. When the newly-elected president finally reached Nacogdoches, he found the place practically deserted. Out of fear of the oncoming troops, not only his own men but the inhabitants of the town had fled. The Doctor himself barely escaped capture. Happily he managed to rejoin his wife and child in safety.

This discouragement did not dash the ardent hopes of Long. Hurrying on to New Orleans, he sought to rally forces to carry on. Felix Trespalacies, a noted exile from Mexico, was among the first to throw his fortunes with the zealous leader. A goodly number of fighting men rallied at their call; supplies were obtained without great difficulty. The new patriot army was soon aboard a vessel making its way along the coast of Texas. The expedition landed, and Long, leaving his wife and child at a fort on the coast, struck inland and captured Goliad. His triumph there was short-lived, however; for very soon a force of royalists made a counter attack on the town and forced the republican army to surrender. Long was held prisoner for a time. Then when General Iturbide came to power, he was permitted to go to Mexico to lay his case before the new leader.

Things for a brief season were full of promise. Mexico had won her freedom from Spain. Long's friend, Trespalacies, was made governor of Texas. The Doctor himself was treated as an honored guest. Just as he was in the midst of these uncertain glories, however, the bullet of some assassin cut short his career. Why Dr. Long was slain and by whom has ever remained a mystery. His wife and child, suffering hunger, exposure and cruel anxiety, waited for months in the deserted garrison for their husband and father. Mrs. Long would not leave until news was finally brought of his death; then the heroine returned sadly to her homeland. Another heroic chapter in the story of the struggle for the independence of Texas had been brought to its close.

With the tragic passing of its first and only president, the free republic which had existed only in the hopes and dreams of Dr. Long and his followers passed away. The vision remained, however, in the hearts of liberty-loving Americans and Texans. It was cherished by the devoted, courageous wife, who lived on to see the dream come true, and to become herself one of the honored pioneer mothers of the nation that finally rose under the flag of the Lone Star.

CHAPTER V

HOME BUILDERS ON THE BORDERLANDS

THE real and lasting conquest of any frontier realm is made by its home-building settlers. Pathfinders may mark the trails, adventurers throw open the doors of opportunity; but it is only when fathers and mothers and children come to make their homes, to till the soil, to establish schools and places of worship, that civilization really takes root in any land. The story of the pioneering of Texas, in common with that of every other part of our Country, adds concreteness to this truth. The stable conquest of that great borderland state began with the coming of American colonists in the eighteen-twenties into that still untamed region.

Moses Austin, a native son of old Connecticut, paved the way for this colonization. This enterprising leader, after the Revolution, moved first to Virginia, where in 1793 his son Stephen was born, then to Missouri. Here he became for a few years a citizen of Spain; for Missouri was still a Spanish domain, and the officials required such allegiance from those who desired to enter into the development of the resources of their provinces. Austin's immediate objective was lead mining, and he carried on in that industry through the years of the Louisiana Purchase and exploration, the period of filibustering in Tejas land, and up to the time when Missouri was admitted through compromise into the Union.

In 1820, the year Missouri became a state, this pioneer took the trail on horseback for Texas. It was a man-testing trip through dense woods, across wide rivers, and over prairie stretches. Finally, after following the old Spanish Trail some hundreds of miles, he came to the town of San Antonio. There before the Governor of that region, he stated the object of his long journey. He had come to secure a tract of land on which to settle a colony of American home-building pioneers.

Governor Martinez denied his request, saying that Spain wanted no foreigners in Texas, and ordering this well-meaning American to leave the province. As the discouraged Austin was making his way from the Governor's office across the old Plaza, he chanced to meet Baron de Bastrop, whom he had known in New Orleans. When Austin told his story, this friendly Prussian-Spaniard took him back to the Governor, and urged reconsideration of the constructive proposition. Moses Austin, he told the Chief Executive, had once accepted Spanish citizenship. He had helped in the development of Missouri; he would aid in the building of Texas. His petition for the privilege of doing so should be welcomed and sent to the authorities at the capital of Mexico for a final decision. To this suggestion the Governor agreed, and Austin left for home with new hope in his heart. The arduous journey to Texas and back, so taxed the strength of the courageous leader that he fell ill and died in Missouri before word could come that his mission had been successful. With faith that his petition would be granted, however, he made a last request of his son to carry forward the plan for establishing a colony of Americans in Texas.

Stephen Austin, then in his twenty-eighth year, seemed hardly the man required to head this tremendous enterprise. He was not of the rugged, do-and-dare type, but of gentler mien, with scholarly instincts, and refined tastes. Folk in general would never have thought of choosing him to lead pioneers in the conquest of any land, especially a region of such challenging difficulties as Texas. But folk generally do not know that it takes rare brains as well as brawn to conquer an untamed realm. Pioneering in every part of America has always been under the leadership of intelligent, courageous men of vision. Stephen Austin brought to his heritage of opportunity, energy, wisdom, courage, kindliness, diplomacy, and enduring loyalty.

Before his father died Stephen went to New Orleans to promote the plans for colonization. While there, word came that the authorities in Mexico had acted favorably on the petition. Hastening to Natchitoches he met Don Erasmus Seguin, a Texas leader whom the Governor had sent to find the elder Austin. Stephen had just arrived in this town when word came to him that his revered sire had passed away. The loyal son did not falter, but set forth at once with Seguin for San Antonio to meet the Governor and complete the official arrangement for carrying forward to success. The result that finally came remains an enduring memorial to the vision and leadership of Moses and Stephen Austin.

Times were propitious for their venture in colonization. The long struggle of the patriotic forces to free Mexico from the tyrannies of Spanish government were culminating in victory. There was a welcome for Americans at this time in Texas. The Governor at San Antonio received Stephen Austin cordially and suggested that he look over the land with a view to selecting a tract most suitable for his colony. He finally chose the rich region between the Brazos and the Colorado Rivers —these streams offering means of transportation to the Gulf of Mexico. Austin accepted citizenship in his adopted country, and became an empresario, or contracting colonizer in Texas. The capital of his colony was later established at San Felipe on the Brazos.

Free land was the lure that brought Americans into this region. Under his contract Austin could offer to each man over twenty-one years of age six hundred and forty acres, and increase this by three hundred and twenty more if the man was married. A fee of twelve and a half cents per acre on easy terms was the charge to the settler. The land was tax free. With these generous terms the empresario had little difficulty in bringing some thousands of Americans into his domain. These colonists might travel overland along the old Spanish Trail, or take the water route across the Gulf and up either the Colorado or the Brazos River.

The vanguard of these settlers, gathered by Austin largely in and about the Neutral Strip, was guided by him along the historic way St. Denis had opened about a hundred years before. Another group, recruited by Joseph Hawkins, whom Austin had taken as a partner in the enterprise, shipped from New Orleans on a schooner called *The*

[82]

Lively. Needed supplies and tools for the first colonists were sent aboard this little ship. The plan was to sail to the mouth of the Colorado where Austin had arranged to come and join forces for the pioneering venture. *The Lively* however got into a storm-tossed Gulf, and landed by mistake at the mouth of the Brazos. Finding no Austin there, the band of voyagers explored the vicinity for a few days, then made camp a short distance up the river, and began to plant a crop.

Austin arrived with his band of pioneers in December, 1821. After choosing a site on the Lower Brazos for his first settlement, the leader hastened to the mouth of the Colorado to meet those who had shipped on *The Lively*. No vessel appearing at the appointed place, he finally gave up and returned to his colony. Though greatly handicapped for want of tools he had hoped to get from the schooner, he set to work with his settlers to build cabins and to till the soil. These Pilgrims of Texas, like those that had landed on the bleak new England shore two centuries before, did not return to their old homeland, but worked on to lay the foundations of civilization and freedom in this new land of promise.

While they were working that first year a revolution occurred in Mexico. The old Spanish régime was overthrown and a new Republic rose in North America. Austin, surprised to learn of this change when he went to report progress to the Governor in San Antonio, decided to leave for Mexica City immediately and have his grant reconfirmed by the new government. His colony was left to the leadership of Josiah Bell, of South Carolina, who had brought a girl from old Kentucky as his wife into the pioneer realm.

The trip of the empresario not only brought the desired results but proved the diplomatic genius of Stephen Austin. His previous experience as legislator and as a judge in Missouri doubtless helped him greatly in the new and difficult situation he had to face in this disturbed country. Though he had to remain for a year in the Mexican Capital while political adjustments were being made, he succeeded better than others were able to do in getting favorable action from the new authorities. Meantime he was winning among the leaders of the newly-born Republic, friendships which were to prove of value in the after years. There is no doubt too that Austin, schooled in things American, gave valuable counsel during this troublous time to those who were in the throes of setting up a free nation. The constitution adopted by Mexico in 1824 showed the effect of American influence; it was modeled in great measure upon the pattern of our own Constitution.

His mission successfully accomplished, Austin hastened back to his struggling colony. His long absence had disheartened some of his followers, but a faithful few had gone forward with courage. The reappearance of their leader with his heartening news gave new zest to the pioneers. It was good to feel that they had moved from one free country to another, and that the contract made with the previous government had been renewed and strengthened. They could go on building with greater hope and confidence.

Austin, as empresario, exercised firm but fair and kindly rule. Prosperity began to come to those who had cast their lot with him in this borderland. More and more, families came to build homes and to develop farms and ranches. Austin's good friend, Baron de Bastrop, was appointed to survey the lands, and to assist in issuing deeds to the colonists. The town of San Felipe de Austin was officially made the capital of the new domain. From his offices there the American-born leader gave himself whole-heartedly to the interests of his settlers who were laying the foundations of a nation and great state of the future. Austin was never blessed with children of his own, for he never married, but he justly won for himself the title of Father of Texas.

It soon became necessary to expand the colonization. Austin's prompt and successful fulfilling of his first contract to settle three hundred families in his grant of land, made it easy for him to win a second contract for five hundred more families and later a third contract. Within eight years the empresario had succeeded in bringing into Texas some twelve hundred families—approximately six thousand souls. When one considers that the original Puritan group that settled New England numbered about twenty-five thousand, one can better appreciate the magnitude of the pioneering of Texas launched by the stalwart son of old Connecticut, and carried forward with such humanitarian statesmanship by his loyal son.

Whence came these pioneers of Texas? They were from all America, and from countries overseas. Not a state then in our Union but was represented many times over by those that made the Land of Tejas their new home. And they came, bringing not only their basic tools for the conquest of the soil and the building of homes, but with a love of freedom burning in their hearts. They came bearing those essentials of modern civilization: love of home, desire for education, civil righteousness, and reverence for God. Some among them were of course of the "black sheep" caste—no pioneer community is ever without its wild ones. But the rank and file of most of the settlers were

honest and industrious, neighborly and helpful—
just good citizens for any country. For the most
part these pioneers of Texas believed in the "Golden
Rule" to a point that they were ready to fight for
its observance. Square-dealing, fair play, and freedom were their watchwords.

Austin's colonies were not the only ones that
were established during those pioneering years in
Texas. Others inspired by his successful leadership,
sought to become empresarios themselves; and a
number of able men succeeded in getting land
grants under similar terms. Among these were
David Burnet of New Jersey, who afterward became president of the provisional republic of Texas;
Lorenzo de Zavala, a Spanish leader who had rebelled at the tyranny of Spanish officials and fled
to America to dedicate his life to the cause of freedom; Colonel Benjamin Milam, a veteran of the
War of 1812, who later made the supreme sacrifice
for Texas. Under these and other empresarios
who followed the lead of Austin, colonies were
spread over the gulf plain of that then Mexican
province.

Not all the ventures in colonization had smooth
sailing. Difficulties arose over land grant boundaries and there were conflicts between the unstable
of different races. One of the first of these was the
trouble between the De Leon and the De Witt

colonies. These two groups, the De Leon made up of families brought from Mexico, and the De Witt of American families, found themselves claiming in part the same ground. Stephen Austin was called in as a disinterested party to help settle the difficulty. He played the rôle of peace-maker admirably, effecting an amicable adjustment and winning added respect for his fairness and wisdom.

Other controversies that arose during this period of colonization were not so readily settled. In the case of one colony planted near the Louisiana boundary in 1825, the difficulties that came out of the assignment of lands flamed finally into open conflict and resulted in the expulsion of the empresario in charge. The involving of Americans with Mexicans and Indians at this time brought a serious aftermath of trouble.

One Hayden Edwards had succeeded in getting a large grant of land in Eastern Texas with the right to settle eight hundred families within the domain. Nacogdoches, founded by Barbo in 1779, was to be the capital of the Edwards colony. Naturally there were a good many Mexicans and others living round this old town, with property rights which the new empresario had been expressly instructed to respect. Edwards on coming with his new settlers into this region, ordered that all that held certificates showing ownership to the

land they were occupying, present them to him
that he might pass upon their validity. The order
was accompanied by the warning that those who
did not substantiate their claims in this way, would
be dispossessed. This blunt show of authority
brought angry reaction from the Mexican settlers.
They were resentful enough of having an American
placed over them; his preëmptory demands incited
open protest.

Another act that threw fuel on the flames was
the election Edwards called for the selection of officers of the militia and for alcalde—or judge. This,
his opponents held, was stepping beyond his rights.
The election was carried through despite all objec-
tions; and the empresario's son-in-law was declared
the new alcalde. At this, the Mexicans, protesting
that the election was fraudulent, carried their case
to the political head at San Antonio, and gained
from him a decision that their candidate was entitled to the office. The son-in-law of Edwards relinquished the judgeship to his opponent. Further
trouble followed. It was speedily found that all
the decisions made by this official were in favor of
the Mexicans.

Edwards, during these troubles, obliged to return
to the United States on business, left his colony in
charge of his brother. In the face of thickening
difficulties, this brother made appeal to the Gov-

ernor of Coahuila and Texas—then one province—
for redress of grievances. No reply, only a series
of disturbing rumors to the effect that the Edwards
land grant was to be annulled, reached the colony
by the time his brother returned. Then came a
letter from the Governor confirming these rumors.
The empresario was charged with exceeding his
authority, his contract was annulled and he and his
brother were ordered out of Texas.

This action brought serious trouble. After in-
vesting all the wealth he could gather in this venture, Edwards was ready to fight for his rights.
His decision was made forthwith to defy the Mexican government and set up a free one of his own.

The settlers of his colony for the most part rallied
at his call. Two leaders of the Cherokee Indians,
with grudges against the Mexican rulers, joined the
rebellious empresario. Adventurers from the old
Neutral Strip, always ready for a fight, threw their
lot with him. A convention was called straightway, and out of its deliberations came the "Republic of Fredonia." In the formal declaration the
eastern part of Texas was severed from Mexico and
divided between the Americans and Indians. This
of course meant war.

An appeal was made to all the other colonies to
join in this fight for freedom. Austin refused
to lend his aid to so volatile a group. The other

empresarios likewise withheld their support. Even
the Indians, who had been so quick to align themselves with the movement, were as quickly lured
away by promises of land made by an emissary of
Mexico. Edwards soon found himself standing
practically alone in the leadership of a hazardous
enterprise. A force of Mexicans was dispatched to
end the rebellion. Austin, using his good offices for
peaceful settlement, induced its commander to extend an offer of pardon for all Fredonians who
would lay down their arms; and to give to Edwards
freedom to appeal his case to the authorities in the
capital of the Republic. This offer was haughtily
rejected, and Edwards, with the faithful few who
had stood by him, was forced to flee across the
boundary line into the United States. Through
the dividing of his grant among Burnet, De Zavala,
and Vehlien, the settlers whom the fallen empresario had led into Texas were able to get some
redress for what losses they had suffered.

The unfortunate affair did not end with this
settlement of the property rights involved. Its
effects were to carry on with increasing malevo-
lence. The officials of the new Republic that was
just trying to get firmly established were made
suspicious. The oft-repeated warning that Americans were intent on making Texas an independent
state began to look prophetic. The cordial rela-

tions that had obtained between Austin and other dependable empresarios and the rulers in Mexico grew somewhat strained. In their place came distrust and other ominous signs of approaching trouble.

Despite these warnings that pointed toward difficult days ahead, the colonists went steadily on with their constructive conquest of Texas. Each year saw more homes built, more land made fruitful, more cattle grazing on the rich ranges. Old trails were becoming easier to travel; the waterways and the harbors were showing gradual improvement. Lines of communication were being made safer and surer. Public education and free worship were retarded, for by terms of the colonization, there could be no common schools and no religious liberty. For these precious privileges the home-builders had yet to fight.

There was an alluring picturesqueness about the life in old Tejas Land. Indians were still roaming over these wilds. Often they would come to trade with the settlers, bringing their warm buffalo robes and tanned buckskins and furs to barter for knives and guns and bright cloths and beads or other commodities. With the more peaceful red folk the pioneers had little trouble; but marauding bands from the wilder tribes would sometimes raid and steal and kill. The settlers had ever to be wary, and prepared to ward off such attacks. It took patience on the part of the leaders to keep the redmen and the whites at peace.

The blend of races added to the color and romance of life in early day Texas. A large proportion of the population was Mexican. About one-third were army officers, merchants and Mexican officials. The others were mostly poor and unoffending folk—though some of them were of a banditti type. Then there were the Spaniards—a goodly sprinkling of the descendants of those who had come from the Canary Islands in the long ago days. They maintained the fine culture of old Spain in this frontier. Added to these were the Americans of various types—Puritan and Cavalier —frontier folk—plantation owners—all mingling with the other racial elements that made up the people of the Lone Star Land.

The American pioneers that helped to make this varied group came from a rich heritage. They were largely the sons and daughters of those who had founded our nation. They brought the traditions of New England homes and of the Southern mansions together with those of the frontier cabins. They blended the qualities that make the truly American character—earnestness, courage, dependability, frankness—and magnetized it all with a burning love of freedom. All the letters and books of this period record that Texas had an unusual number of educated men and women. It was men and women of this character and spirit that followed Stephen Austin and other leaders as colonizers and founders of Texas.

CHAPTER VI

HISTORY REPEATS ITSELF

THE clash between the forces of democracy and those of autocracy in the land of Texas was inevitable. With twenty thousand Americans settled in that borderland, and with a group of liberty-loving Spaniards and Mexicans who had felt the heel of Spanish tyranny through the years, mingling with them as neighbors and friends, and bound in some instances with ties of marriage, there could be no other outcome. The thought of government by royal decree to these frontier-trained folk was hateful; and dictatorship in every form intolerable; yet because they loved peace and because they stood for law and order and loyalty to their superiors, these folk endured oppression at the hands of tyrants for years before they threw themselves into an open fight for freedom.

[95]

Their revolutionary war came only after every other means of obtaining justice and right-dealing from the tyrannical officials had been exhausted. When the republican forces had triumphed in 1821 in their war to free Mexico from Spain, the hope for good government rose high. With the adoption for the reborn nation in 1824 of a constitution that was based on the same fundamental principles as that of the United States, there was great rejoicing especially among the American settlers in Texas. They had yet to learn that a dictator can find devious ways to annul any compact, however sacred.

Mexico, though ostensibly free, was still ruled by men whose training had been under the old Spanish régime. It was a republic only in name, and this through no fault of the patriots that fought heroically to make it really free. These good people had not had practical experience for years, as had our own, in the art of self-government. Groping out of the gloom of tyranny, they could easily be made the prey of clever and unscrupulous leaders ambitious for political power.

General Iturbide was the first to seize this opportunity for self-promotion. When the patriotic forces triumphed in 1821, this military leader got himself elected Emperor, and then began to rule with autocratic hand. Again the fighters for freedom rose, overthrew the usurper of their hard-won liberties, and set up a republican form of government. A solemn compact was drafted to give assurance against further dictatorial rule; and yet the old tyrannies, like Banquo's ghost, would not down.

Americans in Texas were first to feel their force. Their background of training in democratic government doubtless made them more keenly sensitive and resistant to autocracy however disguised. More than this they had speedily become the main target of these tyrannies. There was a waxing hate among the dictatorial politicians of the supposed-to-be republic, for things American. They felt—and there were good reasons for the feeling—that the Americans wanted to achieve the independence of Texas.

It was no secret that many folk in the United States believed that the land should either be given its freedom, or better, be added to our realm. John Quincy Adams as president tried vainly in 1825 to have the Florida treaty so modified that we would get at least part of Texas. Later our country made an unsuccessful effort to acquire some or all of it through purchase. Andrew Jackson, who had come into intimate contact with the whole southwest during the War of 1812 and the Indian Wars, was keenly in sympathy with orderly efforts that would finally bring Texas into our Union. Still, as President, he maintained a consistent "hands-off policy" and let the Texans fight through the cause of freedom and annexation for themselves. Our nation kept neutral, however close the ties, through that struggle.

This is not to say that individual Americans were inactive in promoting movements to free Texas. Singly and in groups they did give help in various ways through a good many years. The story persists that Aaron Burr included that borderland province in his plan—if he made one—to set up an independent republic in the Southwest. Whatever was thought or done regarding such an ambitious scheme by this political leader, seems destined to remain in the realm of conjecture. His co-worker, General Wilkinson, it is reported, did play hand-in-glove with the Spanish on that frontier, taking pay regularly from them while he was yet in the United States army. This collusion may help to explain his readiness to agree with General Herrera in declaring the Neutral Strip, which became, as already shown, a breeding place for various filibustering expeditions aimed at achieving independence for Texas. All these efforts, however sincere of purpose, were ill-timed and unsuccessful save for one main thing; they did help to keep the torch of liberty aglow through the dark years until the final war for freedom came.

The tyrannies that led to the Texas Revolution were basically like those that brought our own War for Independence. The constitution of 1824, like the English constitution, was violated. There was a studied effort to curtail the liberties of the colonists. Texas was not permitted to govern herself, but was kept as part of Coahuila, whose capital, being south of the Rio Grande, was practically inaccessible to Texans, and whose governor was always Mexican. Taxes and duties were laid arbitrarily and collected in the same spirit. Mexican soldiers were stationed at various points throughout Texas, ready to enforce the will of the rulers. It was decreed that Mexican convicts should be settled in Texas. The carrying out of that order would have made of the region a kind of Siberia. All these autocratic acts aggravated the growing enmity between the Texans and the Mexican officials.

Finally came the decree of 1830, which practically excluded foreign folk from settling in Texas. Though this law applied to all outsiders, it was clearly aimed against Americans, and its hardships fell mainly on that group. Many from our country who had already made sacrifices to join their relatives and friends in the Texas colonies found themselves suddenly shut out. Plans were disrupted, and progress checked. This unjust decree, added to the other abuses of power on the part of Bustamente—then president of the Mexican Republic—and his petty officers, brought protest from the Texans and then open revolt.

The first outbreak was touched off, strangely enough, by an American, Captain John Davis Blackburn, in the service of the Mexican government. Acting under directions of General Teran, who had taken issue with the newly-elected Governor of Coahuila, Blackburn began to execute orders like a petty tyrant. When the people made complaint, the pugnacious Captain ordered all the ports except Anahuac, over which he personally had charge, closed. This in effect was declaring a blockade against the colonists.

Blackburn was speedily waited upon by a delegation of determined settlers, authorized by their people to demand the revocation of that order. He tried to pass the demand on to his superior, Teran; but the Texans would stand for no delay. Fearing the outcome, the arbitrary official yielded to the extent of opening another port. Then he threw more fuel on the embers of the Texan wrath by declaring the ten-mile strip, reserved by the government along the coast, under martial law. After

ther assurance that they stood with Santa Anna in the fight he was waging for the Constitution and the cause of liberty. The best interests of Mexico, the Colonel felt, were safe in the hands of these people. Thus impressed, he returned to Mexico, taking practically all the Mexican soldiers with him.

Great rejoicing followed this demonstration of friendliness and confidence. It brought the colonists actively to the support of Santa Anna, who was promising to do so much for the people. The feeling grew that with Mejia carrying back so fair and favorable a report to this rising leader, the time was ripe for Texas to act in her own interests. A definite and respectful statement of what her people desired, and to what by natural and constitutional right was theirs, should be set forth. Texans must be brought together for their own protection and for the promotion of their common welfare.

A convention of delegates representing all parts of the province was called to act upon these sensible suggestions. October 1, 1832, was set as the opening date, and San Felipe named the place for this meeting, the first of its kind to be held in Texas. Every district except Bexar was represented among the fifty men that participated in this historic assembly.

The convention, with Austin as chairman, dealt squarely with the issues then disturbing the Texans. It drafted a memorial reaffirming allegiance to the republic as founded on the constitution of 1824. It recommended that Texas be made a separate state with privileges of self-government under the provisions of that compact. It also requested that basic commodities essential to the development of the colonies be admitted into Texas for three years free of duty.

The need to keep Texans informed and ready for unified action was met by effecting a more permanent organization. This consisted of a Central Committee with headquarters at San Felipe, and a sub-committee for each of the various districts of Texas. Further, it was provided that all males between the ages of sixteen and fifty be enrolled and trained for military duty. Here was something akin to the "Sons of Liberty" and the "Minute Men" of our Revolutionary War days.

These activities, aimed honestly at promotion of the common welfare, not only of Texas but of Mexico, were bitterly resented by the Mexican leaders. Those of autocratic mind denounced the acts of the convention as treasonable, and as directed solely at achieving the independence of Texas. Austin was warned by certain of these authorities to desist from participating in such movements. He calmly replied, "If Texas does nothing for herself, she is lost."

The petition of the Texans was ignored. Instead of its bringing redress to the tried colonists it brought only added tyrannies. The puppet raised temporarily to the presidency when Bustamente was deposed, simply dispatched a force of soldiers into Texas to hold the audacious citizenry there in check—and this on the advice of Santa Anna, the pretended champion of the liberties of the common people.

The answer from Texans to this autocratic action was another convention held during April, 1833, in San Felipe. Delegates, roused by the ignoring of their petition and by the return of troops, were ready to make a definite stand for their rights. Among this history-making group were not only the clear-thinking, courageous Austin, but also the stalwart David Burnet, whose sire had seen service with Washington in America's War of Independence, and hard-hitting Sam Houston, also descended from Revolutionary forebears, and with a background of practical experience in frontier fighting and political leadership that made him "a man of the hour" in the oncoming crisis.

Under the skillful leadership of men of this stamp, the convention did some clear-cut, forward-looking work. One committee headed by David

Burnet, drafted a cogent memorial petitioning first that the obnoxious law of 1830, barring Americans and others from settling in Texas, be repealed; and second, that Texas be given separate statehood. Another committee under the chairmanship of Sam Houston proceeded to write a constitution for the proposed new state.

The plan set up for Texas followed somewhat closely the state constitution of Tennessee, over which Houston had once presided as governor. Echoing through it all were the basic things upon which free government is founded—right of trial by jury, freedom of speech, right of petition, and suffrage. What these earnest Texans were struggling to get was just the privilege of helping to govern themselves. They were redrafting the old "Bill of Rights." To these men born and brought up under such a system of self-government as they were proposing, this was the reasonable and sensible thing; but to the rulers of Mexico schooled in autocratic practices, it was quite a different matter.

The memorial and the constitution were speedily adopted by the convention, but how to get the approval of the Mexican Republic was the problem. W. H. Wharton, who had presided over the gathering, J. B. Miller, and Stephen F. Austin were appointed as a commission to carry the documents to Mexico City and win if possible their adoption by the authorities there. For some reason, Wharton and Miller found it inconvenient to go, so Austin, at his own expense, carried through alone.

Despite earnest and persistent efforts, this leader was able to accomplish little for Texas in the Mexican Capital. Santa Anna, though elected president, had turned over, for the time, the affairs of state to his vice-president, Farias. Things were in confusion, and slight attention was paid to the Texan emissary. When he finally did gain brief audience with the acting president, he chanced to make a remark that later was to help bring official wrath upon his head. In urging the separation of Texas from Coahuila, Austin expressed the fear that if this reasonable request was not granted, Texans would take things into their own hands. Following this, a letter that Austin had written, advising his friends in Texas to go forward hopefully with their plans for statehood, was forwarded by some ill-wisher of the cause to the vice-president. Putting one and one together, Farias chose to misconstrue these expressions as treasonable, and angrily ordered the arrest and imprisonment of the empresario.

For three months Austin was kept in solitary confinement in a dungeon. Then, though given somewhat better quarters, he was still held a political prisoner through over twelve more dragging months. These lines from a little journal he kept secretly during his dungeon days, give a flashlight view of a great soul in captivity. "March 2 (1834) —I obtained today a little book called yes and no. I prefer bread and water with books to the best of eating without them. In a dungeon, the mind and thoughts require more aliment that the body." *

News that their leader had been cast into a foul prison brought anger and dismay to Austin's followers. Only the thought that any outbreak on their part in his behalf might bring injury to him, held them from acts of retaliation. And this was perhaps just the main reason why this leader, innocent of wrong thinking or wrong doing, was being subjected to incarceration. The Mexican officials were probably holding him as a hostage to assure good behavior on the part of the Texans. Santa Anna may have been back of the plot, but he was adroit enough to keep himself under cover if he was implicated in it. He allowed the onus of it, as of other things, to fall on his vice-president.

During the spring of 1834, the wily Presidente resumed his duties connected with this high office. Some time thereafter he called together a council to consider matters pertaining to Texas. Austin, brought out of prison to present his case, was materially aided by that loyal friend of freedom,

* From Austin's Journal, published in *Texas Historical Quarterly*, January, 1899.

Lorenzo de Zavala, who was an official member of the council. The two succeeded in getting the hateful law of 1830 revoked, but they could not win approval of separate statehood for Texas. The other members of the council held with Santa Anna that Texas was not strong enough to govern and protect herself. Garrisons of federal soldiers must be stationed there to keep law and order. The Presidente was careful not to reveal whose law he expected to be obeyed. Ostensibly he was going to uphold the constitution under which he had been elected, and defend the rights of the common folk as he had promised. Austin was willing for the time to believe him, and wrote home hopefully to his people. He was by nature a peace-maker, and strove to the very last, even in face of bitter criticism by Texans themselves, to keep down the rising rebellion.

Santa Anna's promises, it was soon to develop, were only a mirage. When in a position of power, he began to reveal all his innate tyranny. Yet once in a while he seemed to show a different nature and perform some humane act, as he did when he finally freed Stephen Austin and let him go back to Texas.

What rejoicing there was when this leader returned home! The heart of all the loyal people of that land was poured out in welcome to one who had suffered so much for them. In this expression of love and confidence for him was some compensation at least for what he had endured. It renewed his strength for the man-testing days that were just ahead.

CHAPTER VII

TEXANS FIGHT FOR FREEDOM

THINGS that had happened during Austin's absence were driving straight towards war. Texas herself was divided on the question of peace or conflict. Austin, still counseling peace, was unable to hold those who felt that freedom would come only through fighting openly for it. Santa Anna sensing that rebellion was in the air, dispatched his soldiers to seize and punish those who were inciting it. Bitterness waxed between Texans and those who stood with the dictator. A crisis was imminent, and in the year 1835 it came.

Anahuac was the scene of the opening outbreak. Soldiers had been placed at this port to police the collection of duties. The colonists, charging injustice and high-handedness on the part of the collectors and the soldiers there, mustered in under the command of Colonel William B. Travis and forced the Mexicans to vacate the port. This was an invitation to serious trouble, and trouble was not long in coming. Santa Anna ordered the arrest of Travis and other leaders in the revolt. The Texans refused to yield these men, and the enraged dictator dispatched more soldiers to crush out the rebellion.

A large army under General Cos, Santa Anna's brother-in-law, was ordered to San Antonio. Rumors were rampant among the Texans that this force intended to dispossess and drive out every American, and turn Texas into an armed camp. Santa Anna had just given a tragic example of what he would do with those that defied him. The freedom-loving people of Zacatecas, one of the mountain provinces, who had challenged his right to set aside the Mexican constitution, had been mercilessly crushed under his iron heel. It was another blood-letting like that at the battle of Medina, where Santa Anna as a cadet was trained in the Arrendondo method of dealing with rebels. Now that the pseudo-champion of the people had thrown off his disguise, the patriotic forces who had helped to put him in power knew just what to expect at his hands.

Peace and war parties in Texas banded together in the common cause of defeating this tyrant. All the American colonists, together with many of the Spanish families, and also a goodly number of Mexicans who hated tyranny, joined in the fight to liberate their land from the rule of Santa Anna and his satellites. When the president had turned dictator, the valiant De Zavala and other patriots left Mexico to throw their strength with the Texans.

This was no clash of peoples of different races, but another age-old struggle between the forces of autocracy and those of democracy. The same spirit that had backed King John against the wall and made him sign the Magna Carta, that had challenged the "Divine Right of Kings" and cost Charles the First his head, that had made our American colonists battle on from Lexington to Yorktown, had risen again in the land of Tejas to fight for the God-given rights of man to "life, liberty, and the pursuit of happiness."

Vital events followed in swift succession. Mexican soldiers, carrying out orders to disarm the people, demanded of the inhabitants in Gonzales the surrender of two brass cannons that had been granted them some years before to help them protect themselves against Indian marauders. The answer to this demand was, "Come and take them." The fight that ensued has been called "The Lexington of the Texas Revolution." It went badly for the soldiers of Santa Anna. War was on.

Leaders of the Texans were speedily brought together. Sam Houston was made commander-in-chief of the armies of east Texas, and Stephen Austin was placed in command of the volunteer forces that had gathered for the fight at Gonzales. This force was being augmented every hour with more volunteers from all the surrounding country.

Victory at Gonzales spurred the Texans to strike at other places. Some of the volunteer settlers decided to capture Goliad. As they were making their way—not more than fifty in number—to attack this town, they happened by good fortune to come upon Colonel Ben Milam, who had just escaped from a Mexican prison. The empresario, happy to get a chance to even up the score with his enemies, joined with zest in the fight. A surprise attack on the Mexican garrison there soon brought the surrender of Goliad.

Heartened by this new triumph, the Texans determined to drive on and take San Antonio. This was a far more serious undertaking; for Cos with a large force of trained soldiers had entrenched himself in the old town, and would put up a hard fight to hold that strategic point. Undaunted by such anticipation, however, the Texans began to gather for the big battle. With his volunteer army greatly increased right after the victory at Goliad, Austin took up the march during October, 1835, for the new objective. Encamping with the main force on Salado Creek, he sent Colonel James Bowie and Captain Fannin forward to find some spot nearer San Antonio to be used as a base for the attack.

These leaders chose the old Mission Concepcion, not many miles distant from the town, and quartered their troops within its protecting walls. Before daybreak the next morning, roused by rifle shots, they found themselves surrounded by the enemy. There was a hasty getting into boots and a scrambling for rifles. Volleys were coming from the rapidly advancing infantry and cavalry. The Texans took things more deliberately. Frontier-trained marksmen that they were, each one picked out his human target carefully and generally got his man. The lively battle lasted only half an hour, but at its close the forces of Cos were on the run for San Antonio, leaving a good many of their number on the bloody field, and listening to the roar of some of their own cannon that the Texans had captured. Though the enemy outnumbered them and were better armed, for this open battle, the fighters for freedom had won a signal victory. It was all heartening for the harder days ahead.

Austin coming up with the main body of troops, had difficulty holding Fannin and others from pressing on to the capture of San Antonio. He managed to keep these ardent ones in check, however, while his thrown-together troops could be shaped into some semblance of a fighting force, and given a little "first aid" drilling in the art of soldiery. Then came a call that took this leader off to Washington, D. C., as one of a commission appointed to seek aid of the United States in this war for independence. Edward Burleson was chosen to succeed him as commander of the volunteer army.

The new commander prolonged the delay until his soldiers grew restive. They had volunteered to fight, not to hang about a soldier camp. They wanted the job done "pronto," so that they might get back home to their families, who were more in danger from Indians than from the soldiers of Santa Anna. While this sort of talk was going on, into the camp came the New Orleans Grays, a fine group of boys from Louisiana who had volunteered to help their neighbor Texans win freedom. Then came the scout "Deaf Smith," the wise Sam Maverick who had escaped from San Antonio, and Ben Milam eager for the fray.

One day Milam focused the desire in the hearts of all by shouting, "Who will follow old Ben Milam into San Antonio?" The shout was taken up, and plans were quickly made for the attack. A swift drive into the heart of the old town followed by some desperate fighting that cost the fine life of

Milam and a few other brave Texans, finally
brought General Cos to terms of surrender. He
made solemn agreement, if his life was spared, to
leave Texas with his troops, and never again to lead
soldiers against its people. The populace saw him
begin the keeping of that peace pact when he
marched away with his disarmed men along the old
Spanish Trail towards Mexico. It seemed that the
freedom of Texas was in sight; but the word of
Cos, at the demand of his autocratic brother-in-
law, was to be speedily broken, and Santa Anna's
wrath was yet to be faced.

Overconfident as a result of the series of un-
broken victories, the Texans relaxed their efforts
during the winter days that followed the capture of
San Antonio. The volunteer army for the time was
practically disbanded, only a small garrison being
retained to hold the surrendered town. The promise made by Cos, together with the fact that any
other formidable force at Santa Anna's command
was then south of the Rio Grande, made fears of a
return attack before a good many months had
passed seem absurd. The Dictator could not possibly cross the wide plains which lay between that
river and San Antonio, with any large body of
troops, before spring. Why worry?

But the defeated Cos had hardly reached the
Mexican border when Santa Anna met him. En-

raged by the report he brought, the Presidente ordered his brother-in-law to right-about-face and march with him to heap punishment on the insolent rebels. While the Texans rested in fancied security, their foes were coming steadily back with an augmented force of well-armed, well-fed and colorfully clothed soldiers ready to obey the iron will of an angered commander.

Meantime the cause of freedom was suffering not only from inaction but from dissension. Some of the Texans wanted to declare independence and fight for it; but more at this time wanted to carry on the struggle to make Texas an independent state under the Mexican constitution. The constitutionalists had their way for a time, but the wrangling that ensued over this and other vital problems threatened disaster to the whole cause. Henry Smith, governor of the provisional state that had been set up, tussled vainly with a refractory council to bring about the strengthening of the depleted forces at San Antonio. General Houston was having an uphill job organizing an army. A force under Johnson and Grant, dispatched in an ill-advised attempt to capture Matamoras, had been annihilated. The Texans were in an almost utter state of unpreparedness when Santa Anna with the vanguard of his well-equipped fighting force ap-

DAVY CROCKETT ARRIVES AT THE ALAMO

peared before San Antonio during late February of 1836.

Here was a crisis that had to be met with all the fighting spirit that brave men could pour into it. The tyrant must be stayed or the cause of freedom was lost. What force could hold the Dictator at bay while the Texans could rally their forces to carry forward the fight to victory? The answer came from the heroic band at the old Alamo.

Only about one hundred and fifty Texan troops were still in San Antonio when the forces of Santa Anna reached the outskirts of that town. These were under the command of Colonel James Bowie, who was stricken at the time with illness, and Lieutenant-colonel William Barret Travis, who, with Bowie's counsel, was in active charge of the band of fighting men. When the Mexican army came upon the scene, the Texans left San Antonio and made the old Mission Alamo their fortress.

The courageous band set at work to strengthen the crumbling walls and buildings of this historic place. Couriers were dispatched to bring in more men with arms, ammunition and supplies. There was no thought of retreat, no suggestion of surrender. The preparations were all made with the thought of fighting it out with the forces of the tyrant, no matter what the odds.

Suddenly into the midst of the little fighting

force came Davy Crockett. The picturesque frontiersman and noted bear-hunter, defeated for an
added term in Congress because he had dared to
oppose "Old Hickory," had bade good-by to that
state with a remark to the effect that his opponents
could go to hades, he was going to Texas. And
shouldering his rifle, "Betsey"—a gift from his political admirers in Philadelphia—he had struck out
for that frontier realm with determination to help
its people win their freedom. On his way, he had
picked up a beehunter and a deft-fingered fellow
whom he called "Thimblerig." Straight to the old
Alamo these three musketeers went, ready for a
fight or a frolic. The band of Texans welcomed
them with a roar that echoed through the old
Mission.

In a diary kept by the remarkable Crockett during the crowded hours that followed his advent at
the Alamo, we are given a closeup of one of the
most heroic and thrilling events in history. With
grim humor, he sketched vividly the waxing fight
against overpowering odds. Here are a few flash
views from his moving picture: "February 22
(1836) Mexicans, about sixteen hundred strong"
marching on to San Antonio, headed by the Dictator and General Cos, who "has already forgot his
parole of honor,"—The decision of the Texans to
withdraw to the Alamo, "and defend it to the last

extremity."—The raising there of "a large national flag, composed of thirteen stripes red and white alternately on a blue ground, with a large star, of five points in the center, and between the points the letters TEXAS."—Then the demand from Santa Anna for unconditional surrender, with the threat that every man would be put "to the sword in case of refusal." The only answer from Travis "a cannon shot" which sent Santa Anna's messenger back "with a flea in his ear." The dispatching of an express to Colonel Fannin at Goliad to send reinforcements to the besieged but determined band in the old Alamo.—Following this, the wounding of the strange Thimblerig, and his grim remark, "lead is getting scarce, and I'll lend this bullet out with compound interest"—and after his keeping of that word by killing six of the enemy, his saying, "That account's settled."—Following this the continual day after day fighting, with Colonel Bowie still ill, but the stricken hero crawling "from his bed every day, that his comrades might see him," his presence alone "being a tower of strength."

One entry from this priceless record gives a flash view of the central object of all this heroic struggle, and of the spirit of the men who were giving their lives to attain it: "March 2. This day the delegates meet in general convention to frame our Declaration of Independence. That the sacred instrument may never be trampled on by the children of those who have freely shed their blood to establish it, is the sincere wish of David Crockett."

Another revealing entry tells how the beehunter, after bringing down three of the enemy with his unerring rifle, finds a bullet in his Bible he had carried in his breast pocket, and remarks, "I am not the first sinner that has been saved by this book."

One flash view of the terror Santa Anna's coming has brought to the home builders of Texas: "Hunters out for food, bring back word that the settlers are flying in all quarters, in dismay, leaving their possessions to the ruthless invader, who is engaged in a war of extermination—sparing neither sex, age, nor condition. . . . Santa Anna appears determined to verify his threat and convert the blooming paradise into a howling wilderness. For just one fair crack at the rascal, I would bargain to break my Betsey, and never pull trigger again."

Such was the spirit of the men who fought the forces of tyranny at the Alamo. Travis voiced the soul of his dauntless band when he penned this letter:

Commandcy of the Alamo
Bejar, Feb. 24th, 1836
To the people of Texas & all Americans in the world:
 Fellow Citizens and Compatriots—I am besieged by a thousand or more Mexicans under Santa Anna—I have sustained a continued bombardment and cannonade for 24 hours and have

not lost a man—the enemy has demanded a surrender at discretion, otherwise the garrison are to be put to the sword, if the fort is taken—I have answered the demand with a cannon shot, and our flag still waves proudly from the walls —I shall never surrender or retreat. Then I call upon you in the name of Liberty, of patriotism, and everything dear to the American character, to come to our aid, and with all despatch. —The enemy is receiving reënforcements daily & will no doubt increase to three or four thousand in four or five days. If this call is neglected, I am determined to sustain myself as long as possible & die like a soldier who never forgets what is due his own honor & and that of his country—Victory or Death.

WILLIAM BARRET TRAVIS,
Lt. Col. comdt.

P. S. The Lord is on our side—when the enemy appeared in sight we had not three bushels of corn—we have since found in deserted houses 80 or 90 bushels & got within our walls 20 or 30 head of Beeves——

TRAVIS

A few men broke through the cordon thrown by the enemy around the Alamo, and joined the embattled ones in the fight to death. Bonham, one of the couriers dispatched for help, ran the dangerous gauntlet to rejoin the gallant Bowie, Crockett, and Travis. No other help, it seems, could be sent. The calls coming from everywhere for protection of mothers and children against the savagery of Santa Anna held back any reinforcements that might have been available.

In the final entries of Crockett's journal we have a vibrant firsthand record of the courage and the superb fighting qualities of this beleagered band in the face of their desperate situation. The lines this brave man wrote with Death bending over him, portray with simplicity, concreteness and spirit some of the closing hours of that history-shaping struggle. Slightly condensed the record reads:

March 3. We have given up all hopes of receiving assistance from Goliad or Refugio. Colonel Travis harangued the garrison, and concluded by exhorting them, in case the enemy should carry the fort, to fight to the last gasp and render their victory even more serious to them than to us. This was followed by three rousing cheers.

March 4. Shells have been falling into the fort like hail all day, but without effect. About dusk we observed a man running towards the fort on foot, pursued by about half a dozen of the Mexican cavalry. The bee-hunter immediately knew him to be the old pirate who had gone to Goliad, and calling to the two hunters, he sallied out of the fort to the relief of the old man, who was hard pressed. I followed close after. Before we reached the spot the Mexicans were close on to the heel of the old man, who stopped suddenly, turned short on his pursuers, discharged his rifle, and one of the enemy fell from his horse. The chase was renewed, but finding he would be overtaken and cut to pieces, he now turned again, and to the amazement of the enemy, became the assail-

ant in his turn. He clubbed his gun, and dashed about them like a wounded tiger, and they fled like sparrows. By the time we reached the spot . . . we saw that our retreat was cut off by another detachment of cavalry. Nothing was to be done but to fight our way through. . . . We dashed among them and a bloody fight ensued. They were about twenty in number and they stood their ground. After about five minutes a detachment was seen issuing from the fort to our relief, and the Mexicans scampered off leaving eight of their number dead upon the field. But we did not escape unscathed for both the pirate and the bee-hunter were mortally wounded, and I received a saber cut across the forehead. The old man died without speaking as soon as we entered the fort. We bore my young friend to his bed, dressed his wounds, and I watched beside him. He lay without complaint or manifesting any pain until about midnight when he spoke, and I asked him if he wanted anything. "Nothing," he replied, but drew a sigh that seemed to rend his heart as he added, "Poor Kate of Nacogdoches." His eyes were filled with tears as he continued, "Her words were prophetic, Colonel." And then he sang in a low voice that resembled the sweet notes of his own devoted Kate:

"But hame came the saddle, all bluidy to see.
And hame came the steed, but hame never came he."

He spoke no more, and a few minutes after, died. Poor Kate, who will tell this to thee?

March 5. Pop, pop, pop! Bam, bam, bam! throughout the day. No time for memorandums now. Go ahead. Liberty and Independence forever!

So died the men at the old Alamo—fighting to the very last breath—making the forces of tyranny pay almost ten-fold for every defender of freedom who fell in that fight. And every one of the dauntless band made the supreme sacrifice.

The night of March fifth fell upon the old mission with a strange quiet. In San Antonio the victors were reveling over the costly outcome of the days of struggle; but stillness reigned within the ruined walls, broken only by the wailing of a few women and children who had lived on through the nights and days of terror. On March sixth, the Alamo fell. Afterwards the Dictator spared these, sending the one white mother among them with her babe on to tell what had happened to those who had defied him; the others were ordered out of his sight. As for the bodies of the band of the heroes of the Alamo, they were heaped upon a funeral pyre and consigned to flames.

> That was a torch of living fire,
>   Touched by relentless foe,
> When the men who died in American pride
>   Were burned at the Alamo.

> In flames of lurid light it leaped
>   Up to a darkened sky,
> And set a Lone Star blazing there,
>   Whose light can never die.

The gentle winds their ashes keep;
But in our hearts aglow,
A golden flame to their undying fame,
Burns the light of the Alamo.

Dark days came in the wake of this victorious defeat. Santa Anna's unleashed forces were spreading terror throughout the land. One army under General Urrea, after cutting to pieces the little force Grant and Johnson were leading to Matamoras, marched on to recapture Goliad, and to enact there the blackest of all the chapters in the story of the Texas Revolution. Colonel Fannin and his men, fighting till their ammunition, food, and water were exhausted, finally had to surrender. A few days afterwards these prisoners of war were marched out of Goliad and shot down without mercy, a mere handful of them escaping this cold-blooded murder, which Santa Anna had ordered.

These were tragic and uncertain days for Texas. With many of her fine fighters laid low, with the merciless soldiers of Santa Anna carrying death and destruction everywhere, and with confusion of counsel among even her own leaders, the cause of freedom seemed almost utterly lost. Yet it was during the gloom and terror of these same days that a new Texas rose. Out of the sacrificial heroism of the Alamo had come her battle cry, while the stark tragedy of the Goliad had filled her heart with righteous wrath that boded ill for the minions of tyranny.

While Santa Anna, held at bay by the fighters at the Alamo, was losing time and men, the Texans were uniting and strengthening their forces. The convention of which David Crockett had written in his diary, was held, and a Declaration of Independence breathing the spirit of that of 1776 was adopted. A provisional government for the new republic was organized with David Burnet as President, Lorenzo de Zavala as Vice-President, and Sam Houston as Commander-in-Chief of the Army.

It was no easy task that General Houston faced to gather and shape and equip an adequate fighting force during these dangerous days. The settlers were widely scattered, and many of them were in flight. Arms, ammunition, food and clothing were hard to obtain. With the fall of the Alamo and the Goliad, attack on Gonzales by the triumphant enemy was imminent. The best way to evade such an onslaught while the Texans were in this state of unpreparedness, Houston decided, was to withdraw from that outpost and lead his troops eastward into more favorable territory.

In late March the retreat was ordered. Gonzales was left in flames. Santa Anna would find no comfort there. It was a rather bitter thing for the Texans to give ground before their hated enemy;

but Houston was not ready to risk a battle until he felt more assured of victory; so he kept retreating week after week before the oncoming Mexicans. The trail taken by the little Texan army was filled with refugees—mainly mothers and children—on foot, on the backs of animals, in wagons and in carts—all fleeing they hardly knew where to escape from the ruthless Santa Anna.

Would General Houston never turn and strike back at the enemy? There was growing restiveness, even open resentment from the men who wanted to "give the devil his due." Yet the commander-in-chief bided his time until he led the foes of freedom into a trap. Then the righteous wrath of the Texans burst forth. With "Remember the Alamo!" "Remember Goliad!" ringing all along their charging line, these fighters for liberty struck like a thunderbolt. In twenty minutes hundreds of the enemy were killed, hundreds more taken prisoner while the remnant of the routed forces were in wild flight. The proud Presidente himself was made captive and brought before General Houston to beg for life. The battle of San Jacinto had ended in a glorious victory for the cause of liberty.

The Lone Star had really risen over the land of Tejas. Days to come might obscure it with clouds at times, but it was destined to shine on with ever-increasing luster through the years. The victory at San Jacinto was a turning-point in history and one of the decisive battles of the world. It brought a new nation into the world, and also faced the new-born republic with the serious responsibility of maintaining itself as the independent, self-governing country it had declared itself to be.

Santa Anna, held a prisoner, was compelled to make terms with the Texans. Under these he was to order cessation of hostilities and the withdrawal of the Mexican armies to the south of the Rio Grande; further he was to recommend recognition by his government of the independence of Texas. This done, he would be freed. There was an outcry from some of the Texans against liberating the Dictator on any terms; he deserved death, these vengeful ones felt, for the bloody cruelties he had heaped upon the people. General Houston, President Burnet and other leaders, however, would not blot the escutcheon of their young republic by executing the captive Presidente. They accepted his solemn promises and sent him on to Washington with General Bee for an international conference with Andrew Jackson. Afterwards he was sent in a Mexican warship back to Vera Cruz.

Meantime the people of Texas were wrestling with the serious problems that had come in the wake of their Revolution. The settlers were back in their homes, rebuilding those that had been destroyed, and planting their crops. The leaders were kept hard at work setting up orderly government and financing the new nation. Though the war had been won, there were many serious problems to be solved, many obstacles to be overcome. The situation was very similar to that which came immediately after our American Revolution with its soldier troubles, land difficulties, border fighting, and political readjustments all pressing upon the men who were guiding the young nation through the breakers into a safe harbor.

We can only glance here at the swiftly moving events crowding the years that followed the winning of the war for freedom. During an election held in September, 1836, Sam Houston was chosen president of the new Republic. Austin, though defeated by the hero of San Jacinto in this race, took the decision with magnanimity and became, at the solicitation of Houston, Secretary of State. The arduous work that came with this new position kept Austin, always rather frail, and still weakened from his imprisonment, in too close confinement. While performing with conscientious care his new duties, he was taken ill of pneumonia, and in December he passed away. In the hearts of the people he will be ever held as "The Father of Texas."

Troubles thickened right after the closing of the

year of independence. There was a great influx of
settlers. Some of ruffian caste gave the authorities
serious difficulty to hold them within bounds. The
Santa Fe expedition, authorized by the second president of Texas, Lamar, for trade and to extend to
New Mexico an invitation to join the new Republic,
ended in disaster. Reaching Santa Fe after a grueling journey, the men who made this venture were
seized by the Mexican governor of the province, and
marched away to the prisons of Mexico. Following
this came raids by Mexican soldiers on San Antonio,
which twice fell into the hands of these marauders.
These are believed to have been instigated by Santa
Anna, who was again in the presidency of Mexico.

All this stirred the fighting spirit of the Texans,
who, denied help from their government, then almost bankrupt, took matters in their own hands.
A band of them invaded Mexico and attacked the
town of Mier. Surrounded by Mexican soldiers,
these adventurous Texans suffered an even more
tragic fate than those that had gone to Santa Fe.
The forces were divided, and, by order of Santa
Anna, sixteen of the hundred and sixty men were
executed, the victims deciding which ones should
die by drawing lots. The rest of the men were
marched off to the dungeons of Mexico City.
There were Indian troubles too, along the Northern
border. Along the gulf coast also further difficul-

ties arose, the Mexicans threatening to blockade the
ports. This danger was met by providing a small
navy for the young republic. Its cost was stagger-
ing for the struggling nation; but the little war-
ships kept open the doors to the world.

The question of annexation to the United States
brought international complications. Most of the
Texans, being of American birth, wanted Texas in

the Union. Fear of an extension of slavery, however, caused Congress for a time to vote against all
measures that might have led to the annexing of
this great realm of the southwest. England also
played a diplomatic rôle in keeping Texas independent. Coveting the trade, or even the young
republic itself, this over-seas nation used her influence against permitting it to be added to the do-

main of the United States. Yet that choice borderland was finally made part of our great nation,
and the Lone Star took its rightful place in our
flag.

War with Mexico followed the ratification of
this uniting of the two sister republics in 1846. It
was a conflict of but brief duration yet it brought
far-reaching results both geographically and his-
torically. By the Treaty of Guadalupe Hidalgo,
which officially terminated the conflict, the United
States was brought up to the Sabine, and also on
westward to the Pacific Ocean, the vast provinces
of New Mexico and of Upper California being
added to the possessions of our Country. The vex-
atious problem of boundary lines between Texas
and Mexico was finally settled by that international
compact.

This did not mean however that the troubles
along the borderline were forever settled. Texas
had one thousand miles of frontier still to protect.
Marauding bands of Mexicans and of Indians and
outlaws must still be held in check. It was a task
that challenged the bravest and best of men—and
such men were found in the Texas Rangers. These
mounted scouts, playing their courageous rôle of
peace-keepers of the wilds, have won high place in
the romantic story of America's making.

The building of Texas went on through the pi-

oneer 'forties and 'fifties. Under the guidance of
Sam Houston, who consistently and persistently
held Texas to the path of her destiny, and with the
able help of other stalwarts who gave invaluable
leadership in her building through the trying years,
the great state went steadily forward. Her population increased by leaps and bounds, her farms and
ranches spread farther and wider, her commerce
added to the comforts and luxuries of the people.
There was promise of increasing prosperity in the
land of the Lone Star.

Then came the whirlwind of war which rent our
nation. Sam Houston stood firmly against secession; but he was overruled. He would not accept
the offered hand of help from Lincoln to hold his
state against the will of her people, but retired as an
old man to his home in Huntsville, while the conflict was fought out through the four long tragic
years. The flag of the Confederacy waved during
this time over the state. That war, with its aftermath of "Carpet Bag" government, gave to Texas
some of the bitterest suffering in all her history,
but her courageous people rose out of the defeat
and humiliation to new and more glorious heights.

Today the Lone Star shines again more brightly
than ever in our starry flag. The proud state it
represents stands justly proud of all its heroic past.
Its farms and orchards spread over the wide rich

valleys; its herds of pure bred cattle feed in meadows and on grassy hills. Oil wells by the thousands spout their liquid gold. Hundreds of villages, towns and cities have grown up at strategic spots along the old trails marked first by the wild animals and followed by the Indians, the hunters, and the humble priests. Some of the old missions still stand to help us recall the stories of the long ago.

The men and women who played their parts in winning freedom for Texas, and in laying the foundations of that frontier state are no longer here to tell of those long-ago days. While they lingered among us, they hardly realized that they were makers of history and weavers of romance. Nor did many of their children, or those who were privileged to know these pioneers as old neighbors and friends, appreciate the real life stories these old folk liked to tell to those who cared to listen. A rugged mountain close at hand is for most folk just a craggy pile; but viewed from a distance in the glow of sunset, it becomes a stirring picture.

Happily some among us did see the romance of reality in the lives of our nation-builders before they all had passed away. A few even had the forethought to save some of their real life stories. Sheer joy in hearing a good story, coupled with the added satisfaction that comes from sharing it with others, doubtless inspired and sustained this effort. Whatever the impelling interest, it has been of invaluable service. These true stories of the founding of our free country add concreteness to our definitions of courage, fidelity, and liberty.

We are glad to be able to present in this little volume, dedicated to the pioneers of Texas, some of their firsthand stories. They are part of a priceless heritage that belongs not only to those who live in the land of the Lone Star but to all America.

PART TWO

Pioneers Bring Back Heroic Days

CHAPTER VIII

SEÑOR GARZA RECALLS OLD TIO JUAN

THE boys and girls of the Bowie School in San
Antonio were getting a bit drowsy one warm
September afternoon when suddenly a pirate appeared right in the doorway. Something akin to an
electric shock swept through the classroom, bringing the youngsters up in their seats and causing
many of them to rub their eyes to make sure they
were not dreaming. There was no mistake about
it: a pirate—with a bright red sash round his head,
red velvet pantaloons, green velvet jacket, ear-
rings, silver bracelet and cutlass and pistols—
stood before them. Just what the excited young
Americans were going to say or do in this emergency was a problem until one keen-eyed boy,
recognizing his Spanish teacher in the costume, ex-

claimed, "Oh, it's Señor Garza! I know! He's going to tell us a story."

An outburst of handclapping greeted this announcement. Then the pirate doffing his hat with a bow to the teacher, said, "At your service, Señorita; at your service, *niños*. I come at the invitation of your teacher, who wishes me to turn a few pages of stirring history for you, just as old Tio Juan used to turn them for me when I was a boy."

"Who was Tio Juan?" asked one.

"A filibuster and a privateer. He was one of those who helped to open the way for Mexico and Texas to win their freedom from Spanish tyranny. I knew him as an old man. This was some years after Texas had joined the Union. My father had found Tio Juan in need, and had brought the aged patriot to our home, where he was cared for the rest of his life. One reward that came to me from this kindly deed was to get from Tio Juan, or Uncle John, some thrilling history straight from the lips of a man who had lived it."

"You called Tio Juan a patriot," spoke up one of the boys. "I thought that a filibuster was a lawless fellow, and that a privateer was just a pirate."

"A good many others have the same idea," returned Señor Garza; "but I am sure if you could have known Uncle John, you would have had this twist taken out of your history. It is true that some privateers did become real pirates, and that some filibusters did do lawless things at times; but others performed a patriotic service for our country, no matter by what names they were called— and old Tio Juan was one of these.

"I wish I could bring back to you Tio Juan's actual words and spirit. It was easy to tell that he was an educated man. Tio Juan was not Spanish, but American. He was born, I was told, in Boston. perhaps it was some of the blood of the Minute Men in his veins that made him quick to join with the Mexican patriots who were fighting for freedom."

"But how did he happen to get to Mexico?" asked one of the class.

"He ran away to sea when a boy, and sailed into many foreign ports. In 1810 he happened to land at Vera Cruz. It was just at the time when the heroic priest, Hidalgo, who felt keenly the sufferings of the Mexican people under their tyrant Spanish leaders, sounded the *grito*—or call to fight for freedom. Tio Juan caught the cry from one of Hidalgo's leaders—Bernardo Gutierrez—and joined the cause of liberty. Shortly afterwards, when Hidalgo fell a victim to treachery and was slain, Gutierrez and Delgado, two of his commanders, made their escape into Texas where they hoped to raise reinforcements to carry on the struggle. Delgado was captured by Spanish Royalists and killed. His head, put on the end of a pole, was set high in front of the Alamo as a warning to those who defied the Spanish authority. Gutierrez and Tio Juan barely escaped with their lives into the Neutral Strip that lay between Texas and Louisana.

"It was in this 'No-man's Land'—the rendezvous of adventurous spirits—that Gutierrez met another young American—Lieutenant Magee—whom he won to the cause. Together they organized the Republican Army of the North—a band of about fifteen hundred men—gathered from not only Mexican and Texan exiles, but also from Louisiana, Tennessee, Kentucky, and other states. Tio Juan, who, after saving his head from the wrath of the Spanish, had gone on to New Orleans, heard of the new army and hastened to enlist with the fighters for freedom.

"As the band of crusaders marched across the border into Texas, Colonel Gutierrez issued a stirring call to bring others to his standard. Old Tio Juan would often recite this appeal, and he had me learn it by heart. Here is one part of it I still remember:

"'Soldiers and citizens! It is more than a year since I left my country. I have overcome many difficulties and have made many friends to aid us in throwing off the insulting yoke of the insolent despots of Spain. Rise en masse, soldiers and citizens! Unite in the holy cause of our country. Many of

our friends have been unjustly slain by the sword of the
tyrant. Their blood cries out from the grave for vengeance.

"'I am marching now to your succor, with a respectable*
force of American volunteers who have left their homes to
take up our cause. They are descendants of men who fought
for the independence of the United States. They feel the
force and worth of Liberty as did their fathers in the war with
Great Britain. As brothers and inhabitants of the same con-
tinent, they have drawn their swords in the defense of the
cause of humanity.'

"Americans and others who responded to such an
appeal as this might be called filibusters; but they
certainly had the blood of true patriotism in them.
They were ready to fight and die to free a people
from tyranny. Old Tio Juan's eyes would always
light up when he heard these stirring words. And
when he told of the struggles and tragedies he became a young man again in spirit. He had a fine
sense of humor too—saw the funny side of things as
well as the serious.

"I can hear him yet telling how the little army
marched out of the Neutral Strip and across the
Sabine into Texas. Reaching Goliad, they attacked
and captured the place. Then Lieutenant Magee,
stricken with pneumonia, or 'quick consumption,'
died. Colonel Kemper was elected leader of the
Americans—about eight hundred in number. Besides these, there were nearly two hundred Mexicans under the command of Captain Menchaca,

and some four hundred Indians under Colonel Gaines.

"The little army, flushed with victory, struck on for San Antonio. A fierce attack and the place was captured. Governor Salcedo, Governor Cordero, and other Royalist leaders were taken prisoners by the Republican Army.

"I'll try to tell old Tio Juan's story in his own words, just as he used to tell it to me:

"We were riding high, now, and we might have kept on gaining victories but for a tragic mistake that was made."

"What was that?"

"These Spanish leaders were brave men and of fine education but revenge was a part of their code and they reaped the consequences.

"You see we had in our forces young Delgado, son of the man whose head had been stuck up on that pole in front of the Alamo. Well, when he saw that gruesome sight, naturally his blood boiled. I heard him and Gutierrez swear revenge when we passed that spot. And I sympathized with him deeply. The head of Gutierrez and my own head came near being there too; but for all that I wasn't ready to do what these Mexican leaders did.

"I was suspicious that something tragic was in their minds when Gutierrez suggested that the prisoners be sent to New Orleans in charge of Captain Delgado. Menchaca objected to the proposition; he wanted the Americans to guard the captured Spaniards. The Americans, not suspecting anything wrong, let Gutierrez have his way, and the two governors with about ten others were marched to their death. About a mile out of San Antonio, the prisoners were killed. It was an 'eye for an eye and a tooth for a tooth'—the motto in those days among the Mexicans and Spaniards. Young Delgado had avenged his father's death.

"What shocked us Americans was the breaking of our word with prisoners of war. They had been treacherously executed. Some of the Mexican leaders in our forces felt outraged as we did and even defied Delgado and branded his deed as inhuman, and one that would make the Americans desert the cause. Captain Menchaca had warned against trusting the prisoners in Delgado's hands. But the evil deed was done and evil days for us followed it.

"Captain Delgado, brought to trial by the Americans, made an impassioned defense:

"'My father was killed by Governor Salcedo, and not content, he set his head on a pole. You saw the hideous sight. Can I forget it? Your leader, Gutierrez, would have shared the same fate if he had been found. They fought under Hidalgo. We may yet share a similar fate. I beg you not to *blame Gutierrez. These men were a scourge to my race and my country. Why spare them?*

"'The Americans are my comrades-in-arms, but would you have let the traitors go? Why? To return and cut our throats. Your decree for them was perpetual exile, you remember.

"'It is true that Gutierrez turned the prisoners over to me for safe escort. We took them from the Alamo. I pointed to my father's head as Salcedo mounted his horse. We rode silently as far as where the San Pedro flows into the San Antonio River. We tied each prisoner to a tree, and then cut their throats.

"'I told Salcedo, "You sent my father to eternity without the consolation of religion and I do the same to you."

"'I seek not clemency by saying, I acted under orders. Spaniards set this rule of death for all prisoners. Read the history of my people in Mexico. If any American here has reproof, let him arise.'

"Delgado and Gutierrez were acquitted, but the Americans left the army in disgust. Many returned to the United States. It was their way of giving reproof to the Mexican leaders who had betrayed a trust. The Spanish code of honor was not the American code.

"I left with the other Americans but soon returned. Texas had a fascination for me. I joined another filibustering expedition under Perry, and we whipped the Spanish under Elizondo. The victory went to our heads.

"Don Jose Toledo, a Spaniard, was then elected

as head of our army. He was Republican in sympathy, had helped Magee with money and supplies; but the Mexicans wanted no full-blooded Spaniard as their leader. In spite of the feeling, our army was ordered to march to an attack on the Royalists. We struck the enemy at Medina. The Spaniards fired and ran with our men right after them.

"Suddenly we found ourselves in an ambush. Toledo ordered a retreat, but it was too late. The Spanish cavalry were right on top of us. Our men were thrown into a panic, and only ninety-three Americans escaped.

"About eighty prisoners were taken. A great pit was dug and logs placed across. The captives were tied onto these and shot. Captain Delgado was the first victim. Toledo was wounded, in the fray, but he managed somehow to escape and to make his way to Louisiana. While the fighting was going on I was wounded and fell into the Medina River. As I came up I grabbed the branch of an oak tree that was hanging over the stream, and worked my way up into the branches. There I lay watching the Spaniards kill Captain Delgado and the rest of the captives. That terrible experience made my hair turn white. In my sleep I still dream of Colonel Delgado's head in front of the Alamo and see his son falling into that pit.

"That night I wandered round in the darkness

half crazy with my wounds and the terror of it all. I don't know how I came to escape being seen by the bloodthirsty Spaniards; but I managed somehow to get to the jacal of a poor Mexican mother and she hid me in her home and took care of me until I was well enough to get out of that dangerous region. Then, disguised in the dress of a Mexican woman, I made my way to the coast of Texas."

"The Mexican women," said Señor Garza, "were full of sympathy for one in distress. Most of those in Texas were loyal to the cause of liberty. When the Spanish leaders found this out, they tortured these poor women terribly. In San Antonio Arrendondo imprisoned five hundred of them in the Quinta, an old adobe house and garden. He made them grind corn for his army until their hands bled. As a boy I often heard the story from the old Mexican mothers who had suffered this torturing experience. A priest warned Arrendondo to desist or the women would kill him. The other tyrant leader of the Spanish forces, Elizondo, was shot down by a Mexican lieutenant who went insane over the terrible cruelty that the tyrant meted out to the mothers and children. The patriots were crushed for the time under the iron heel of Spanish tyranny.

"Tio Juan used to say that the tyrant Arrendondo's

report of the battles of the Medina was full of praise for Arrendondo. He did ask some rewards for some of his officers who helped him in his fighting and his cruelty. One of these was Cadet Don Antonio Santa Anna, the future dictator of Mexico."

"What happened to Tio Juan, after his escape?" one of the pupils asked the story-teller.

"I think I can answer that question best by again letting the old man tell the story as nearly as I can in his own words:

"When I got down to the coast I lived by fishing and hunting. One of the poor settlers there would lend me his gun, and I divided the game I got with him and his family. After a while a trading boat came by and I worked my way in it along the shores until at last I reached New Orleans. There I came in contact with some of Jean Lafitte's band of privateers. Many folk thought that Lafitte was just a pirate, but he wasn't; he was a real patriot and what he did for the American cause proves it. Even 'Old Hickory' turned to let Lafitte help him fight the British in the battle of New Orleans.

"One thing that Lafitte carried in his heart was an undying hatred of the Spanish. What had happened to cause this I do not know. He would never talk of his life. There was a story among the men that Lafitte had married a beautiful woman. At one time he set sail with her on one of his richly laden vessels for France. The ship was captured by a Spanish man-of-war; and Lafitte with his wife was left on a barren sand bar. An American schooner, so the story went, rescued them, but Lafitte's wife died from the effects of this inhuman treatment. How much truth there was in this tale no one knows; but it is certain that Jean Lafitte hated the Spanish to the end of his days, and was ever grateful to America.

"It is my private notion that one thing that kept this French leader fighting the Spaniards through the years was his loyalty to Napoleon. There was no doubt of his devotion to 'The Little Corporal'; he even wore a hat like Napoleon's. He gave his means to help the cause of the French Emperor; and he was never the same man after the downfall of the great leader. Some say that Lafitte was a relative of Napoleon.

"He hated the British for bringing about the defeat and imprisonment of Napoleon. That and his love for America made him spurn the bribe the British officers made to him when, flushed with their victory at Waterloo, they landed their troops for the attack on New Orleans. Lafitte would have nothing to do with them; instead he proffered his services to General Jackson.

"Jackson was a bit haughty at first about accepting help from our chief. You see, he had got into his head that Lafitte was a pirate; but he soon came down off his high horse and took our powder and bullets and us privateers to help him trounce the British."

" 'Didn't we do it though?' old Tio Juan used to say with glee. 'Why, boy, we rode alligators through the bayous to get a shot at the Redcoats.' "

"Oh, what a yarn!" broke out the listening youngsters.

"Yes, it was a great yarn," responded Señor Garza; "but old Tio Juan was entitled to his fun. He had certainly gone through enough in his fighting during the years for the liberty of Mexico and Texas and our America.

"After the War of 1812, Tio Juan kept on with the privateers—helping settle old scores with the Spanish. When the cause of the heroic Hidalgo was won, and Mexico was a free nation, the old privateer drifted back into his beloved Texas to help Austin with his colony. Again he met my grandfather. They had fought for freedom together. He came to our home when I was a child, so that I grew up on Uncle John's stories."

"Did he wear that pirate suit you have on?" asked one of the girls.

"No; Tio Juan was never one who liked gaudy costumes. He did have a green velvet jacket like this one. It was the kind, he said, that Lafitte wore. This very bracelet, too, was one that Tio Juan wore; and this cutlass was one that he carried."

"My!" exclaimed a wide-eyed boy. "I wonder if he ever killed any one with it!"

"Well, really, I do not know. Uncle John never boasted about his exploits as a fighter. He always talked of the bravery of others rather than of his own."

CHAPTER IX

OLD RECORDS YIELD ROMANCE AND ADVENTURE

THADDEUS SMITH, white-haired clerk of the County of Bexar in Texas, one day was thumbing through a time-worn record book in the archives over which he had charge, when his eye caught a marriage entry that held his interest. It was that of James Bowie, one of the heroic leaders who died at the Alamo, and Ursula de Veramendi, daughter of the Lieutenant Governor of the Province of Texas. The simple record touched off a train of memories in the old man's mind.

Thaddeus was not merely a county clerk, but a keeper of human records. Practically all his days had been spent in historic San Antonio. His parents were pioneers in the Lone Star Land. By inheritance and by his daily work he had been brought into intimate acquaintance with nearly every family—Spanish, Mexican, American—that had ever lived in the town. He spoke Spanish, French and German and for years and years he had recorded in his careful penmanship their marriages, births, deaths, deeds and wills. These official entries meant for him, however, not merely names and dates, but stories out of real life. And here was one recorded long before his time, that was vibrant with romance.

An adventurous American had won the heart and hand of a beautiful señorita of one of the first Spanish families to come to the land of Tejas. Thoughts of their courtship brought pictures of dark eyes through latticed windows, music of the guitar, a pretty fan, old lace, and moonlight streaming down through the flowering trees and vines of the patio. As to the wedding, a well-penned, stately record of the ceremony may still be seen in the "Second Book of Marriages" of the old San Fernando Cathedral in San Antonio. Translated from Spanish into English it reads:

In the City of San Fernando de Bexar * on the 25th day of April 1831, I the priest Don Refugio de la Garza, pastor of this city, having performed the investigations prescribed by the Canon Law, published the banns on three consecutive feast days—"Inter Missarum Solemnia," during the high mass to

* Old name of San Antonio.

wit, on the 11th, 17th, and24th of said month, and having found no canonical impediment, even after the lapse of 24 hours from the last publication of the banns, I married and blessed at the nuptial mass—"In Facie Ecclesiae"—publicly in the church, Don Santiago Bowie, a native of Louisiana of North America, legitimate son of Raymond Bowie and Albina Yons, and Miss Ursula de Veramendi, legitimate daughter of Don Juan Martin de Veramendi and Doña Josefa Navarro. Their parents stood as sponsors and Don Jose Angel Navarro and Don Juan Francisco as witnesses. In witness whereof I have hereunto affixed my signature.

REFUGIO DE LA GARZA

Pictures of the wedding festivities in the grace and elegance of the Veramendi mansion came to the mind of the old clerk as he perused the record. From boyhood he had known of the Veramendis, the Navarros, and other families of "old San Antonio" who had brought Spanish culture to this frontier land in long ago days. Descendants of these first families had been his playmates and schoolmates. It was rather easy for him, therefore, to recreate that joyous wedding day.

As for James Bowie, he had been one of the first heroes in the memory of Thad Smith. Often during his schooldays, Thaddeus and his companions had whittled out wooden "Bowie knives" and used them to fight imaginary Indians and to reënact stirring scenes from Texas history. He knew by heart the story of Bowie at the Alamo.

"We boys used to play round the place," he said. "Sometimes we would go and look into the old tunnel there, which, according to legend, was a secret passage through which the priests and the people could get into and out of the old Mission. But we never dared to penetrate too far in this passage; we were afraid of a cave-in, or of the rats that infested the tunnel. You see," he added, "we were just plain boys, not heroes."

Mr. Smith's interest in the story of Bowie stirred him to search for other facts about this hero's life. He dug further into the old records, and he gathered from oldtimers more of the story. The quest led him back into the times of the Revolutionary War and on into the days when members of the Bowie family joined Texas in her fight for freedom.

The youngsters and patrons of the Bowie school had a glad welcome for the county clerk when he was introduced to them one colorful October day. In presenting him, the teacher had said that Thaddeus Smith was "a walking volume of true history. He can tell you all about the hero after whom our school was named," she concluded.

Responding with a smile to this introduction and to the applause of the pupils, the old clerk began in a gentle voice:

"Yes, I know most of you and your fathers, and

BOWIE MEETS HIS SPANISH SENORITA

some of your grandfathers. You see, I have been a keeper of our county records for years, and there are many interesting stories hidden in these records. They can be found if one knows just how to hunt for them."

"Do the records tell the story of Bowie?" asked a pupil.

"Not exactly, my boy," was the reply; "these records are generally very brief, you know—a line or two of names and dates and other facts. So it is with those about Bowie; his marriage with Ursula Veramendi is recorded briefly there. Think though what a charming story must be hidden between those lines. Then there are other entries telling about Bowie's land transactions. Perhaps these hold interesting stories too. Bowie, we feel sure, was a young man who had ambitions to become wealthy and influential. Had he lived longer he might have realized these dreams. At any rate he did win undying fame for himself and his family by his heroism at the Alamo.

"This was but adding to the honors his father had won, fighting for our freedom in the War for Independence. Wounded in one of the battles of the Revolution, Raymond had been nursed back to health by a Southern belle. A pretty romance and a wedding were the sequel to this experience. In time James Bowie was born.

"The old marriage record in the cathedral has it that he was a native of Louisiana. This is hardly correct. James Bowie was born in Maryland. He did spend part of his life in Arkansas and later in Louisiana, where his father had a large estate. By this time there were a number of children in the family. Three of the brothers—John, Rezine, and James—finally came to Texas.

"Rezine Bowie, not James, was the inventor of the 'Bowie knife.' This noted weapon came out of the necessities of pioneer days for a strong knife that would serve all-round service in camp, on the hunt, and in hand-to-hand fighting. It became a popular companion of the rifle and has carried the Bowie name through the years. Because of this knife which connected with their name, it was commonly thought that the Bowie boys were bold and quarrelsome. This is far from the truth. The Bowies used their knives, outside of everyday needs of pioneer life, only when they were fighting for what they deemed was a righteous cause. Rezine Bowie, the inventor, after indirectly helping Texas to win her freedom, fell fighting at the battle of Monterey in the Mexican War. The Indians called Rezine Bowie, 'Little-man-hold-on-your-heart.' Perhaps they gave him that name because they feared him and his famous knife.

"Though James Bowie grew up on the frontier,

he was gracious in his manners. As a boy he had been given the best of schooling the days afforded; and he was reared in a home of culture. The family shield bore this motto, 'What not, for God and Country?' Bowie was tall, with light complexion and keen gray eyes—quite in contrast to the dark-eyed señorita whose heart he had won; but love seems to delight in contrasts.

"Just when Bowie first came to Texas is not certain. It was some time around 1820, however, that he is first heard of in that region. About that time it is said he ventured there with some slaves. Later he took part in the filibustering expedition under Dr. Long. It was during this struggle on the part of Americans to win back Texas, which they felt had been unjustly relinquished by our country to Mexico in the settlement of boundary lines, that Long was captured and killed. Bowie was also taken prisoner and held for a time in a Mexican dungeon. How he finally escaped we do not know.

"In 1830, the American adventurer was again in Texas. There he met Veramendi, the newly appointed Lieutenant Governor, and his family. Soon after this James and Ursula were married. In time two children were born to them. Then came a tragic ending to their happiness. They went to Monclara, Mexico, to visit relatives. An epidemic of cholera broke out. The lovely young wife and both their children were stricken and died. Bowie, broken-hearted, seemed almost to court death after this bereavement. He threw himself into dangers with little thought of consequence to himself.

"One thing that was engaging his attention at this time was the famous San Saba silver mine. Legend had it that somewhere there in Western Texas was to be found a body of fabulously rich ore, and Bowie had determined to find it. Even before his beloved wife was taken from him, he had made two trips to try to discover the mine. When she had passed away, he bent all his efforts to make this venture successful, organizing a well-equipped force of men to assist him in the enterprise.

"Back of this story of the silver mine lies some intriguing history. Coronado in searching for the famous Seven Cities of Cibola, had explored the San Saba Valley. Later, it is said, Spaniards had discovered rich silver ore there and had opened what they called 'La Mina de la Amalgres.' In 1756 a mission with a presidio was established in the valley—both for the purpose of converting the wild Apaches, and as an outpost against the French. The Apaches had welcomed the Spaniards in this region, not for any interest in the religion the priests brought, but because the white men made strong allies for them against the roving Comanches. The Apaches did so much boasting, indeed, about their new friends, that the rival tribe, angered about it, gathered their forces, and struck, two thousand strong, to rid themselves of this coalition. All but one priest and two soldiers fell in the fight. These, in badly wounded condition, managed to survive to tell the tragic tale. The Apaches gave no help to their white friends, but fled to the sheltering mountains. The mission, a wooden structure, was burned to the ground.

"A force of five hundred soldiers under the command of Parillo was dispatched to punish the murderous Comanches. In keeping with their policy, the Spaniards tried to stir up inter-tribal warfare to kill off the Indians the self-sacrificing friars had failed to bring into the fold of the Master. The attempt was fruitless. The mission, however, was rebuilt—this time of stone; but even this fortress was taken by treachery. The Comanches, pretending they wanted to attend mass, were permitted to get inside the mission stronghold. Suddenly they drew the knives they had concealed, fell upon the soldiers, priests and the few followers. Children were taken captive, and some of these in after years told the terrible story. After the massacre, the savages set fire to the buildings, but the stone withstood the flames. In later days, the pioneers in the San Saba Valley made use of some of these stones in building their houses. Part of the ruins of the old mission still stand, however, as a mute witness to the blood of martyrs."

"What about the silver mine?" asked one of the class.

"There is so much legend about the mine that it is difficult to get at the truth of the story. Some folk say that the Comanches made their attack on the mission to get back possession of the rich mine. For years, so the story goes, these Indians had used the ore from this mine to get silver for the making of their bracelets and other silver ornaments, with which they decked themselves, and their bridles and saddles. There may be little or no truth in the tale. This we do know: that the stories that have sprung up around Bowie's mine are as numerous and various as those about the hidden treasure of Captain Kidd.

"Whatever the truth in any of these legends of the lost silver mine of the San Saba, we may be sure of one thing: Bowie did make an earnest attempt to find it. Some folk say he wanted the treasure to help Texas win her freedom; that is probably just the thought of one who admired the man who gave his all for liberty. Anyway we do have record of Bowie's expedition into this country, his fierce fight with an overwhelming force of Indians, and the astounding victory he and his little band won over the horde of redskins.

"The background of that fight lies in another Indian story. Bowie felt certain the Indians had knowledge of the mine he wanted. The tale was that after the second massacre at the San Saba Mission, the Comanches, in order to hide the mine, had filled it up and kept the secret of the place of this fabulous wealth to themselves."

"Do you think that the mine is still there?" asked one of the eager boys.

"Well, I do not know," returned the old clerk; "and no one else knows. Many Texans believe there never was such a mine; others have searched and searched in vain for it. I believe that the mine exists, for the old Spanish records tell of a rich mine near San Saba, and reports were made that rich silver ore was sent on the backs of burros from there to Mexico City. Bowie surely believed the mine was there, else he would not have risked his life to find it.

"The story goes that he got the secret of the mine from the old Lipan chief, Xolic. This aged Indian leader had broken his leg somewhere in the wilds; Bowie found the chief and nursed him until his injured leg was well. Afterwards it is said that Xolic brought his tribe to San Antonio and camped for a time at San Pedro Springs. Here, in gratitude for what Bowie had done, the Indians made him a member of the tribe. There was great Indian pomp and ceremony.

"Shortly after this adoption, Bowie accompanied the tribe to the San Saba Valley. His skill in shooting made him most helpful to the Indians in their buffalo hunting and in their battles with the Comanches. When Bowie had thus gained the complete confidence of his red brothers, Xolic, after swearing the white tribesman to secrecy, revealed to him the location of the Lost Mine.

"Unfortunately for the plans of Bowie, Xolic died, and Tremanos, an inveterate enemy of the whites, became chief of the Lipans. Knowing that Bowie had the secret, Tremanos plotted to kill him. Discovering the plot, Bowie felt that he was absolved from his oath of secrecy. Then, despite all the dangers he must face, Bowie gathered his forces to win the wealth hidden in the fabulous mine.

"Thirty-four white men and five Mexicans enlisted at the outset for the venture. All but eleven of these, however, backed out. Nothing daunted, Bowie went on with his reduced band, and a negro servant, who later played a brave part for his master. The little party was well-armed and had ample supplies for the expedition. Each man rode a fine horse and each had two heavily laden pack mules. Out of old San Antonio they rode full of confidence.

"Near the site of the present Mason City, one camp was made with some friendly Indians. These redmen warned Bowie that Tremanos with two hundred braves was on the warpath looking for him. The hostiles had boasted that they would get Jim Bowie if they had to capture and sack San Antonio to do it. His red friends begged the white adventurer to turn back, but Bowie went on towards San Saba. Within a few miles of the place they caught sight of Tremanos and his warriors. The white men changed their course, and under the cover of darkness stole three or four miles away to a creek. Here they camped in the timber for better protection in the fight they knew was coming.

"The next morning Bowie, on guard, saw the Lipan chief and his men approaching the camp. Rezine Bowie, who was with his brother, tried to appease Tremanos, but to no avail. The Indians opened fire, and Buchanan, one of the white band, was shot in the leg. Rezine rescued his comrade, and then dashed into the fray. The fight was on— eleven whites against more than one hundred and fifty Indians. Tremanos was among the first to

[167]

fall victim to the unerring aim of the frontiersmen. Another chieftain took the place of the
fallen leader. Charley, the negro servant, kept
loading guns for his master, and the Indians kept on
falling one after another. Another white man,
Doyle, was wounded, and one by the name of Mc-
Caslin was killed. The redmen paid so dearly for
these casualties that finally they drew back. Then
the redskins attempted by circling the camp to get
at the band of white fighters from the rear. Bowie
ordered his men back into the timber, and from the
vantage points there they kept up their firing at
the redskins. Each time a shot was fired the
frontiersman would jump way from his place.
The Indians became so puzzled as to where the bullets were coming from that they finally set fire to
the grass and carried their dead and wounded away
under cover of the smoke.

"While the fire was raging, Bowie and his men
threw up a kind of breastworks to help them ward
off another attack. Charley, the negro, attending
to the wounded, kept running through the fire to
the stream for water. The flames finally got so
close that the men did not dare to open their powder flasks. It began to look like a 'last call' for
them. Behind the rude fortress a council was held.
The suggestion came that they make a break

and every man fight it out for himself; but the wounded were there and the decision was to protect them at all costs. The men turned to strengthening their breastworks with dirt dug up with their bowie knives.

"As the flames died down the battle began again. It went on fiercely until night came. Then the Indians, cut down to about one-third of their original number by death and wounds, gave up the struggle. The white men slipped away in the darkness bearing their wounded companions on with them to San Antonio. They had not found the lost silver mine, but they had proved themselves fighters of the finest brand.

"The days were near when these same men would show their mettle again in the battles for the freedom of Texas. Some of them followed old Ben Milam when he led on to the capture of San Antonio. Some of them died fighting by the side of James Bowie at the Alamo. Rezine Bowie fought on through until Texas had gained her liberty and then played the hero's part in the fight at Monterey where he lost his life.

"The death of James Bowie at the Alamo closes the story of the 'Lost Mine.' He was the only white man, it is said, that knew the secret. The fierce Indian fight would not have deterred him from finding that mine; he was gathering new forces to carry through his plans when the war for the freedom of Texas broke out. Into this war he plunged with his splendid force, and dying for liberty, won undying fame."

CHAPTER X

AMERICAN PIONEERS SETTLE IN TEXAS LAND

DREAMS of a new home with broad acres of rich, virgin soil were the lure that brought most Americans into old Texas," remarked the pioneer minister. "It was the same impulse that had sent thousands upon thousands of them across the Alleghanies to the conquest of the woodlands and prairies of the Northwest Territory. The purchase of Louisiana lured a host of them into that new domain; and many of these later crossed the Spanish border to become pioneers in the land of the Lone Star. These youthful, adventurous spirits hailed from every one of the thirteen colonies and from all the other states and territories then in our country."

It was Dean Richardson, one of the spiritual leaders of San Antonio, who was giving his reminiscences to a group of friends round his fireside.

"My father," the Dean continued, "was born in Mount Desert, Maine. He was one of the many Easterners who joined Stephen Austin in his colonization venture. Stephen, you remember, was carrying on the work of his brave, far-seeing sire, Moses Austin, a native of old Connecticut, who had opened the way for Americans to settle in the great Southwest.

"I've often wondered," mused the old minister, "why these fine men and women, who were well established in good homes, with comforts and some luxuries, with schools and churches, would suddenly cut loose and strike out into far-away, untamed regions to begin building all over again. The Lord surely had something to do with it; for the inborn instinct that impels folk to seek new adventures and new experiences has doubtless been the main driving force that has extended our Land of Freedom 'from sea to shining sea.' Our pioneers, strong in body, with clear heads and pure hearts, carried forward the American frontiers, adding new stars to our flag, and developing not only the country they settled, but something far more precious—the American character.

"As I recall some of the struggles of my own father and mother," the Dean went on, "I marvel at the courage and cheer with which they took the grinding toil and the difficulties and dangers that came with pioneering this borderland. Just their unswerving faith in God gave them such fortitude. And the thing that helped to leaven their lives through all the pioneer hardships was the talents and culture they brought with them.

"The too common notion that our American pioneers were an uncouth folk needs correcting," the old philospher continued. "Simply because our early settlers had to wear homespun and buckskin, and live in rude cabins, is no reason for one to think of them as uneducated and uncultured. Of course there were some such untutored folk among them —and some even who were of the desperate and wicked type; but such characters were few in number. The majority of our pioneers were honest, hard-working, God-fearing folk. Remember, some of the brightest and wisest of our leaders have come out of such conditions.

"Education and culture—a love of books and music, the drama and art—could be easily carried even in flatboats and covered wagons. The pioneers of our country took an ample supply of these best things of life along with them into the conquest of new lands. Many of the first cabins were not only homes but places of entertainment, of education, of worship. There were no public schools for some years in Texas; the Mexican government would not establish them; and it would have none but Catholic churches."

"Won't you tell us, Dean Richardson," said one

of the listeners, "something more about your father's experiences as a pioneer in Texas?"

"I was coming to that," was the response, "but you know we preachers have to sermonize a little—just natural for us. The experiences of my father," he went on, "were typical of most of the Austin colonists—a series of ups and downs. He was never a man to do much talking about his own exploits; so I have not so much directly from him to tell; but I did gather some incidents of his life; and what mother and others have told me of those old days, together with a little I have lived through myself, may help me to give you something of a concrete picture of the days of the Austin colony as my parents lived through them.

"Austin as a colonizer, or 'empresario'—as the Mexicans called him—by 1821 had brought three hundred families into the wide region granted him by the Mexican government. This was only the vanguard of the fifteen hundred families he could under his contract bring into his colony. Father was one of this vanguard. He was closely associated with Austin; and he knew other empresarios—Burnet of New Jersey, Ben Milam, the veteran of the war of 1812—and several other Americans who like Austin had contracted with the Mexican government to establish colonies in Texas.

"When these pioneers came, the country was wild. Indians of all sorts were around them—the clam-eaters along the coast and then those that had been more or less converted to Christianity by the faithful mission fathers. Besides these there were Lipans, Comanches, Apaches and others that roved the plains and sometimes raided the settlements to kill and steal. The colonists often suffered loss of their much-needed cattle and horses, and at times even of their friends and loved ones, at the hands of these red raiders.

"Mexico was not simply generous in her desire to have Americans settle in Texas. The Mexican leaders knew full well that the American colonists would help hold the warlike Indians in check, as indeed they did. Forts were built by the pioneers; and their men were soon trained to hold their own with the redskins.

"Fear of the Indians kept the first settlers from any extensive farming. Only a few acres close to the towns and forts were brought under cultivation. Austin of course encouraged his followers to extend this fruitful acreage, and he even tried to get the friendly Indians to raise crops. Father used to tell us how the empresario once gave to Chief Carita a supply of seed corn for his tribe to plant. The chief straightway had the squaws grind the corn and make bread of it. He told Austin afterwards, 'Great Spirit heap good.'

"Scarcity of farm foods made the settlers turn to hunting to round out their supplies. Happily for them the country at that time was full of game. Wild turkeys, geese, ducks and other fowl were plentiful. The woods abounded in deer; and on the plains were buffaloes. In the streams, the lakes and the gulf were fish of all kinds. The pioneers were not strangers to the art of hunting and fishing; many of them were adept with the Kentucky rifle. The Indians too were helpful in teaching the younger white boys new tricks at getting fish and game.

"One way we learned to hunt was by 'shining the eyes.' The hunter would attract the wary animals by a torch placed on his head. As the deer gazed with wide-open, shiny eyes, the fatal shot could be fired."

"Would you call that fair sport, Dean Richardson?" asked some one.

"No, it was very unfair, but you must remember that a hungry family was waiting at home. It wasn't good sportsmanship as we think of such things today; but in those earlier days getting food was a matter of life or death. To bring home the game was the thing that mattered; and we usually brought it.

"There was not quite so much suffering in our colony as in others. Those who came with Austin were generally better supplied with a good start in foodstuffs, seeds, clothing, tools and weapons than were some of the other groups of settlers. One pioneer of those days told me that in his settlement the folk went for half a year at one time with no corn or flour at all. Sometimes about all the settlers could do was to tighten their belts, huddle in the forts and live on in a half-starved state until better days came—as they usually did. The Lord didn't forget those hard-working, God-fearing folk, even though He did put them to some severe tests at times to try their mettle.

"The pioneer homes were built at first of logs or clapboards. Usually they were of two large rooms with a broad passageway roofed over between the rooms. This passage served as a kind of sitting room in pleasant weather. It was made rather picturesque with skins hanging on the side walls, firearms, and rough home-made furniture. In the other rooms there was often better furniture which had been brought from the States. I remember we had several pieces of old mahogany—heirlooms from my mother's family. Besides she had some silver that was the pride of her heart. I still cherish one of the spoons that was made in Boston in 1785. Perhaps Paul Revere designed some of this silver;

he was a silversmith, you know, when he made his famous ride. At any rate the silver I possess is a relic that has a real story in it whether it links with this noted 'Son of Liberty' or not.

"Pioneer homes in the beginning had few decorations. Mother, who made an art of weaving, had created some pretty drapings for the windows of our home. We had no door except one heavy affair at the front entrance. Our bedding was also mainly homespun made by mother and her negro helper.

"Clothing was of various kinds and patterns. A gentleman 'held back' his best suit, shirt and stock for rare occasions. The men often wore leather breeches and leather jackets. These were fringed in great style. A man could be quite a 'dandy' when dressed up in clean, artistically trimmed leather. It was a sensible and durable outfit. A few had 'store clothes' left from their life in the states. Clothing materials were rather costly—calico selling as high as seventy-five cents per yard, and other cloths in proportion.

"My mother had two calico dresses of the 'Dolly Varden' style. This means, as you may know, prints, or calico with sprays of flowers on it. Mother's flowers were pink. I thought her the prettiest lady in the land in these 'Dolly Varden' frocks.

"Mother used to tell me that the settlers hired some of the tame Indians at first to do their hunting. It saved time and powder—and probably gave greater assurance of getting the game. The pioneers came to be much attached to their hunters; and often the white boys would go into the woods with these keen-eyed redmen. In this way the youngsters were taught much Indian lore and secrets of the chase that helped them in many ways afterwards.

"I remember no scarcity of food in our home. We had plenty of fish, fowl, and venison. Our bread was generally not so varied, however. It consisted for the most part of just 'hoe-cakes.' Such cakes were a compound of cornmeal, water, and a pinch of salt. They were cooked on the griddle or in the ashes. They were delicious with wild honey. Bacon, beef, eggs, milk, and sometimes butter helped to enrich our larder. Later we got sorghum from the cane fields of Louisiana to help sweeten things up a bit. There were wild fruits and nuts too, that were gathered from the woods. Oh, it wasn't so bad as I remember it. My boy appetite helped always to make it taste good. I never could make the molasses and the hoe-cake come out even.

"The pioneers had many good times despite all the hardships. It was recreation they created for themselves; but that is the best kind after all. Now and then there was a dance of the old-fashioned sort. The Virginia reel and the 'square dance,' or plain quadrille, with all its variations, gave everybody good fun. Young and old mingled in the pastime—shuffling and double shuffling, promenading, and swinging their partners to the tune of the lively fiddle. Picnic parties and socials, home dramatics, barbecues—all added to our enjoyment. When the men were away at their work, the women had their quilting bees. All of it was recreation of a hearty and happy sort.

"Once in a while we were given another kind of excitement. Father used to tell us how in 1823 word came that the Indians were going to raid the settlements. A man named Dewees was dispatched like Paul Revere to warn the people. All the women and children were gathered together at San Felipe —the capital of Austin's colony. They had hardly got to the place of protection when eighty redmen in warpaint and feathers appeared. They said they were Waco Indians on a foray against their enemies, the Tonkaways. However, they stayed several days at the settlement, and demanded the settlers' cattle for food. When their demand was refused, they danced some kind of war dance, and threatened the colony; but much to the relief of all, they did not make an attack. Perhaps they were afraid that the men might give them too hot a fight if they did carry out their threat. At any rate, the band finally left with no harm done except a big scare for all.

"The incident brought to father's mind an experience when he was a lad in his teens in his home town of Mount Desert, Maine. It occurred during the War of 1812. Fearing that the Britishers might attack the harbors along the coast, the leaders called meetings in the various places to organize 'Minute Men.' At one of these gatherings held in my grandfather's house, father's boyish enthusiasm impelled him to enlist. The night before he left home he dreamed that he was in a battle, and that dark-skinned men fled before the onslaught. The War of 1812 and his term of enlistment passed without his being in a single fight, except at New Orleans. Here he heard so much of Texas that he brought his family from Maine.

"They drifted slowly to the Southwest. He taught school in Shawnee Town on the Ohio for a time. Then he went down the Mississippi on a flat-boat to New Orleans, where he became a merchant. One of his customers was Lafitte. Father traded with this noted privateer both at his rendezvous on Galveston Island and later at Tampico. Things were getting prosperous with the Yankee merchant, when suddenly he met with a reversal of fortune. On his third trip back from Tampico, he was shipwrecked at the mouth of the Brazos River and lost everything he had. This misfortune came to him on Christmas Day in 1822.

"The vanguard of Austin's colonists were coming into Texas at this time. Father saw an opportunity in this venture to mend his fortunes, so he joined the band of pioneers. He turned again to 'keeping school,' as he used to say. Certainly he did keep the boys and girls at their tasks while he was teaching. I hear that this good old word *task* is somewhat out of fashion in school these days. I hope that is not true, for studying hard helps to put backbone into boys and girls. My father was a strict teacher—one who believed that Solomon was right when he said, 'Spare the rod and spoil the child.' But for all that he was not a harsh man; he was always just and kind even if he was firm. I am glad now that he held me to the learning of my lessons. I pay tribute now and always to my parents for the good training they gave me both in home and in school.

"School teaching in those days meant so many sacrifices and such poor pay that father was obliged to turn to other ways of making a livelihood. This time he tried merchandising and stock-raising at the same time. The store failed because of too generous credit; and the stock died from drought and disease. All that father got out of this double venture was some more rich experiences.

"Evidently the people had full confidence in him; for they elected him as mayor, or alcalde, of San Felipe. The position took much time and paid him about enough to get his salt. Like some of the other ventures, its main returns were in added experience. He went on courageously, however, through all his tasks and his ups and downs; and mother stood bravely by him.

"His next enterprise was lumbering. The first mill he built was on the Chocolate Bayou about ten miles from the present town of Alvin. It was made to go by water-power, and it went. Before the mill even got started, there came a terrible storm and the whole thing, dam and all, was washed away. I don't mean to give you just 'hard luck' stories but they have to come into any true picture of pioneering.

"The sheer pluck of my father was shown by his starting right over again to build a mill. Not a board of the first one was left to give him a beginning, yet he plunged into the work; and soon the sawmill was humming away. This time he did not trust to water-power; he used patient oxen. They had to travel the treadmill he made, and the wheel had to go. Thousands of feet of lumber were supplied by this pioneer mill for the building of homes in old Texas. There was no money in the communities with which to pay for the lumber; so father took his pay in barter and in land. We couldn't eat or wear the land, so we did not feel at all rich. I still have some of the old land scripts he received for this hard work."

"Why didn't he farm the land?" came a question.

"Indians were one reason. Another was that there was no market for farm products; almost every family was producing enough for its own needs. You have heard about being 'land poor.' Well, we were certainly getting in that condition fast. Land was worth next to nothing in Texas in those days. But we managed to live along through the hard work and hard times in our simple pioneer way. We found joy too in our labors. There were no serious troubles to vex our souls—at least until the war with Mexico broke out—and then we had some real trouble on our hands. But that brings us to another—and a more thrilling part of our story."

CHAPTER XI

THE TEXANS TAKE SAN ANTONIO

WHAT brought the Texans into an open conflict with Mexico back in those stirring 'thirties," said Dean Richardson, "is too long and involved a story to tell at one sitting. I think, however, that I can bring you close to it all by giving you some incidents connected with my father's part in the struggle.

"It was just a clash, he used to say, between two different ideals of government—Spanish autocracy, upon which the leaders of Mexico had been brought up; and American democracy, in which the sons and daughters of the Revolution had been reared. The colonists from the United States were not long in sensing the difference once they had settled in Texas and accepted Mexican citizenship.

"Mexico had won her freedom from weakened Spain in 1821 just after Austin had launched his colonization there. Naturally the American settlers were happy to feel that they had come into a region that was no longer to be under the Spanish yoke," the Dean continued. "They were happier still when Mexico, after unseating the tyrant Iturbide, in 1824, set up a free Republic fashioned in large measure after that of the United States. What they had yet to learn to their own sorrow was that the new Mexican government was a republic in name only. Underneath all the outward forms of democracy, the old autocracy was still at work.

"Tyranny in various subtle and even open forms kept showing itself. Little if any respect was shown the new constitution by the Mexican officials. They became a law unto themselves. There was bitter resentment, particularly in Texas, not only among the thousands of Americans who had settled there, but also among many of the high-minded Spanish who had fought with Hidalgo and other patriots to free Mexico from tyranny.

"Certain things began to cause the Mexican leaders to suspect that the Americans wanted to free Texas from their domination. They were doubtless close to the truth in that suspicion; for many Americans did feel that the Louisiana boundary

should have been set along the Rio Grande. Dr.
Long with James Bowie and others had even started
a fight to put it there in the old filibustering days.
They were not successful; but the fire of their cause
kept smoldering on through the years. Tyrannical
acts, aimed mainly at curbing the American in
Texas, finally made these embers burst into flame.

"Father came into active participation with the
movement that finally resulted in freeing Texas
when he was sent as a delegate to the second convention at San Felipe de Austin," the old minister
went on. "This was in 1833—just after Santa
Anna had been elected president in Mexico. The
Texans, thinking that Santa Anna was going to
right some of the wrongs that they had suffered
in the previous years of injustice and misrule, had
supported his candidacy; but they soon found him
a greater tyrant than his predecessors. He even followed the example of King George the Third by
sending an army into the Texas colonies to enforce
his will.

"The Texans met this challenge to their liberties
by calling this second convention of their repre-
sentatives in the capital of Austin's colony: this in
face of the fact that a like convention held there the
year before had been branded as treasonable by the
Mexican leaders. Austin had been advised by these
officials to take no part in this second convention;

but he replied, 'Texas is lost if she does nothing for herself. I must follow the dictates of my conscience.'

"He was there and my father was with him," said the Dean with just a touch of pride in his tone. "Sam Houston was there too; it was the first time father met this rough and ready American who had cast his lot with the Texans. Houston was made one of the committee that drew up at this time a constitution for the hoped-for state of Texas. Along with this constitution, which was adopted, a memorial was drawn petitioning the Mexican Government to repeal a decree made in 1830 that barred Americans from coming as settlers into Texas. The memorial also petitioned that Texas be created as a separate state of the Republic of Mexico. At that time it was just part of the state of Coahuila.

"Stephen Austin was chosen with two others to present this memorial to the Mexican Congress. The other members of the committee did not go, but Austin, even though he felt it unwise to press these claims at this time, took this mission upon himself at his own expense. The petition he carried was ignored, however, and Austin was seized and thrown into prison where he was kept for two long years.

"When this beloved leader did return, pale and haggard from his cruel confinement, his friends flocked round him with tears of joy in their eyes. Father with other strong men wept unashamed. Down in the hearts of all there came resolve that Texas must be freed from such tyranny. Austin had tried with all sincerity to settle things without bloodshed; but the clash of armed forces had already come. Texans were determined to carry through to victory.

"The die was cast when General Cos, brother-in-law of Santa Anna, marched with a large force of Mexicans into San Antonio," the old minister went on. "Then came a skirmish at Gonzales—the Lexington of the Texas war for freedom—and the whole land was set on fire. The Texans determined to take San Antonio from Cos; and they gathered as the Americans had done years before when they drove the British out of Boston.

"Stephen Austin, with my father as his aide, organized a little army of volunteers and struck out for San Antonio. The two had been intimate friends for years—Austin having even stood as 'best man' when father and mother were married. My elder brother remembered vividly father's kissing him good-by and starting off with this leader and friend into the war for freedom. As the little army hurried on towards San Antonio—it was joined by other colonists eager to get into the fight.

"The advance guard was ahead under Bowie and

Fannin. At the Mission Concepcion on the outskirts of San Antonio, the Texans camped. Here they had a skirmish with the Mexicans and won. One Texan named Andrews was killed in this fight. Dissension then rose between the two leaders of this advance guard. Fannin, a West Point man, knew more of military tactics, but Bowie was the more popular leader; and this brought trouble that caused Bowie finally to resign.

"About five days after this, Austin with father and their volunteers reached the scene of action. A council of war was called, at which father and Austin were present. Some of the hot-headed fellows like Bowie and Fannin wanted to attack San Antonio at once; but the majority thought it wiser to wait for more volunteers. New men were coming in every day. Deaf Smith, a famous scout, joined the ranks. He was a native of New York who had come to Austin's colony and settled in San Antonio.

"Help came also from the outside. New Orleans sent two companies of fine young fighters to our army. They were called 'The Grays.' There was a host of friends of our cause not only in Louisiana but in all the other states. Feeling that active support might be won, Austin was chosen as a commissioner to go into the United States to get such help as he could get from the people and the American government. After he had gone on this mission, Edward Burleson was chosen by the soldiers to take Austin's place as commander of the army then gathering for the attack on San Antonio.

"While the forces were assembling, not much occurred to break the monotony except the 'Grass fight,'" the old minister went on. "That gave the Texans some hearty fun, because it promised so much and yielded so little. How it happened was this: The Texans caught sight of some Mexican soldiers on the Alazan Creek with bags on their horses. Word was passed that these soldiers were loaded with money. A group of them under Bowie dashed out on their horses to capture the band. The Mexicans, dropping their bags, struck back for San Antonio on the run. They had been out cutting grass for the cavalry horses, and the bags were filled with the fresh fodder.

"What a laugh went up when the raiding party came back to camp. Anyway the Texans had sent some of the enemy flying; and my father, who took part in the skirmish, came back with a fine horse he had captured from a Mexican officer. He always said that his dream as a young soldier in Maine about being in a battle with dark-skinned men and putting them to rout came true with this 'Grass Fight.'

"The Mexicans were not all on the side of Santa Anna. Some of these folk were real Texans at heart, and these patriotic ones did brave service for the cause of liberty. While still in command at San Antonio, Austin authorized Captain Seguin to raise a volunteer company of native Mexicans 'for the defense of the Constitution and the Federal Government.' This high sounding language, which I found in one of Austin's books recording this important event, shows that up to this time the Texans were fighting not to free themselves from Mexico, but for their rights as Mexican citizens. Their 'Declaration of Independence' did not come until after the war was well under way. Here again we have a parallel to the story of our American fight for freedom.

"Captain Seguin and his Mexican boys did fine service for our cause. They kept scouring the country for horses and cattle for our army. Many of these animals were taken from the big ranches owned by Mexicans sympathetic to the Texan cause. Some of these ranchmen lost all they had for that cause. Seguin and his men also gave good help to Travis and Fannin who were kept with their companies on scout duty capturing horses, ammunition or other supplies intended for Cos and besieged forces.

"While the rest of the Texans were encamped round the old mill, my father and Valentine Bennett turned their training in the War of 1812 to account by drilling the raw Texans in the arts of soldiery. It was rather a difficult task; for every day new faces would appear in the ranks, and old ones would be missing. No lack of patriotism caused these men to leave the volunteer army. Those that did go went because of threatened danger to their families at home. Word came that the Mexicans under Santa Anna were inciting the Indians to go on the warpath; and some of the men whose wives and children or parents were in places most likely to be attacked by raiding redskins, left to give these loved ones protection.

"All the men waiting to starve Cos and his forces into a surrender, or lure him out to an open fight, began to get restive as the days dragged on. The spirit to carry the battle to the enemy grew. Burleson, feeling that Cos was strongly entrenched within the city, hesitated to risk the attack. The volunteer army grew angry at the delay. Then some prisoners that had been taken by Cos escaped. They brought word that the Mexican army was having its dissensions, and that it was not in so strongly fortified a position as had been reported.

"At this juncture Ben Milam, a veteran of the War of 1812—and one of the old fighting filibusters,—appeared on the scene. About ten years before, while fighting to overthrow the tyrant, Iturbide, Milam had been captured and thrown into a Mexican prison. When the Mexican republic was established, he got free and set up a flour mill down in Mexico. Later when Santa Anna began to play the dictator, the miller got himself jailed again by talking too much about liberty and against the new tyrant. Escaping from this second imprisonment he had made his way straight for the Texan army that had Cos bottled up in San Antonio. And here he was," the old minister went on, "ready to even up the score with tyranny. The Texans gave him hearty welcome to their ranks.

"Burleson and Milam went immediately into conference. It was not long before Ben appeared with orders to go ahead. Swinging his hat he shouted, 'Who will go with old Ben Milam into San Antonio?' A rousing cheer came from the soldiers. About three hundred of them volunteered to make the attack. My father was one of them," added the Dean proudly.

"Before daybreak on the morning of December 5, 1835, the band gathered quietly at the old mill to get Milam's orders. Two divisions were assigned to the attack—one to be led by Milam himself, the other by Frank Johnson. Another body of the Texans under Colonel Neill was to feign an attack on the Alamo as a ruse to draw the attention of the Mexicans away from the soldiers who were stealing upon the town.

"The Alamo stood at that time some distance out of the city. The men under Neill, who had dashed ahead of the main body, set up such a lively firing at the old Mission that they ran out of powder," continued the Dean. "A fellow by the name of Ingram sped half a mile to the camp of the Texans, grabbed up a keg of it, and ran back to his comrades. All the while the Mexicans were shooting, but none of their bullets touched him. This was just one of many heroic incidents that occurred during this battle of San Antonio. Our boys were ready to dare anything for their homes and liberty.

"During the excitement around the Alamo, the Americans got right into the town. Milam led his men down Acequia Street and Johnson headed with his force along Soledad. They almost reached the Veremendi house before the Mexicans opened fire with some pretty good cannon they had, and with their rifles. It is likely that more of our men might have been killed in the fight if their leaders had not decided on a new way of attacking the town under the protection of its own buildings."

"What way was that?" some one asked.

"By digging through the walls of the houses," came the reply. "The Texans got off the streets about as soon as the Mexicans began to shoot, and with picks and crowbars broke through the walls. It wasn't very hard opening manholes in adobe dwellings, you know. Men stood ready to clear the way the moment openings were made. House by house they fought their way through. Red-headed Karnes, one of the big-muscled Texans, and other strong men played the part of battering-rams while others guarded and fired every time they sighted an enemy.

"This kind of fighting took time but it saved men. They were five days working through to the Main Plaza. Not many Texans were killed, but among the brave fighters that had gone down was the heroic old Ben Milam. The veteran had run along a trench dug by our forces and had reached the door of the Veremendi house. My father, who was in the patio of that dwelling at the moment, yelled, 'Stand aside, Milam. That is a dangerous place!' The old veteran started to heed the advice, but fell dead. A bullet from the rifle of some sharpshooter had pierced his brain. It could not have been a chance shot.

" 'We buried the hero where he fell,' father said," added Dean Richardson. "Later his remains were laid away under a monument in Milam Square. He had made the supreme sacrifice for the cause of freedom. It was a serious loss to the Texans when this leader went down; but they set their jaws and fought on to victory.

"The Mexicans had taken to the San Fernando

Cathedral when our men broke out into the Main Plaza. Its tower gave their sharpshooters a chance to get in more of their deadly work. The weather was so bitterly cold—remember it was just before Christmas—that it was hard to load the rifles; but our boys kept up the fighting with their frost-bitten fingers. Finally Deaf Smith and some others managed to reach the roof of a house near the Cathedral. Half the men who attempted to scale the buildings with him were shot down. The Mexicans there were dislodged, and some of them withdrew to the Alamo. At last on December 9, a white flag appeared, and San Antonio was ours.

"Now the fighting was over, father could wipe off the grime and dust of the battle. 'About the first thing I did,' he used to say, 'was to take a good bath in the limpid San Antonio River. Then without eating, I threw myself down by a battered wall of an adobe building and dropped off into a sound sleep. Five days of fighting had left me plumb exhausted. I might have slept on until doomsday,' he would add, 'if a Mexican woman who was helping to find the dead and wounded had not given me a hard shake to find out whether I was alive or not.

" 'The first word I heard when I finally came to my senses was that Cos had signed papers officially surrendering San Antonio and agreeing to leave the soil of Texas. It was cheery news to me.'

"General Cos lived while in this town in a little adobe building which still stands on Villita Street. Father saw and talked to him there. The General conversed freely and seemed to bear no animosity against the Texans for what they had done, even though he must have known how his brother-in-law Santa Anna would take the defeat. The sequel of this story shows how bitterly the Dictator did take it.

"But that again is still another story which I must leave for others who know it more intimately than I to tell," concluded the old minister.

CHAPTER XII

HEROIC HOURS ROUND THE ALAMO

MISS SARAH SUTHERLAND for many years had treasured an old manuscript. It was doubly precious to her, first, because it had been written by her own grandfather; and secondly, because through him she was also a granddaughter of the Texas Revolution. Within the faded pages was a story of some of the stirring events connected with the heroic fight at the Alamo. It was from this—and from her father's own words—that she obtained the first hand account of this historic event.

"My grandfather, Dr. John H. Sutherland, was one of the scouts of the Alamo," Miss Sutherland told a group of friends one day. "He had ridden away at the request of his commander, Colonel Travis, to bring help to the heroic band of Texans holding the Mexican horde in check; and thus escaped being among those that fell fighting at that old mission. His nephew, William Sutherland, and his friend, William Wells, did fall with those heroes. Grandfather carried in his mind vivid pictures of those thrilling, tragic days. Occasionally his children and his friends would be given the story from his own lips. He did not write anything about it, however, until once he was stirred by what he felt was a warped, second-hand account of the battle of the Alamo, and then he 'put his pen to paper'— 'just to help keep the history of that fight for freedom straight'—as he said.

"Virginia was his birth state. The Sutherlands had come to the 'Old Dominion' way back in colonial days. They were from one of the 'first families' in England. I did not get this from grandfather. He, like many of the other earlier American pioneers, rather felt family pride to be one of the sins. This I think was both right and wrong. We should know our ancestors so that we may emulate their virtues and avoid their errors. Anyway I have taken some interest of late in looking up my genealogy—it is rather fashionable in these days—and I find that the Sutherlands have an honorable lineage.

"Grandfather certainly upheld the family name and tradition. He was a gentleman in all the word implies. Educated in the common schools and in college, he rounded out his work with a course in medicine, and entered that profession. He was a physician of the old school—a pioneer country doctor, who gave generously of his time and skill to helping his neighbors and friends. Though he did not get much money for his services, he did win the hearts of a great many good people.

"Some time in 1835 he went to Texas with a view of making his home and carrying on his practice there. The first thing he found was an opportunity to join a struggling people in their fight for freedom. Coming as he had from the State that gave us Washington, Patrick Henry, Thomas Jefferson and many other leading spirits in our American Revolution, it was just natural for him to join the Texans in their fight against tyranny. Acknowledging allegiance to the provisional government that they had just set up, he enlisted at once in the Texan army. On January 18, 1836, with Captain Patten and ten others he reported to Colonel Travis for duty at San Antonio. From that time forward he was in the thick of the storm then gathering about the old Alamo.

[201]

"There was some distress in and around the town when grandfather arrived. Lack of food and clothing and adequate shelter from the winter storms caused a good deal of suffering and illness among the citizens. The Texan army, too, was on scant rations and ill-equipped.

"There was no thought then of any immediate recurrence of trouble with the Mexican forces. Even if the Dictator, Santa Anna, should attempt to recapture the city, it was felt certain he could not get an army from the Rio Grande across the plains to San Antonio before spring. With this feeling of assurance, most of the volunteers, after the surrender and departure of Cos and his troops, had left for their own homes. They feared the depredations of Indians more than they did the possible return of the Mexicans. The gentlemanly conduct of General Cos in making his treaty had made the Texans over-confident.

"The strength of the little army of patriots left at San Antonio was depleted also in other ways. An ill-fated expedition to Matamoras drew away from San Antonio men and badly needed arms and supplies. Dissension among the leaders of the Provisional Government left the town that had been captured at such heroic cost, with just a handful of poorly-equipped men to defend the place.

"The enemy on the other hand was gathering

new forces to strike. When General Cos reached
the Rio Grande with his defeated troops, he was
met by Santa Anna at the head of a fresh, well-
equipped army. The enraged Dictator, brushing
aside the pledge of honor made to the Texans by
Cos, ordered the General to turn back and help
him crush the patriots. These men, upholding the
constitution of the Mexican Republic, had dared to
rebel against its autocratic president who was nul-
lifying that solemn compact.

"Word of the movements of the Dictator was
slow reaching the leaders of Texas and the little
band stationed at frontier San Antonio. The first
rumors that Santa Anna was leading his army to
recapture the town were not credited. Serious attention was given to such reports only when Captain Seguin's cousin, who had been kept at Laredo
to spy on the enemy, rode post-haste into San Antonio with his first hand report that Santa Anna
had crossed the Rio Grande.

"This messenger reached that frontier town on
Saturday, February 20. A council of war was immediately called. Grandfather was present. It
was a desperate situation that had to be met. Colonel Neill, who had been appointed commander of
the reduced forces still holding the town, was away
on sick leave. Colonel Bowie, second in command,
was also ill, but still at the post. In this emergency,

he had requested Colonel Travis, 'in my presence,' grandfather said, to assume the leadership. It seems that a kind of joint commandership was arranged between them, with Travis, because of Bowie's illness, carrying the brunt of the responsibility.

"Different happenings were soon to verify the message brought by Captain Seguin's cousin. The morning after his coming the Seguin family left San Antonio to get out of the danger zone. The Mexican population of the town was also in complete commotion. Such as had carts were loading them with their household dunnage; others were carrying away all they could on their backs. Numbers had left before the cause of their agitation could be learned. When inquiry was made of any of them, the reply was evasive—usually it was that they were going out on to their ranches to begin preparations for raising their crops.

"The stir was so unusual, however, that the Texans became suspicious. Finally they detained one of the women—Mrs. Ramon Musques, whose husband was known to be unfriendly to the Texan cause, and held her for several hours with her laden carts. It was believed that she and other Mexicans knew more about the movements of the enemy than they would divulge. The feeling grew that Santa Anna's forces were getting close to the town.

"A friendly Mexican finally told Colonel Travis

what had happened to cause the commotion. Word had been secretly passed to the Mexicans in San Antonio for them to 'vamoose.' Santa Anna's cavalry, fifteen hundred strong, was encamped on Leon Creek—not far from the town. The plan had been to make a surprise attack on the Texans; but a heavy rain held the dragoons back.

"Grandfather happened to be out of town while this excitement was on. He and Captain Lewis, not anticipating any immediate trouble, had gained permission to ride out with a Mexican to look over some land they had purchased from him. On their returning to San Antonio, the Captain was called to testify in court, and grandfather, while waiting for him, climbed the tower of the San Fernando cathedral and took a look over the town and its surroundings. The ladder with which Deaf Smith and the other Texans had scaled the wall during the Battle of San Antonio was still there.

"After talking with the sentinel up in the tower, grandfather was making his descent when suddenly the old tower bell was set clanging. Then came a yell, 'The enemy is here!'

"The Mexicans left in the town made a scramble to get behind trees or other protection. A number of Texans rushed to the belfry to chide the sentinel for giving a false alarm. Colonel Travis appeared on the scene, and grandfather proffered to ride out, if some one who knew the lay of the land would go along, and do some scouting to determine whether the enemy was really near. John W. Smith volunteered.

"This plan was arranged with Colonel Travis. If any of Santa Anna's forces were sighted, the two scouts were to come back on the run. If none of the enemy appeared, they were to ride back slowly.

"Away went the two horsemen—the anxious Texans watching them from the walls and house-tops. Nothing of moment happened until they had reached Alazan heights some miles away. Then the eager watchers saw the scouts wheel their horses and start back on the dead run. The Mexican cavalry in all its color and glitter had been sighted. Suddenly a mishap stopped the messengers. Grandfather's horse slipped and fell on the rain-soaked road, seriously injuring its rider's leg and arm. The excited Texans saw Smith rein up his horse, leap off and help grandfather back into the saddle; and then the two came crashing on with the word that the enemy in formidable numbers was just beyond the heights making ready to attack.

"Reaching the town they found the Texans rushing to the Alamo. This old stone-mission with its walled outer courts and corrals offered some substantial protection for the little band against the host that Santa Anna was gathering for his onslaught. A few women and children were brought into the fortress. All the preparations for safety and defense that could be made quickly were being made.

"When grandfather reached the Alamo and tried to dismount, he could not use his leg at all. Colonel Travis was sympathetic, but the emergency called for fighting back pain and carrying on. He asked grandfather with his companion to ride on to Gonzales to get reinforcements for the little band of patriots entrenched at the Alamo. The two scouts, responding to the call, rode away.

"They reached Gonzales and rallied twenty-five men. Smith at the head of these hastened back to join the forces at the Alamo. On Cibolo Creek seven more joined him, and with this band he was able to swell the ranks of Texan fighters at the old fortress to one hundred and eighty. Grandfather, because of his injured leg, could not return, but had to remain at Gonzales while these and the other heroes were fighting to the death for liberty.

"When Smith reached the Alamo, Colonel Bowie was seriously ill. This threw the responsibilities of leadership almost wholly upon Colonel Travis. He met the situation most heroically. Grandfather always spoke in the highest terms of both Travis and Bowie.

"Another heroic leader who gave his life for

freedom in this fight was Davy Crockett. This picturesque frontiersman from old Tennessee arrived with his companions upon the scene just before the battle. A great cheer arose when these volunteers came into the fray. Crockett was called on at once for a speech and responded in his characteristic style. The men were kept laughing and applauding at his droll humor and plain Americanism.

" 'And, fellow citizens,' he concluded, 'I am among you. I have come to your country, though, I hope, not with any selfish motives whatever. I have come to aid you all that I can in a noble cause. I shall identify myself with your interests, and all the honor I desire is that of defending as a high private, in common with my fellow citizens, the liberties of our common country.'

"These patriotic words of Crockett brought rousing cheers from the men who were about to face an enemy that outnumbered them twenty to one. All that was needed was just a few more men to back Crockett and Travis and Bowie, and that host of Santa Anna's might have been beaten. That night the Texans expressed their joy over the coming of Davy Crockett and his men in a celebration they held at the old mission. A few days later all of them were fighting it out with the Mexican army the Dictator had brought to crush the rebellion.

"Grandfather had to learn the story of that famous fight from others. The tragic news of the siege and fall of the Alamo seems to have come to Gonzales first by Mexican scouts whom Captain Seguin had left to observe what happened around San Antonio. The Texan heroes—every last one of them—had gone down fighting for liberty; but they had exacted a high price from the tyrant-driven forces for their lives. They were fighting for the Mexican Constitution, which Santa Anna had trampled on. While they were battling to the death, other patriots were in Washington, on the Brazos, drafting the Texas Declaration of Independence.

"One of the saddest things to me in this whole story," said Miss Sutherland, "is that these heroes of the Alamo had no knowledge of the fact that this Declaration had been signed even while they were fighting. No word—no help—it seems could be got to them during those hours when our brave men were making their heroic sacrifice. But their funeral pyre lit the torch of freedom anew and united all Texas to make that Declaration of Independence stand.

"Meanwhile efforts were being made to get more reinforcements to Travis. Captain John W. Smith, after leading the thirty-two men to increase the

forces defending the Alamo, responded to the call
of his commander and rode away to get more. Another group of volunteers joined him; grandfather
meanwhile had recovered somewhat and was gathering men for the fight. On the day the Alamo fell,
these two scouts, leading about forty Texans, were
heading towards the Alamo. As they neared San
Antonio, they heard no cannon shots or other
sounds of battle. The silence was ominous. Scouts
sent out to reconnoiter were chased back by the
Mexicans. The Texans, fearing that the worst had
happened, returned to Gonzales.

"Captain Seguin, the Mexican leader loyal to
the Texas cause, had also gone out to find Colonel
Fannin and ask for help. In this way he missed
being in the fight at the Alamo—for which he often
afterwards expressed regret. The Captain, after
waiting on the Cibolo for the commander he sought,
finally received the word that Fannin felt he
should not go because he and his forces were needed
to defend the Goliad against the Mexican General
Urrea, who at that time was menacing the place.

"Fannin suggested that Seguin go to General
Houston at Gonzales. Grandfather was in that
town when the Captain came. For Captain
Seguin he always had the warmest of praise. The
brave leader had slipped through the cordon that

Santa Anna had thrown round the Alamo and ridden away for help. Despite all he could do, however, he could not gather the needed men. Remember, the country was sparsely settled; and dangers were threatening on every side. There was division too in the councils of the newly formed government. This lack of unity among the Texas leaders, grandfather said, together with the lack of men and supplies, kept Captain Seguin and the rest of us from getting relief to the brave band fighting down to the very last men at the Alamo."

"Wasn't there a man left of all that fighting band of Texans to tell the tale?" some one asked.

"Not a single one," replied Miss Sutherland, "unless we count one man by the name of Rose—a Frenchman, who it is said did not cross the line Travis made with his sword. The story goes that he scaled the wall and escaped being killed. An old rancher afterwards told how this refugee came hungry and ill to his father's ranch. He was taken care of by the rancher's mother and father to whom he told what had happened. Later, however, ashamed of his cowardice, or for fear of the Texans, he denied the story. What is the exact truth in this tale, one cannot say. Every one of the other men under Travis and Bowie at the Alamo died fighting there. The line on the monument afterwards raised to the memory of these heroes suggests their spirit:

"THERMOPYLÆ HAD HER MESSENGER OF DEFEAT—THE ALAMO HAD NONE"

"But were there no others on the side of Texas that survived that battle?" persisted the questioner.

"Yes, there were a few non-combatants—mostly women and children. We cannot be certain just how many or exactly who all of these were. Among them were the wife of Lieutenant Dickerson and their baby, a Mrs. Alsbury and her young sister, Gertrude Navarro, who was related to Bowie through his wife, and the Esparza and Loyosa families with some other Mexican mothers and children. Then there was Joe, the servant of Colonel Travis. Grandfather had some words of praise for this negro boy. In after years, Joe ran away from his new master into Mexico, it is thought.

"When the last fighting Texans had been slain, these survivors were found in the outer parts of the Alamo by the blood-spattered soldiers of the victorious army. They were taken before the Dictator, who spared their lives that they might tell what lay in store for those who defied the will of Santa Anna. The story that did come from the trembling lips of these survivors spread like wildfire over all the land, and roused a spirit that was soon to bring crushing defeat to Santa Anna and end his tyranny in Texas."

CHAPTER XIII

ESPARZA, THE BOY OF THE ALAMO, REMEMBERS

THE principal of the Bowie School one day introduced to her pupils an old Mexican gentleman. The colorful zarape round his shoulders, and the large Mexican hat in his hand emphasized the picturesque.

"Buenas dias, *niños*," he greeted them.

"I am so glad you could come, Señor Esparza," said the teacher as she extended her hand in welcome. Then to the eager group of young Americans: "This, boys and girls, is the man of whom I was just speaking, Señor Gregerio Esparza—the boy of the Alamo. Won't you be seated, Señor?'"

The aged Mexican made a graceful bow, took the proffered chair, and looking over his eager, youthful audience, said, "It gives me great pleasure to see so many bright faces."

"You speak English!" exclaimed one of the girls.

Señor Esparza's black eyes twinkled. "Why not, señorita? I have lived for many years with my American friends. We should know the same language. But before the Americans came we learned how to use the Spanish tongue; so I think in Spanish, and my English words are a little mixed. You must pardon an old man.

"I had many hardships and not the chance for school—not even one day. I did learn by myself to read and to write, and then studied from my children's books. Now I read many hours a day. It is about all an old man can do. I am now over eighty years old and may soon leave my Texas land. While I live I want to tell of my people and of their part in winning the liberty of Texas. Some of us helped the Texans, and it took brave men to face Santa Anna and his resources. We were less than one to a hundred. It shows what right can do against might with the trust in God."

"Do you love Texas more than Mexico?" asked some one.

Señor Esparza shrugged his shoulders and said: "My people have been here—forever. No one counted the ages. We were Indians. Then the Spanish came and other nations. Many of my people are of mixed blood. I am of Indian and Spanish blood. The Indians were the first Americans. We are proud of that ancestry. I know nothing of Mexico but from the tales of old men and what I read in books. My father was killed in the Alamo. He stood by the side of Travis. I saw him die for Texas. I am proud to be a Texan and an American.

"We were of the poor people. There were little riches, and to be poor in that day meant to be very poor indeed—almost as poor as the Savior in his manger. We were not dissatisfied with it. We were very contented. We lived not as the people now live, always seeking happiness in pleasures and much money. There were other things worth while—time to eat and sleep and look at growing plants. We had happy hearts in stout bodies—fresh air aplenty and wild freedom.

"Of food we had not over much—chili and beans, beans and chili. Sometimes my uncle went on a hunt, and then we had venison and buffalo meat; but the Indians were bad and often drove the buffalo far away. Deer along the San Antonio River were as many as the hairs on my head. We planted beans and pumpkins to grow on the walls of the old Alamo. Our jacalita leaned against the ruins— the old wall that came across the Plaza.

"Some of the jacals had a fireplace and chimney. Our chimney was a smoky one, so my mother

cooked outside most of the time. It was very pleasant along the acequia—clear sky and clear water.
Most of the time we ate and slept outdoors. We
were very free and very happy—until my father
died in the Alamo. Then we saw and heard much
we can never forget.

"The Alamo was old and gray and tumbling
when I first remember. It was very large. Near
the west walls the good Padres had built houses for
the tame Indians. Many years had passed after
they had gone. From the tumbling stones of these
buildings we built our jacalita. The old wall of the
Alamo made one side of it. Our roof was of tula
that grew along the river bank, and sometimes of
short grass.

"My father would hunt and fish and farm. The
church allowed us some rich land not far from the
Alamo. The Indians would steal our animals—
often our cows, but we did not worry. We lived
in peace until General Cos came with his army to
drive the Texans out of our country. The Texans
were our friends. We were glad when they came
and drove Cos and his soldiers out of San Antonio.

"My mother sold many tamales and beans to the
Texans. I helped her to carry the earthen jars full
of food. It was a heavy task at times. One day
while I was carrying a jar along the big log that
made a foot-bridge over the San Antonio River, I

slipped and fell into the deep water. Señor Bowie jumped in and brought me out. I could swim from the time I was four years old, but this day I think I struck the log in falling for my head was bloody. I was very fond of Señor Bowie after this.

"My father became a Texas soldier. He belonged to the Benavides company. He was promised much land. He was given a little money—not much. Mother used it to buy some food. She had to work very hard to feed the hungry mouths of her children.

"After Cos left San Antonio, the Texas soldiers taught me a queer tune and some words I did not understand. It was like this:

> 'We are the boys so handy,
> We'll teach Santa Anna to fear
> Our Yankee Doodle dandy.'

I was a very small Mexican boy. When I would sing the song the soldiers would laugh and give me centavos.

"We were poor people but we had many friends. Señor Bowie, Señor Smith, and the rich Señor Navarro. I played with the Smith and the Navarro children. Señor Bowie had no family. His wife, the beautiful Ursula Veremendi, and their two children had died. He was a sad man. One day

[217]

Señor Bowie said to my father, 'Give me Gregerio. I will send him to the United States to school.'

"My father shook his head, and my mother said, 'It is not the will of God, Señor. Gregerio is our son. The United States is far off and is very different. There Gregerio would be like a bird in a gilded cage. We are plain people, Señor, you know —not in your class.' My mother thought that one's place in life was the will of God and it was wicked not to be content. 'Maybe,' as the Americans say, she was right. Now life is hurry, hurry. There is no time to count our blessings. We want more and more—An old man wanders. My life has been long and much time for thinking—Where was I, Señorita?"

"You were telling us of your childhood, Señor."

"Si—Señorita,—forgetfulness—pardon."

"What kind of clothes did you wear?" came a guiding question.

"Not very much and very cheap. A white cotton blouse and cotton pants tied together with rawhide string—no hat, no shoes."

"Was the old Alamo used for worship?" asked some one.

"No, the Alamo was in ruin. It had been that way even before my mother was born. We went to church at San Fernando in San Antonio. The Alamo was almost out in the country. The rich people lived around the Plaza and along the San Pedro River that winds through the town. The poor lived around the Alamo. There were just a few houses between the Main Plaza and the Alamo.

"We thought the Plaza very big and fine. Adobe houses were built all around it, and a grand market place was in the middle of the square. The Indians came here to trade. They brought skins of the deer and the buffalo. The ranchmen brought hides to sell for leather. The hides were worth more than the beef. I have seen hides on the Plaza as high as an adobe house. People came to San Antonio on horseback or in ox-carts and camped on the Plaza.

"On Sunday around the San Fernando Cathedral it was very gay. After mass and vespers there was talking, walking and dancing on the Plaza. The priests lived near San Fernando and sometimes the tame Indians came from the San Jose Mission. They came to mass at the cathedral—Apache, Comanche, Lipans—a few, not many, and old."

" 'You cannot tame an Indian, a rabbit or a parrot'—Señorita—'tis a wise Mexican saying.

"We had many saint days. Then we would visit for a long time with relatives and friends. I had many cousins. We would meet and play together. Then we would join in the fiesta around San Fernando. One time we rode from the Alamo in an ox-cart to the Cathedral to see the Pastores. It was

[219]

very grand to ride and to see this blessed Shepherd
Play. The altar to the Christ Child was bright with
many candles. All over the Plaza shone candles—
the houses were all covered with lights—in remembrance of the 'Light of the World.'

"The first 'villa' in Texas was around the San
Fernando Cathedral. After the Americans came
we called it all—as far as the Alamo—San Antonio
de Bexar.

"As I told you the Alamo was left and it fell into
ruins. When the Texas soldiers came and drove
Cos away, they camped round the old Mission. I
heard some of them say it was too big; they did not
have enough men to hold it. I thought that the
Texans could do anything. There seemed to be
many, many men in the fortress when they
gathered there; but they were only a few when we
think of Santa Anna's army. Anyway I was sure
that these brave men could whip Santa Anna and
all his men.

"There was great cheering when Señor Crockett
came with his friends. He wore a buckskin suit
and a coonskin cap. He made everybody laugh and
forget their worries. He had a gun he called
'Betsey.' They told me that he had killed many
bears. I knew he would kill many of Santa Anna's
soldiers.

"One thing that frightened me was the cannon

the Texans brought. They placed these big guns
on the top of the thick walls and pointed them
every way. The noise they made was terrible to
me.

"Santa Anna had many men and much 'thunder.'
I mean powder. The Indians called it 'thunder.'
A man told my mother he was like a king with
much power and many servants. It was said he ate
from plates made of silver and gold. I could not
believe that, but I have read from books it is true.
He was very proud. He said that the Texans could
not get away from him. A Mexican woman told
this to the men at the Alamo.

"One day Santa Anna demanded that the Texans
surrender. Colonel Travis answered with a shot
from one of the big cannons. Then Santa Anna
ran a blood-red flag to the top of the tower of the
Cathedral of San Fernando. Some one said that
this meant he would kill every one on the side of
the Texans. The Texans did not seem to be excited. At night they would sing and dance. No
fighting came for several days.

"Travis was a brave leader. He had been asked
by Señor Bowie, who was ill, to take command.
Father would rather follow Bowie, because they
were friends. I saw Señor Bowie while he was ill.
The soldiers let me go about among them.

"This good friend did not forget us. When the

mothers and children fled to the Alamo, Señor Bowie had driven in some beeves and found some corn. He gave part of this food to us. We were too scared to think much of eating, but mother made some atole, a sort of mush, for all the children. She ground the corn and boiled it and almost poured it down our throats. Mother was a sensible woman and kept her head. Some of the other women were almost helpless.

"When the trumpets of Santa Anna were heard, we had rushed to the Alamo. When father told her she had better go to a safer place, she said, 'No; if you are to die, I want to be near you!' We gathered up the few things we had—a metate, two chairs, four skins and some cooking utensils. In one bundle was my baby sister. My small brothers and I carried what we could. I was the oldest—nine years.

"We all went into a small store room near the monastery. Here we slept on hay and under hay. With us were other Mexican mothers and children. The women helped by grinding corn and cooking for the men. Mrs. Dickerson and her baby were with us. She seemed not to know what to do in this condition. I heard mother say, 'povrecita,' and take the lady some food.

"At first we got our water from the ditch in

front of the Alamo. Later the enemy cut off this supply and we had to use an old well.

"One night father captured a Mexican who was prowling round, and kept him a prisoner. He was one of Santa Anna's soldiers. During the siege he would tell the Texans what the bugle calls of the enemy meant. I heard that this poor fellow was afterwards killed because Santa Anna thought he was a deserter.

"Then came the days of the terrible fighting. It was all so frightful—but what could one do except just watch and wait? The roof of the old Alamo was off. Along the south side was a dirt wall or embankment up which the Texans would run and fire. Some of them were killed when they did this —Lieutenant Dickerson was among these. His sorrowful wife and babe were left with us.

"Señor Crockett seemed everywhere. He would shoot from the wall or through the portholes. Then he would run back and say something funny. He tried to speak Spanish sometimes. Now and then he would run to the fire we had in the courtyard where we were to make us laugh.

"When Señor Smith came from Gonzales with the band of men he had gathered, there was great shouting. The Texans beat drums and played on a flute. Colonel Travis sent Señor Smith off again to get more men.

"Captain Seguin was also sent for help. I saw him go. The way I remember was he rode Señor Bowie's horse. We were afraid he could not get by Santa Anna's soldiers. They were getting closer and closer to the Alamo. Afterwards I heard that the Captain was stopped by them, but he said he was a Mexican rancher. This was true; and they let him go. He tried to gather men to get back to help the Texans; but the ways were long in those days, and not many men to get. Before he and Señor Smith could return, the battle was all over.

"One brave man that did get back was Señor Benham. He had been sent to Goliad to get Fannin to send help. He rode right past the sentinels of Santa Anna. They fired, but he escaped. My mother knelt and said her beads and thanked the good God. Señor Benham had a white handkerchief tied to his hat. If he was shot while trying to get back to his friends in the Alamo, this handkerchief was a sign he had seen Fannin. Benham came through the danger unharmed. He was one of the great heroes that fell there fighting for liberty.

"At times Señor Travis looked very sad and stern. One day he said to Bowie, 'Help will come.' But help did not come. When he felt that they must fight it out alone, he gave his men a chance to say whether they would stay by him to the end. I saw him draw the line with his sword, and heard him say, 'All who are willing to die cross this line.' I think all jumped across. Señor Bowie said, 'Boys, lift my cot across that line.'

"My heart was in my mouth. My eyes were like coals of fire; but I would stay and listen. Some blame the great Bowie and Travis and Crockett because they did not hasten away. Can men do more than give their lives, Señorita? I heard a great man tell that these heroes of the Alamo saved Texas. If Santa Anna had not been stopped there, he would have marched over all Texas before an army could be gathered to defeat him. This sounds right to me. I did know that these men were heroes.

"At last there came fire and guns and bayonets with many men. The soldiers of Santa Anna scaled the walls to be met by the fighting Texans. It was early morning. I ran out to the courtyard from a deep sleep. I was fastened to the ground. The Texans killed many of Santa Anna's men, but more and more kept coming up the ladders. My father was killed. The brave Travis while shooting a cannon was shot down. I wish I could tell you all the great bravery of these few Texans fighting against that host. It would take great words like in your Bible and in your songs. I do not know these words.

"Santa Anna's men broke down the outside wall and came into the courtyard. The Texans went to the second wall and fought them back. They clubbed with their rifles, and stabbed with their bowie knives. At last the few Texans that were left drew back into the monastery and shot the enemy as they came into the courtyard.

"The women and children had hidden themselves where they could. I crawled under the hay. I would open my eyes and shut them again. I could

not keep myself from looking and hearing. The awful sights still come to my eyes and the sounds ring in my ears. The soldiers of Santa Anna came on thick as bees. Inch by inch they gained ground, but for every Texan they killed five of them fell. Poor fellows—many of them cared not to fight. It was the will of their tyrant leader. Mexico builds not one statue to Santa Anna. It is a lesson to all. He was a self-seeking, cruel ruler.

"I did not stay in the courtyard. I was afraid. Long before this I had heard Señor Bowie tell Señor Smith, 'We must hold the Alamo. We must keep Santa Anna back from Gonzales. If we don't even the women and children will be murdered.' I had kept close to Señor Bowie. He knew my language and I could feel his strength. Though he was ill I felt he would yet find a way to overcome Santa Anna. When he and the other brave fighters were slain fear seized me.

"I hid with other frightened children and their mothers. Some of Santa Anna's men shot into the room. One boy was killed, but the rest of us escaped alive. We could see little in the dark corner where we had huddled. As soon as it was light enough, some of the soldiers came searching through the rooms.

"One of them put his bayonet against my mother and said, 'Where is the Texans' money?'

" 'If they had money, find it,' she said.

"The soldier struck her and I screamed. An officer appeared and ordered the soldier to go and leave the women and children alone.

"When it was broad daylight, the families were sent to the home of Don Musquiz at the southwest corner of Main Plaza. A servant there gave us coffee and tamales. We were very hungry. That afternoon we were taken before Santa Anna. He had his headquarters on the Plaza. I saw a pile of silver on the table where he sat.

"Mrs. Dickerson was more excited than any of the other women. My mother was very quiet and very sad, but not afraid of Santa Anna. I was scared. The Texans had told me that he would cut off my ears if he ever caught me. I did not cry out, but I clung to my mother. Santa Anna, I remember, was dressed up very fine and he had a pleasant voice; but he looked angry. He thought us traitors. He was kind to Mrs. Dickerson, at least his voice sounded different when he spoke to her.

"He asked the Mexican women, 'Why do you fight your countrymen?'

"'They are not our countrymen,' my mother answered; 'we are Texans.'

"'I suppose if I let you go you will raise your children to fight Mexico.'

"'Yes,' my mother said. Her sorrow over the death of my father had made her not afraid to die, I think.

"'You ought to have your ears cut off,' he replied.

"This made me and the other children scream.

"'Get the mob out!' Santa Anna said. 'Give each woman two dollars and a blanket.'

"The officer led us away. As we were going out he said in a low voice, 'Vamonos.' We did.

"Mrs. Dickerson sat there before Santa Anna when we left. She was crying. Señor Travis had a negro slave named Joe, who was also standing there. We heard afterwards that Santa Anna sent Mrs. Dickerson on a horse to Gonzales with Joe to help her along. Deaf Smith and some of Houston's scouts met her on the way. After hearing the sad story from her, some of them hurried on to Gonzales with the news.

"We stayed in San Antonio with my uncle. He had taken no part in the war. He was too old. Uncle found my father's body among the slain and buried it. It took three days for the soldiers of Santa Anna to gather up their dead and bury them. In after years I was told that six hundred of them had been killed by the one hundred and eighty-two Texans who died fighting at the Alamo."

"Did you see them burn the bodies of these Texans, Señor Esparza?" some one questioned.

"No, but I heard that they did burn the bodies. Later, when Santa Anna had been defeated, I learned that Captain Seguin had come to San Antonio and gathered up the ashes of these brave men and given them honorable burial near the spot where they had died fighting for freedom. Alcalde Ruiz helped to burn and bury many of the bodies.

"After the battle of the Alamo we moved away to San Pedro Creek. I was frightened until Santa

[229]

Anna had left San Antonio. He did not stay long. We were all happy when he was beaten in battle by General Houston.

"The old Alamo was left in ruins. It stood like a haunted place—full of many memories for me."

"Do you know how many Mexicans were in the Alamo fighting as Texans against Santa Anna?" came a question.

"I heard Guerrero, an old man, tell that the names were Fuentes, Loyosa, Jimenes, and my father; also Captain Badilla of Nacogdoches. Guerrero was there, too, I was told, but escaped because he said he was a prisoner of the Texans. It is a sin for a man to carry a lie to his grave.

"There was a monument made and the names on it were many, but I heard that no Mexican name was cut in the marble. My father and other Mexicans died for Texas. These of English tongue could do no more, so why not every name? Yet I blame no one. It was thought by too many that all people with dark faces and foreign tongues were wicked like the cruel Santa Anna.

"That is not so. Many of my people loved liberty just as did the Americans who came to help settle Texas. I am glad to tell this story of the Mexicans who gave their lives for freedom. It is good to come and tell it to you American boys and girls.

"Gray hairs cling to old memories. I live by the soil and with the soil. I talk to few about the Alamo and the old days. Some believe me not; some know it all. I talk now and then to friends of understanding and sympathy."

CHAPTER XIV

A SURVIVOR OF THE GOLIAD TELLS HIS STORY

AFTER the Alamo, came the Goliad—the darkest tragedy, I feel, in the Texas Revolution." It was Laura Steele, one of the daughters of Texas, speaking. "The Alamo was a heroic fight to the death," she continued, "the heroes of the Goliad were victims of a treacherous massacre after they had made an honorable surrender. It was one of the blackest of the black pages in the story of Santa Anna's tyranny; but it was to prove the darkest before the dawn.

"My uncle, John C. Duval, was one of the precious few that escaped to tell the tale, so I have it from a first hand source," Miss Steele went on.

"He did not care to talk much about it for the memories were bitter ones; but sometimes he would give us the story as he knew it. There was little dwelling on the painful details—just a straightforward account of what he had experienced during those tragic days that came right after the battle of the Alamo. In later years he wrote the story with others of his early days in Texas. The copy I had of that book has disappeared.

"Uncle was with Fannin's little army that had been held at Goliad to keep back General Urrea. Events were moving so swiftly it was hard to keep up with them. The Declaration of Independence for Texas was signed on March 2, 1836. The Alamo fell on March 6. General Houston, with his title of Commander-in-Chief of the Texan Army reconfirmed by the new government, had hastened to Gonzales to rally the forces for freedom. News of the fall of the Alamo had come to him there. It was naturally expected that Santa Anna would drive on to crush others who had rebelled against his autocracy. The people were panic-stricken.

"Orders were sent to Fannin to retreat, but there were helpless women and children to protect at Refugio. Fannin delayed his departure, sending Captain King to lead the inhabitants of Refugio out of the danger zone. Then Colonel Ward with his hundred and twenty-five men had to go to the relief of Captain King and the women and children.

"Fannin waited in vain for Colonel Ward within Goliad. Earthworks had been thrown up around the old Mission. It became in name and spirit— Fort Defiance. It was decided, however, best to leave this fort to the advancing enemy. On March 19, the little band of Texans evacuated the fort, and crossed the San Antonio River intending to hasten to Victoria by Houston's orders. While they halted on the prairie, Urrea's army—outnumbering the Texans ten to one—suddenly appeared.

"Uncle John said that Fannin formed his men in a hollow square and the battle began. The Texans fought desperately for a time against the overwhelming odds. Here is one episode just as Uncle John used to tell it:

" 'One Texas woman, Mother Cash, was with us. She had refused to leave Goliad when danger was threatening, and was now with our army. She traveled in a cart. While the fighting was going on, a boy, Hal Ripley, son of General Ripley of the War of 1812, climbed onto the cart to fire at the enemy. He was wounded and called to Mother Cash to help him down. That night the Texans had seven killed and sixty wounded. How many of the enemy we had brought down, no one knows; but we did our best to make them pay for it.

" 'The next morning Mother Cash took her own son and went to General Urrea to beg for water for the wounded. Urrea looked at the boy and said, "Woman, why bring a child into battle?" At which the boy answered, "I am here fighting for my rights and for Texas. We mean to get our rights or die." Urrea looked at the boy and then pointed to a white flag that had been raised by the Texans.

" 'Fannin and his men, without food or ammunition, had decided to surrender. Those who lived to tell the tale said that Urrea made favorable terms with them; Urrea claimed that the terms were not accepted by Santa Anna. Whatever the truth here, it is known that Urrea was impressed with the bravery of Fannin and his men; and also that he did try to get food to them after they were made prisoners.

" 'The order came from Santa Anna, however, that these prisoners of war were to be shot. Urrea claimed that he was never asked to execute this brutal order. The message, he said, went directly to a lesser officer who passed it on to Colonel Garay. This Colonel Garay—evidently more humane than his superior—contrived through various excuses to save a few of the condemned men.

" 'While all this was happening, General Urrea was in Victoria. It was Palm Sunday. The Texans, who had been told they were to be sent to New Orleans, were cheery enough. They had been singing songs of home the night before. All night they had slept without fear, and many of them were laughing and talking when they came the next morning at sunrise to take them away.

" 'The Texans were ordered to march out. None of the men suspected what fate was in store for them until about three-quarters of a mile away, the order came for them to kneel. Then some one cried out, "Boys, they are going to kill us!"

" 'Hardly had the cry come when the soldiers began to shoot the brave, helpless fellows down like dogs. While the massacre was going on, Señora Alvarez, the wife of one of Urrea's officers, rushed upon the scene and denounced Santa Anna. All her denunciations and pleadings for mercy did not stop his brutal will from being carried out. Nearly every one of Fannin's little army fell in that slaughter.' "

"What became of young Hal Ripley and the son of Mother Cash?" some one asked Miss Steele.

"Both were shot down with the rest."

"How did your uncle manage to escape?" came another question.

"In a rather remarkable way," was the reply, "and I'll tell this part of the story in his own words:

"As we were coming out of the prison, I overheard some Mexican women saying in pitiful tones, 'povrecitos'—poor fellows—but this did not arouse my suspicion. It was not till later that the horrible truth burst upon us.

"We were marched away in three divisions. The one I was in happened to be led along the road near the San Antonio River. When we were halted I heard firing. This made me alert. Suddenly the devils turned on our men and began to shoot. I was at the rear of the column. The man right in front of me was struck, and in falling knocked me down. Some of the men had broken into a run for the river, with the Mexicans after them. I jumped up and made the race for life too. Luckily I got to the bank without getting hit by the bullets that were flying all round us. I dived into the water, and being a good swimmer, kept myself under until I was well across. As I came up for air the bullets spattered around me, but did not find their mark. I kept diving and coming up for a second at a time. On the other bank I grabbed a hanging grapevine, but a bullet clipped it off just above my hand. Finally I managed to get out on the bank unharmed. Here I found two other Texans who had also escaped. We hid in the timber and watched Santa Anna's assassins kill five of our men the cavalry had pursued and caught.

[237]

"We three companions secreted ourselves in a ravine until night fell. Then we traveled all night. In the morning we caught sight of some Mexicans and Indians scouring the country, but the grass was high. By lying down on the wet ground for hours we eluded our blood-thirsty pursuers. There was plenty of game all round us, but we had no guns. We wouldn't have dared to fire them under those conditions anyway. It was just a case of starve it out until we could get on safer ground.

"For several days we wandered round more or less in bewilderment and getting hungrier and hungrier. Finally we tried eating the fruit of some cacti we found. It helped a little but it gave me a high fever. After five days we came to the Guadalupe River. Here a wild mother pig and five little ones happened to seek the same shelter we had. Here was desperate need. I grabbed up a club and killed the little pigs. The mother ran away. We made a fire and had a feast on young pork. This gave us new strength and made us sleep well. After several more days of wandering in search of Texas friends, we suddenly came upon some more of Santa Anna's soldiers.

"In giving these soldiers the slip we all got separated. That night as I was going on alone I happened on a deserted house. In it I found some corn and bacon. Besides this food I found some preserves. It was the home of some Texas settler whose family was then fleeing from the army of Santa Anna. My heart went out to these poor refugees, but I felt that I could help them best by filling up on the food they had left behind in their haste.

"These people must have been refined folk. They had a good library in their home. There were a number of fine dogs about the place. One of these took to me and followed me everywhere. I called him Scout. When I left the place he would go with me in spite of the thrashing I gave to make him stay at home. I was afraid he would betray me to any of Santa Anna's lancers who might be on my trail. Once indeed when I did sight some of these soldiers, I had to choke Scout to keep him quiet. Every day I would sight some of these lancers, but they seemed not to be very alert, for they did not find me.

"Farther on I came to a bayou. I decided to put that between me and any lancers who might be skulking about, so I swam it. Scout was right at my heels. When I got to the other bank I found that I had lost my knapsack with what little food I had. In searching for more, I finally came, wet and weary, to a cabin. No one was at home so I decided to build a fire. While I was there searching for something to eat, Scout suddenly jumped through the open window at a man.

" 'Call off your dog,' he yelled at me.

"I rushed out to meet two Texans. They were scouts of the Texas army fresh from the glorious victory at San Jacinto. We had some real stories to tell to one another that time."

"What became of the two companions that escaped from the massacre with your Uncle John, Miss Steele?" came a question.

"They managed to escape with their lives," was the reply. "Uncle John had a joyous reunion with them some years after that thrilling adventure. How they found their way back to friends and home I never learned."

"What about Scout?" some one else asked.

"Uncle John gave him to one of the Texans whom he met at the cabin. The man afterward lived at Austin, Texas.

"As for Uncle John himself," continued Miss Steele, "he decided he had had about enough of Texas and returned to his 'old Kentucky home' for a time. It was not for long however. The lure of Texas brought him back there in less than a year. In after years he wrote several books about his experiences in Texas. They were called 'Early Times in Texas,' 'Big-foot Wallace' and 'Young Explorers.' I had them all when I was a child, but lent them to others and finally lost them. I'd give a good deal to possess those old books today. I did not appreciate them, I fear, when I was young.

"When Uncle John used to tell us stories, I was always more interested in his funny experiences and his jokes about Cudjo—the old negro—than about the Fannin massacre at the Goliad. That seemed too sad to me. Anyway, Uncle John did not care, himself, to talk so much about it; the memories were too tragic, I suppose. It was certainly a terribly treacherous and cruel thing. But one thing sure, the Goliad, added to the Alamo, made superhuman fighters of the Texans who fought at San Jacinto. Those tragedies hastened the downfall of the tyrant.

"Some years after his escape from the massacre at the Goliad, Uncle John happened to go to this tragic spot again. He had found a friend in Texas by the name of Pitt, and proposed that they take an exploring and hunting expedition together. On their way they chanced to pass through the Goliad. Near the place they came upon a skeleton which Mr. Pitt felt certain was that of his own brother who had been slain there. They buried the skeleton. Soon after this they met some Mexican peons, and Mr. Pitt flew into a terrible rage. Uncle had all he could do to hold the excited man from killing these Mexicans. It was difficult for him to feel that these people were not responsible for the deeds of their tyrant leader, Santa Anna.

"With my uncle on this trip was the negro, old Cudjo. Near the Hondo they saw signs of Indians. And here also Uncle John had an encounter with a cougar. He barely escaped with his life from the beast. The lion ran away, however, after being wounded.

"That night their horses stampeded. They had been teasing Cudjo, the cook, about the dangers of the country. After the stampede the negro was nowhere to be found. While they were discussing his possible whereabouts, some one remarked, 'Do you reckon Cudjo was dragged off by that lion and killed?'

" 'No, dat he ain't,' said a voice from above, 'Dis chile am too smart for dat.'

" 'Come down here, you black rascal,' Uncle John called.

"Cudjo skinned down the live-oak in a hurry. Then scratching his woolly head he said, 'Clar to goodness, I clum dat tree when I was fas' asleep. I dream' dat Mexican lion was right after dis niggah.'

"There was a hearty laugh at the old negro's story. He was joked a good deal about it during the days that followed. The time was soon to come when he showed himself no coward but a real fighter.

"On the return to San Antonio, the exploring and hunting party camped at the head of the Frio

River. This part of the country is picturesque and broken up into many small canyons. Game was in abundance and the party feasted on deer and buffalo meat.

"One day 'Big Drunk' and some of his Choctaw Indian band came to the camp and reported that the Comanches were not far off. To reconnoiter a bit the hunters mounted their horses and followed the friendly Choctaws up one of the canyons. Here they found clear cold springs bursting out of the canyon walls. On the cliffs, too, as uncle used to say, was 'an Indian Art Gallery.' The redmen had painted many pictures of deer, buffalo and other animals on the rocks. One scene was a picture showing a battle with redmen winning a victory over the white men.

" 'They never drawed that pictur' from nary scrimmage I ever seed,' dryly remarked Seth, an old scout who was with the party.

"The company did not stay at this picturesque spot very long. They needed better grazing for their horses, so they went down the canyon. About noon they saw a signal smoke and soon after, three smokes.

" 'The Indians know we are about,' said Seth.

"In the afternoon the party reached a green valley. The luxuriant mesquite grass was a treat for their tired horses. The water was clear and cool and full of fish. The party decided that here was the place to camp. It offered safety too in case of an attack by the Comanches. 'Big Drunk' sent out some of his band to see whether any of the hostile Indians were near. In about two hours they rode in with the word that they had sighted a Comanche encampment not far away.

" 'Wal, the sooner we fix fer 'em the better,' said old Seth. 'We don't want to be caught nappin'. This place is perty safe with water on three sides and chapparal on the other. A thousand Comanches couldn't rout us here unless our grub gives out. Let's git to work and fix our fire irons. Where's Cudjo? Ask him about the food stuff.'

"Cudjo had disappeared, but Uncle John, suspecting he had hidden under the blankets, gave them a kick. Out came the old negro, his teeth chattering.

" 'Excuse me, Marse John,' he said; 'but I'se got a misery in my back. I wish I'd stayed at home. Dis rampagin' ober the whole country ain't got no sense in it. It's jes' temptin' de Lord, dat's what it is!'

"Just about that time Uncle John said they heard the notes of many birds and the cries of various wild animals.

" 'Maybe so Comanches come now,' warned the Choctaw chief.

"The redskins did not appear immediately, however. It was about two hours before there was any warwhoop. Cudjo disappeared in the chaparral the moment the attack came. There was brisk firing on both sides. Several Comanches were wounded.

Suddenly old Cudjo dashed back in a panic yelling, 'Oh Lawd, dey's done killed Cudjo! I'se shot clean through.'

"The scared negro had been struck sure enough, but his wound proved only a slight one in the leg. Seth soon had the injured limb bandaged. Cudjo was mad clean through—raring to fight the redskins. 'I'se gwine to get even wid dem debbils,' he yelled. And he surely did. All the savage in him was let loose as he leaped into the fighting.

"The Choctaws yelled their delight to see the black man firing at their enemies. 'If Big Drunk had been killed,' Uncle John used to say, 'I really believe the tribe would have made Cudjo their chieftain.'

"After a few hours, the Comanches left. And wasn't Cudjo set up in his feelings. 'Dar were five hundred of 'em,' he said proudly; 'and we jes' sent 'em scootin'.' Uncle John said that 'about eighty were in the band of hostiles. They left because they probably felt that the Choctaws had reinforcements coming; rather than because we had whipped them. But we gave them a right good scrap while it lasted; and Cudjo certainly did his full share of the fighting. That bullet made him a changed being.'

"The hunting party stayed a while longer on the Frio. Then, if I remember rightly, they had a big buffalo hunt on the San Saba. It is my recollection that they did a little searching for Bowie's silver mine while there."

"What became of old Cudjo?" some one asked.

"My remembrance is that he lived on until after the Civil War. Then even though he was set free, he stayed on with his master. He was a good old darky, but he spent most of his time in the after years telling about that big fight 'the 'splorers had wid de wild Comanches on de Frio Ribber.'

"As for Uncle John, he would rather tell funny stories than dwell on the tragedy at Goliad. That sad chapter in the fight for liberty was too close to his heart."

CHAPTER XV

SAM HOUSTON STRIKES AT SAN JACINTO

LIFE began for me in 1816—at old Natchez in Mississippi," said Captain Edward Miles, a gray-haired, upstanding veteran, who was telling a Texas audience something of his life story. "I was born there just a year after General Jackson had defeated the British at New Orleans. My parents were well-educated and rather well-to-do for those days. They gave me the best of schooling the times afforded. I had conquered the "three R's" and some Latin by the time I was thirteen years old. My father and mother, in common with most of the pioneer builders of America, believed in schools; and they did everything they could to give their children an education.

"When I was in my 'teens, father's health failed. It was felt that a change of climate might help bring back his strength, so a trip to Texas was planned. I begged him and mother to let me go too, and they finally consented. Oh, what a joyful boy I was when we mounted our horses and rode away to the southwest. All my young life I had heard about that country with its Mexicans and Indians and buffaloes. Now I was going to see it, and have some thrilling experiences. I little dreamed at that time what the years immediately to come would bring to me.

"After many days of travel we struck the old Spanish Trail and followed it to San Antonio. The country was picturesque, the climate was delightful. The soil was fertile too, and cheap. Father decided that here was a good place to make our new home; so he bought a tract of land at the amazing price of fifty cents per acre.

"The thing in which I was most interested, however, was not the climate nor the soil, but the adventures I was having. One of these was a buffalo hunt; that was full of excitement for me. At another time father let me go on a trip with others to catch wild mustangs. These animals, which then were plentiful over Texas, gave one a thrill to catch them—and many a thrill afterwards in breaking them to ride. Another adventure which nearly turned out tragically was one I had with some javelinas—or wild hogs.

"It happened that we had camped with a family

named Brown. One of the boys named Bill was about my age. Father was ill and while Mrs. Brown was giving him such care as she could, Bill and I tried to do our part by bringing in game. We shot a good many wild turkeys and some deer.

"One day I saw a javelina. It was an ugly-looking beast with black bristles and big tusks; but we boys decided to try to capture this wild boar. I threw my lasso at it and missed. Bill was more successful. He got his rope around the brute's neck but unfortunately did not pull the noose tightly enough. The enraged hog rushed at Bill's horse and ripped it savagely with its sharp tusks. Bill grabbed for a limb to lift himself out of danger but missed. His horse broke away with the hog after it. Meanwhile I had spurred my horse up to Bill. He sprang on its back behind me, and we all sped back to camp. The wounded horse had reached there before we did. Of course we reported what had happened and took the licking that was due us. In those days they did not 'spare the rod and spoil the child.'

"After some time in Texas we returned to our home in Mississippi. Father had not regained his health. It was not long before he passed away. Later with mother's consent I yielded to a longing to get back to Texas. By this time I was seventeen —a man in size—and ready, I felt, to take care of myself. When father and I had left Texas in 1829, everything was peaceful there. In 1833, when I returned, serious troubles had broken out between the pioneers there and the Mexican government.

"There was no welcome for me or any other Americans in Texas at that time. A law, indeed, had been passed the year after father and I left, forbidding any more Americans settling in Texas. Unjust taxes too were levied on the settlers there. And to make bad matters worse, an American named Blackburn had hired himself to the Mexican government to enforce these laws. He immediately closed all the ports of Texas except one. Such a fiery protest arose from the Texans over this, that Blackburn was directed by a Mexican official to withdraw the order.

"Then two Texans, William B. Travis and Patrick C. Jack, played a joke on Blackburn. He flew into a rage and threw these men into jail. The Texans rushed to arms, and I joined them. We had a skirmish and killed five Mexicans under Blackburn. Colonel Piedas came upon the scene at this juncture and ordered Blackburn to release the two prisoners. This settled the matter temporarily, but it had aroused bitter feelings and distrust between the Texans and Mexicans.

"These feelings went from bad to worse under the dictatorial rule of the newly elected President of Mexico, Santa Anna. He played the tyrant and we wouldn't stand for it. That in a nutshell was the cause of all the trouble.

"As a young American, brought up on the spirit of liberty, I naturally was ready to jump into the fight against tyranny. The older men were doing all they could peacefully to maintain our rights. It soon became clear that to win them the Texans would have to fight. I hadn't been in Texas two years until the war of the Revolution was on in dead earnest. Austin's imprisonment was followed by the capture of San Antonio and other towns by the Texans. Then came 1836 with the fight at the Alamo and the massacre at the Goliad.

"The rest of Texas flew to arms. With others, I hurried to Gonzales to enlist with General Houston. We didn't have very good guns, and there was too little ammunition. Our clothes were such as to make us a pretty ragged looking bunch; but we patched our clothes and mended our own boots. We had to forage for food, and sometimes we were on pretty scant rations. One thing we did have, however, was the fire of patriotism and a determination to whip the murderous Santa Anna.

"Things looked pretty hopeless for the patriotic cause during the dark days that followed the fall of the Alamo. That and the brutal work at the Goliad had put the whole country in a panic. While men seized their arms to fight the tyrant,

women and children fled from their homes to seek
safety they hardly knew where. The good horse I
rode into Gonzales was given to help one of these
fleeing families.

"On March twelfth, Houston ordered the town
evacuated. We had not fighting men or ammunition enough to risk meeting the enemy there.
Women and children went with us. As we looked
back we saw Gonzales in flames. On we went to
Burnham, a town on the Colorado. We were heading for the most populous part of Texas to get
reënforcements and supplies.

"It was St. Patrick's Day when we crossed the
Colorado River, and in faith we needed the blessing
of the God of Patrick or some other saint to help
us through our difficulties and dangers at this time.
The enemy was right at our heels; at times the two
armies were not more than two miles apart. One
thing that heartened us was the volunteers that
kept coming in. Our forces had increased to
twelve hundred men by the time we reached Burnham. Many in our ranks wanted to turn and fight
Santa Anna right there, but General Houston
ordered otherwise.

"It was about this time that several men who had
escaped from the massacre at the Goliad came into
camp. The story they brought fired our hearts
with hate of our pursuers and steeled them to fight

the tyrant Santa Anna to the death. But something of a panic swept through our ranks too, when thoughts of the women and children came. Many men, fearing the worst, fled with their families on toward the Sabine.

"This greatly reduced our fighting force, but not our fighting spirit. It was difficult for General Houston to restrain that spirit as he kept us retreating, retreating. Finally we reached San Felipe—the capital of Austin's colony—with the soldiers of the enemy not far away. Houston still bided his time.

"For days it rained in torrents. We floundered through mud and water. Men and women died and were buried without coffins. We had smallpox and measles in camp as well as pneumonia. Women grew hysterical. They laughed and cried and even fought at first; but after a time a quiet of desperation came over them. They faced the situation with heroism. Rich and poor, refined and coarse, thrown together, became sisters in misfortune sharing and helping one another—taking care of themselves and the children with bravery that renewed courage in the men. They had to act for themselves, for the fighting force must be kept ready for any emergency. We never knew when the enemy might launch an attack.

"Houston had all he could do to keep his soldiers in hand. They did not take kindly at all to the prolonged retreat. I saw the General during that grueling march through the rain as we left San Felipe. He was riding slowly. The shabby black suit he wore was dripping wet. He was angry too because some scoundrel had stolen his blanket. He told our captain that we were heading for Groces where the hungry army, and the refugees straggling along with it, could get food.

"The sight of that fleeing mass of human beings often comes vividly to my mind. It extended for miles and miles along the rutty, muddy road between the Colorado and the Brazos Rivers: hundreds of women and children walking, many mothers with babes in arms; every kind of vehicle to be had, pressed into service. Dragging through the slush—ill-fed and half clothed—the homebuilders of the frontier trudged on to escape from tyranny. In the bewilderment of the march many of the families had become separated from the Texan army and had fled by themselves on towards the east—anywhere to keep out of the murderous clutches of Santa Anna.

"It was expected and hoped by many of the soldiers that General Houston would turn and strike at Groces. When he did not, but led on with the retreat southward towards San Jacinto, there was increased grumbling in the ranks. Some disheartened men even deserted. Many rushed on towards

"TEXANS, REMEMBER THE ALAMO!"

the Trinity River. I could not blame them; it seemed to be all retreating with the enemy always dogging our footsteps. Would the General never give us a chance to fight?

"One night I saw a group of refugees round a poor campfire. Among them was a woman who was sobbing out a story that held every heart. It was Sue Dickerson—the woman who had been through the terrible ordeal at the Alamo. She sat by a tree and recounted the gripping deeds of Bowie, Travis, Crockett, Benham—the boys who came from Gonzales to die with these men—the cheerful bravado, how it ebbed and flowed—and then the death of her own husband and of the others who fell fighting. Every one listened breathlessly, the resolve growing in each heart to avenge the death of those brave fellows.

"It was a gloomy prospect. Rain, rain, rain— sickness and death round us. The howling of wolves not far away, and a merciless enemy almost within gunshot. Mothers clung to life for the sake of the babes at their breasts. Some of the women told me afterward that they kept close to the banks of the Bayou. If the battle that every one knew must come went against us, they would throw themselves into its waters. Other women told me that if their men were killed they would take up arms and fight until every last woman and child perished.

"The feeling against General Houston for holding us back grew. Some of the men even went their own way when they thought he was leading them on towards the Sabine. They were of course only volunteers and could not be held like regularly enlisted men. So far as I was concerned, I did not care where we went just as long as we finally defeated Santa Anna.

"Deaf Smith, Red-headed Karnes, and other scouts brought word that the tyrant had joined forces with General Sesma and that this enlarged army was heading for Harrisburg to capture President Burnet and Vice-President Lorenzo de Zavala. The Dictator failed to get these leaders in his clutches; but he gave vent to his anger by setting fire to Harrisburg, and then marched in wrath on to New Washington.

"Our army hurried on to San Jacinto. The battlefield that Houston chose there was a prairie bounded by Galveston Bay and its marshland, Buffalo Bayou, San Jacinto River and Vinces Bayou. It offered a natural trap for the army that failed. We were determined that we would not fail. We had to win.

"Santa Anna, with arrogant confidence, took his position in front of the marshlands. Houston chose the higher ground near Buffalo Bayou. Deaf Smith played the part of the Roman Horatius by cutting down the bridge across Vinces Bayou to keep any more reënforcements from getting to the Dictator. It was 'Victory or Death' with us, and somehow we all were happy over the dangerous situation. There was a grim determination in our cheerfulness that gives something of superhuman strength. A spirit akin to hilarity swept through our fighting force. The time was near when we could strike with vengeance for liberty.

"April twenty-first dawned clear. We took that as a good omen. Only eight hundred against double that number. At three o'clock we formed our battle lines. General Houston on his horse shouted, 'Follow your leader!' and we leaped into the fray. 'Remember the Alamo! Remember Goliad!' burst from all our throats.

"The enemy was taken completely by surprise. Into the ranks we charged like fighting demons. Down they went under the fire of our rifles and cannon. We did not give them time to send many return shots. They had bayonets, but our men clubbed the blades aside and cracked the skulls of the tyrant's soldiers with the butts of their rifles. Santa Anna's soldiers could not stand against the terrific onslaught of the Texans—their lines broke and they fled in every direction with our boys hot on their heels. Within twenty minutes six hundred and thirty of the enemy went down never to rise again. We had won a thrilling victory over the tyrant. His men dead and dying were scattered over the battlefield, or running for their lives, with ours in pursuit.

"What an outburst came from our little army over this triumph! We wept and danced. We hugged one another. We swore and prayed. We yelled and kept running and killing. 'El Diablo' the terrified enemies called us. We certainly had a dash of the very devil in us as we kept up our relentless slaughter of those who had fought our men to the death at the Alamo and shot them down in cold blood at the Goliad. All the hate and hunger, the agony and anger of six torturing weeks found vent in these maddened moments in which we crashed through to victory at San Jacinto.

"By nightfall the enemy was completely in our power. Besides the hundreds of dead and wounded, seven hundred of them had surrendered. Twelve thousand dollars of Mexican money had been captured, together with arms, ammunition, and equipment. Against all this gain we had sustained comparatively small losses—two Texans killed and twenty-three wounded. One of these who had been injured in the fight—and rather seriously—was our gallant commander, General Houston. A bullet had struck him in the ankle. As to Santa Anna—the devil who had been responsible for it all—he was not to be found either among the slain or wounded or with the prisoners.

"Capture this tyrant leader we must at all costs. Our scouts were sent everywhere to find and bring him to heel. The first word that came of him was brought by Mr. Vince, whose home was near the bridge Deaf Smith had cut down. He rushed into our camp to say, 'The Mexicans have stolen my son and two of our fine horses.' He had seen, he reported, some Mexicans making their escape from the battlefield and had started to flee from them when one of them called to him in English. 'Don't run; we won't bother you. My name is Almonte.'

"'Just then,' Mr. Vince went on, 'my son Jack rode up on a fine mare we called Quicksilver. Old Whip, another of our horses, was tied to a tree. Almonte took both horses and Jack away with them.' Jack afterwards told us that Santa Anna leaped on Old Whip and dashed away to save his own skin. A fellow by the name of Robert who knew our horse dashed after him, but Old Whip left him behind. Robert turned back, not knowing he was following Santa Anna. Next day, Old Whip was found in the bog near our bridge. The old horse, urged by his scared rider, had leaped onto the bridge and gone down with it. Santa Anna, unable to extricate his mount, had left Old Whip to flounder out for himself while he took to the tall grass.

"Early the next morning a number of our men were sent out to round up any stragglers of the enemy we could find. We had another order, and that was to fetch water into camp. In trying to 'kill two birds with one stone' some of us went towards Vinces Bridge. I happened to be with Lieutenant Sylvester, and two men by the name of Robinson and Bostick. We were about eight miles from the battlefield and near the bridge.

"It was noontime. We were tired and hungry. Lieutenant Sylvester suddenly turned and said, 'Boys, stop here, I want to get a shot at those deer.' We had sighted a few of these animals in the distance. The Lieutenant dismounted and started to creep towards the deer with the rest of us watching. Suddenly the deer bounded away. The Lieutenant returning to us, said, 'Boys, I did not scare those deer. Their heads were turned from me. It was something else. Let's go and see.' Off we went, and not far away we found a man in the grass.

" 'Get up!' commanded Sylvester. The fellow didn't obey.

" 'I'll make him move,' said Bostick, leveling his gun.

" 'Don't shoot,' I said jumping from my horse;

'I'll get him up.' With that I gave him a light kick, for which I am not sorry.

"At this the fellow stood up and said something in Spanish.

"Robinson, who was the only one of us that spoke that language, asked, 'Are you an officer?'

" 'No,' the fellow replied; 'I am a soldier; but I want to speak to your General Houston.'

"Just then I caught sight of a diamond stud on his shirt front, and exclaimed, 'Look, that man is an officer, and rich.' I pointed to the glittering stone.

" 'I am an aide to Santa Anna,' the fellow said.

"Then Sylvester asked Robinson to put a few questions to the prisoner.

" 'Where is Santa Anna?' The fellow shook his head.

"We scanned him closely. He had on a glazed leather cap, a striped jacket, country-made cotton socks, and coarse white pants. His shirt, however, was fine linen, his shoes pointed and elegant. We found out afterwards that he had picked up this coarser clothing in an abandoned house.

"We started him off towards our camp. After trudging a little way, he asked Robinson how far it was.

" 'About eight miles,' was the reply.

" 'I can't walk that far, but I'll go as far as I

can,' he said. After we had gone about three miles, the captive said, 'Kill me if you wish, but I can't walk another step.' We were young, and not very sympathetic.

"Robinson took the prisoner up on his horse. Afterwards he rode behind Sylvester. When we finally reached camp, the Mexican prisoners saluted and said, 'El Presidente!' We had captured Santa Anna himself. I am not sure what we might have done to him had we known before we reached camp who our captive was. It was a crowning feat in the victory to have the Dictator in our power, but we did no bragging about it. The other boys would have ducked us in the bayou if we had boasted. All we had done was just to get a streak of good luck for Texas.

"We took the prisoner straight to General Houston, who at the time was lying under the shade of a tree, his wounded leg bandaged. While we waited there we heard what was said by these two leaders.

" 'You ought to be generous to the vanquished,' began Santa Anna.

" 'You should have remembered that at the Alamo,' said Houston.

" 'It was justified by the usage of war. They refused to surrender,' returned Santa Anna.

" 'Civilized nations have grown more humane,' Houston replied.

" 'But I was acting under the orders of my government,' said Santa Anna.

" 'You were the government of Mexico; a Dictator, sir, has no superiors,' retorted Houston.

"The notorious captive was taken away and placed in irons under guard. Houston, Burnet and the cabinet met meanwhile to discuss the terms that should be meted out to Santa Anna.

"The feeling among the men rose high. Some were eager to put the tyrant to death. If any one ever deserved to die for his cruelty, certainly Santa Anna did. The leaders of Texas, however, felt that the Dictator was worth more alive than dead to the new nation that had just been born. They drew up a treaty that made him acknowledge the independence of Texas. All hostilities should cease. The Mexican troops should withdraw to the south of the Rio Grande. All Texan prisoners should be released. In a word, the war for freedom should be accepted by the tyrant as won. Santa Anna signed that sacred compact and won his own freedom by doing it.

"That night after our victory and after the capture of Santa Anna we gave way to the wildest outbursts of joy. We built bonfires and danced and whooped like Indians. We sang every old song that was set to music and nearly every fellow had some doggerel verses of his own to add. We were half-crazy with delight. The freedom of Texas won! The Alamo and the Goliad avenged! The tyrant in chains! Homes and families restored! Victory with honor! No wonder we were wildly jubilant.

"The Mexicans who had stood by Texas through all the fight for freedom were just as overjoyed as we. A goodly share of the praise for victory was due these patriots. Led by Captains Seguin and Menchaca and Lieutenant Flores, they had plunged into the fight at San Jacinto like tigers. Menchaca's thunderous voice could be heard above the din of battle yelling, 'Give no quarter! Remember the Alamo! Remember Goliad!' Some one said that this big shouting Mexican captain had given Santa Anna the scare that made him run for life. I guess that we all had something to do with the Dictator's panic.

"These Texas-Mexicans knew they could expect no quarter from the tyrant. He had sworn to hang Seguin and Flores and Menchaca and every last one of their followers if ever he caught them. Naturally they were jubilant when the humbled Presidente was brought captive into camp. After his interview with the crestfallen prisoner, General Houston asked Menchaca and Don Rodriguez to prepare Santa Anna a Mexican dinner. These two men had never cooked any kind of dinner in their lives; but they obeyed orders. Some jerked beef and peppers were stewed for chile con carne; and some cornmeal mixed and baked for tortillas. It was rather rough fare for one who had always had the best of his land served, when he was in his glory, on plates of silver and gold. Menchaca and his men had a hearty laugh over that meal.

"Most of the boys seemed to take joy in making things miserable for the man that had brought so much torture to our people. One of the Texans tied a Mexican on a burro. He made this fellow dress up in the general's uniform and led the jack and his costumed rider throughout the camp, yelling, 'Here comes Santa Anna, the Napoleon of the West!' Others of our men raided the tents where the prisoners were, and gathered up all the gaudy uniforms they could get. Decked in these they had a mock parade. Still others found about five hundred candles and using them as torchlights marched back and forth before the tent of Santa Anna singing every old song they could recall—and adding verses of their own for good measure.

"The angered Presidente complained to our commander, but General Houston was too wise to try to check the hilarity. The men had endured much; they were entitled to some such rough and ready outbursts over their well-won triumph. It was slight punishment after all for a tyrant.

"Our victorious soldiers, with thoughts of home,

soon turned their serious attention there. As soon as they could be released, the Texans hastened to find their scattered loved ones. It was no easy task to get families all reunited. Many of the dear ones, indeed, could never return. The difficult days ahead called for sustained heroism; yet there was something that had come out of the fierce struggle that inspired hope and courage.

"Texas was under a new flag. The Republic of the Lone Star had been born. The foundations of our young nation must be laid. There was a call for united effort to make our hard-won victory secure. It is joy to my heart now," concluded the fine Captain Miles, "to feel that the struggles and the sacrifices, made by us old-timers, then in the flush of our youth, were not made in vain. We won the fight for freedom; and we laid the foundation of the great state of Texas. I am happy for what little part I had in this work; and glad too that I still live to help keep it alive for the youth of America today."

CHAPTER XVI

SEÑOR NAVARRO TELLS THE STORY OF
HIS GRANDFATHER

MY grandfather, Don Jose Antonio Navarro, was one of the signers of the Texas Declaration of Independence," said a teacher of Spanish to a group of young Texans one day. "And he was ever proud of the part he played in helping our Lone Star State to win its freedom. I think that none of the courageous men who fought through our Revolution, and afterwards worked to lay the foundations of our state, was more steadfast in their loyalty than he. Liberty with him was a passion. He had caught its spirit from the story of Washington; and he followed its star to his dying day.

"The Navarros came to Texas," continued the

teacher, "with the colony of Spaniards that accompanied the early Franciscan friars. They helped to build San Antonio; and that old town with all the land of Tejas became very dear to their hearts.

"Grandfather was born in San Antonio in 1795. That was while Washington was still president of our Country. His mother was a sister of Don Francisco Ruiz, another of Spanish blood who signed the Texas Declaration of Independence. You see I had both a grandfather and a granduncle among that group of courageous men. Like the great patriot Lorenzo de Zavala, whose name is also on that immortal document, both of them dedicated their lives and gave their fortunes to that great cause. We have never yet recovered the fortunes; but we have a rich heritage in their lives.

"I never knew Grandfather Navarro in life. He had passed away before I was born, his years being cut short, I shall always feel, by the hardships he endured for his country. Yet he has always been an inspiration to me. My earliest recollection is of his picture in our home. His eyes seemed to follow me, chidingly when I was naughty, and looking approvingly upon me when I was good—just a childish fancy, but one that lingers with me.

"All but one of the Navarros stood with grandfather and Texas. His brother Eugene, who was a captain in the army of General Cos, fought on the side of the Mexicans. The conflict divided several of the Spanish families in Texas, setting brother against brother, father against son. It brought no disunion, however, between my Grandfather and Grandmother Navarro. When she was once asked whether she favored Mexico or Texas, her proud answer was, 'A good woman agrees with her husband.'

"My father's cousin, Don Francisco Ruiz, was another of our relatives who took part in the Revolution. As an official of San Antonio, he had some unusual experiences during and after the deadly battle at the Alamo. Following are some paragraphs from a document he wrote which tell a little of his participation in that historic event:

" 'On the Sixth of March about three p. m. General Santa Anna at the head of 4000 men advanced toward the Alamo. . . . The Mexican army charged and was twice repulsed by the deadly fire of Travis' artillery. . . . At the third charge the Toluca battalion commenced to scale the walls and suffered severely. Out of 800 men, 130 alone were left alive. . . . When the Mexican army had succeeded in entering the walls, . . . Santa Anna directed me to call on some of the neighbors to come up with carts to carry the dead to the cemetery and also to accompany him, as he was desirous to have Colonels Travis, Bowie, and Crockett shown to him.

" 'On the north battery of the fortress lay the lifeless body of Colonel Travis on the gun carriage, shot only in the forehead. Toward the west in a small fort we found the body of

Colonel Crockett. Colonel Bowie was found dead in his bed, in one of the rooms on the south side.

" 'Santa Anna, after all the Mexicans were taken out, ordered wood to be brought to burn the bodies of the Texans. He sent a company of dragoons with me to a neighboring forest. About three o'clock in the afternoon, they commenced laying the wood and dry branches, upon which a pile of dead bodies were placed; more wood was piled on them and another pile brought, and in this way they were arranged in layers. Kindling wood was distributed through the pile and about five o'clock in the evening it was lighted.

" 'The dead Mexicans of Santa Anna's army were taken to the graveyard, but not having room for them I ordered some of them to be thrown into the river which was done the same day. Santa Anna's loss was estimated at 1600 men. These were the flower of his army. The gallantry of the few Texans who defended the Alamo was really wondered at by the Mexican army. Even the generals were astonished at their vigorous resistance and how dearly the victory was bought. . . . The men burnt numbered 182. I was an eye-witness, for as alcalde of San Antonio, I was with some of the neighbors collecting the dead bodies and placing them on the funeral pyre.

(Signed) FRANCISCO ANTONIO RUIZ

P. S. My father was Don Francisco Ruiz, a member of the Texas Convention. He signed the Declaration of Independence on March 2nd, 1836.'

"The Spanish families in San Antonio became acquainted with Santa Anna some years before the Texas Revolution. Right after the battle of Medina, in 1813, he had come there as a cadet with the iron-heeled Arredondo. For a time he was quartered in the Navarro home. Stories of his wild escapades in the town during those days became fireside talk. Grandfather Navarro happened to be away at school, so he did not come into close contact with the gay young officer, who later was to play the rôle of dictator. In after years, however, he was to come into a clash with Santa Anna that put his loyal Navarro spirit to an acid test.

"Grandfather it seems to me was hardly one to endure the grueling hardships that came to him. He was of a poetic nature, a student and an orator. He liked white clothing, and always kept himself neatly dressed. His brothers called him the 'White Dove.' He was fond of horseback riding, and had a decided preference for white horses. Unfortunately during his boyhood he had been thrown from a broncho and badly injured. After this accident he walked with a slight limp; yet he ever bore himself with the pride of a true Navarro.

"When his school days were over, grandfather became a lawyer. In the position of Land Commissioner for Texas, to which he was appointed, he settled many disputes between Mexican and American colonists. It was during these days that he came in close contact with Stephen Austin. Their natures and tastes being so much akin, a cordial friendship sprang up between them that was to last through life.

"The most difficult days that came to Don Antonio and to the other Spaniards in Texas were those that followed the Revolution. Their fortunes broken, they could not maintain themselves with the same elegance as before. They had brought, one must remember, the culture and graces of old Spain into this frontier land. To an extent they had blended with the American colonists who followed the cultured Austin into Texas. Some of the young frontiersmen had even found favor in the eyes of beautiful señoritas, and happy marriages had followed. But now came a revolution in all the word implies, bringing not only political but economic and social changes. Into the new Republic came a horde of people. Too many of them were the undisciplined class, ready to sweep aside all the pioneers, and carrying an unreasoning prejudice against everything Mexican and Spanish. Naturally out of this unjust attitude came misunderstanding and trouble.

"One instance connected with my great-uncle Eugene Navarro will help to make the situation clearer. He had been, as I have already told you, a captain in the Mexican forces under General Cos. After the defeat of Santa Anna, he still remained in Texas. It was homeland to him. He reported to

General Albert Sidney Johnston, Secretary of War for the Republic, and was placed at his own request on parole.

"Uncle Eugene, to earn a living for himself, started a store in a corner room of the old Navarro homestead. Being a bachelor he chose to sleep in the store. He took joy in growing beautiful flowers in the patio of the home, and in keeping his place neat and attractive. Grandfather had his notary office in a room next to the store, and lived with his own family in the rest of the old adobe house that then rambled from the corner of Commerce along Flores Street. This Spanish home was famed for its hospitality.

"Well, some time after the Texas War, an American of the trouble-making sort came to live in a house across the road from the Navarro homestead. He had not been there long before he sent a note to Don Eugene saying that he was giving a dinner to some of his friends and would like to borrow the Navarro silver. That silver, a precious heirloom, was as fine as could be had in those days; it was a full table service, solid, and beautifully engraved. My grandmother felt no obligation to lend this treasure to a stranger to make a display in his bachelor quarters. Uncle Eugene as a compromise, or for re-proof, sent a lot of dishes from his store. This angered the man who had made the request, and from that time forward he made Uncle Eugene the target for his race hatred.

"When he found that uncle was an alien, he became more abusive. Grandfather did everything he could to keep uncle calm, and for a time he managed to restrain his proud Navarro spirit. There came a day, however, when the aggressor carried his insults too far, and the end was tragedy.

"Next door to the American newcomer lived an old Spanish woman who had a flock of chickens. These fowl ate some of the corn the American had given to his saddle horse. In a fit of anger the man shot the chickens. The old woman in retaliation secretly cut off the mane of the horse. Growing furious, the owner of the animal accused Uncle Eugene of the act, put up on uncle's store a sign derogatory to his character, and dared any one to take it down.

"My grandfather, happening by the next morning, saw the insulting paper and promptly removed and destroyed it. The trouble-seeker immediately waited on Uncle Eugene, accusing him of tearing off the sign, and threatening to cowhide him. Finally they drew their pistols and fired simultaneously. Both of them fell mortally wounded and soon died. The excitement that flamed up over this affair would have resulted in a race riot had not the calming influence of Grandfather Navarro prevailed. He urged a spirit of fairness. There was no blame in his heart for his American neighbors and friends because of the acts of a ruffian. He sought no revenge for the unwarranted killing of his brother. However keenly he must have felt the tragedy, he firmly set it aside and turned his thoughts upon other matters then before him.

"Just about this time the projected expedition was engaging the attention of the leader of the Texan Republic. The main purposes back of this expedition were to open up trade with New Mexico, and also to induce the people of that province to throw off their Mexican yoke and join the Republic of Texas. Convincing reports had come to the officials of this young nation that the New Mexicans were eager to effect such a union. One other major object in sending out this expedition was to explore the western regions to which Texas laid claim and bring them more securely within its jurisdiction.

"Mirabeau Lamar, then president of the Republic, gave approval against the wishes of Congress, to the expedition. In June, 1841, with the President escorting it for a little way, it set forth on its long, hazardous journey. My grandfather, Don Antonio Navarro, was one of the three hundred and twenty men who joined in this venture. His keen desire to extend the blessings of freedom to others was doubtless the impelling motive in his going on this ill-fated quest. He honestly believed that the people were ready to throw off the yoke of tyranny and even went so far as to prepare an eloquent address welcoming them into the fold of the free republic of Texas. Instead of winning an opportunity to make that address, he won only chains and imprisonment. The expedition ended in tragic failure.

"Only one of its major purposes did it accomplish. The western regions of Texas were more thoroughly explored. Over the vast semi-arid plains and rough mountains there, this band of men made slow and painful progress until they finally reached the borders of New Mexico. This part of our great land became a good deal better known because of the wanderings of those adventurers over it. Those that had joined the expedition for adventure and the pleasures the trip might bring—and there were a goodly number of these—found plenty of adventure, but little of a pleasurable kind.

"The story of the man-testing journey was afterwards written and published by one of the participants, George Willis Kendall, a guest of the expedition. He was an editor of the New Orleans *Picayune*, and went out at this time to build up his health, and incidentally enrich his knowledge of our country. The venture into the then practically unknown western regions of Texas with this expedition challenged his interest.

"Through the pages of the book that came from his pen, one can follow the intriguing story of this misadventure into the wilds, which my grandfather Navarro shared. The earlier days of it were filled with pleasurable excitement. The men ran into great herds of buffalo and feasted on the choice portions of the fat young animals they killed. Later in the journey they regretted their wastefulness of this good meat. At one place called 'Cross Timbers' they had a feast of wild honey.

"Captain Caldwell, a fine scout, and one of the signers of the Texas Declaration of Independence, was with them. It was largely through the eternal vigilance of this leader—'Old Paint,' as he was affectionately called by his men because of his black and gray beard—that the expedition was protected from Indian attacks.

"As they went farther into the northwest, difficulties seemed to multiply. On the arid stretches men and animals suffered intensely at times for lack of water. Food gave out. A fire in their camp wrought serious destruction to their belongings. Two Mexican guides they had employed mistook the Witchita River for the Red River and led them astray; then in fear of punishment at the hands of the Texans they 'vamoosed.'

"While trying to find their own way to the settlements of New Mexico, one small group of the Texans came upon some Mexican sheepherders who directed them on to a ranch. Here the party feasted on mutton until they made up for their long fast. The hosts who supplied them so generously spoke Spanish freely, and to them the Texans explained that they had come into these parts for the purpose of opening up trade. It was further made plain to these people that Texas would welcome the inhabitants of that region to its standard; but if they would not join peacefully, the Republic would not force the issue. Since the New Mexicans were groaning under the misrule of the satellites of the Dictator Santa Anna, who again was in power, the Texans were confident that the response to this invitation to join a free Republic would be favorable.

"No expression other than one of fear of the consequences came. The ranchers warned the party to look out for treachery, but the Texans would not listen. They went on to a little town named Chico. The inhabitants there trembled at their coming, but the kindly-hearted Mexican women cooked food and fed the hungry strangers. When the next village was reached, another warning came that Governor Armijo was waiting at San Miguel with Mexican troops.

"This San Miguel," explained the Spanish teacher, "was a town of small adobe houses on the upper Pecos River. The Pecos is a beautiful stream that comes sparkling and dancing down from the snowy mountains near Santa Fe, which is about fifty miles to the northwest. In earlier times, San Miguel was a port of entry, the tax officers of New Mexico coming there to meet and to collect fees from all trading caravans. Governor Armijo used to assess every wagon five hundred dollars. He was a cruel and ignorant man who had won his place of power because he had helped the tyrannical rulers in Mexico to crush down the Pueblo uprising; and then he had lorded it over his own New Mexican people. It is not generally known that the Texans were wrongly blamed by the Mexican leaders for the uprising of the Pueblos. Armijo, anxious to court further favors with these rulers, eagerly seized this chance to get a band of Texans in his clutches.

"When the vanguard of the expedition neared the little village of Cuesta, it was suddenly surrounded by more than a hundred Mexican soldiers. The captain of the band, Salezar, suavely asked them who they were, and what was their purpose in entering New Mexico. On being told, he politely but firmly insisted that the Texans give up their arms, assuring them that these would be returned. Then the brute, marching his captives into the village, summarily ordered their execution. It was only through the prompt interference of the son of the alcalde of the place that this cold-blooded murder was averted. The prisoners, upon his pleading, were finally taken on to San Miguel for a hearing before the high-handed Governor Armijo.

"The haughty official spared the lives of the band that Salezar had sent to him, but ordered them back to prison in San Miguel. Two others of the Texan band who had been previously taken, and who, breaking out of their miserable jail, had made a heroic attempt to get word back to their comrades, were not so fortunate. Recaptured, they refused, even on promise that their lives be spared, to betray their companions, and were taken into the public plaza and shot to death. The other Texans who were in a prison overlooking the place of execution saw the whole bloody affair.

"Another even blacker happening occurred a little later when Lewis, one of the other captured Texans, to save his own worthless hide, did turn traitor, and effected the surrender of the rest of the expeditionary force to Armijo. Grandfather Navarro was told by the Mexicans who came bringing gifts and uttering words of pity for the unarmed prisoners that they would all be killed. Armijo, they said, was a tyrant. He did not go to such lengths, in his brutality, however; but he did put his captives to most inhuman treatment, ordering his cut-throat Captain Salezar to march them off to El Paso. Not even Mr. Kendall, who had Mexican passports to assure his safety, was freed.

"Of course from their own viewpoint, these Mexican officials were acting within their legal authority. The Texans had come, they felt, into their province to alienate the people there. The Texans on the other hand claimed part at least of what is now New Mexico. There was, moreover, no warlike intention on the part of the Texans. It was to be a peaceful conquest if any; and the chief objective was to open trade between Texas and Mexico. Willingness to lay down their arms and to accept the assurances of the New Mexican leaders, should have convinced Salezar and Armijo of these friendly intentions. The best that can be said of the Governor and his brutal captain is that they were unsportsmanlike, whatever the legalities in the case.

"Salezar continued to act the part of a savage during all the long march to El Paso. One of the prisoners who fell exhausted died on the way. Another whose feet became terribly swollen refused to try to march farther, whereupon Salezar threatened to shoot him unless he hobbled on. 'Shoot then!' the brave fellow retorted, flinging back his blanket. The brutal Salezar whipped out his revolver and added another murder to his crimes. A third weakened soldier was frightened to death by a Mexican soldier who kept snapping his rifle in the face of the emaciated man.

"Acts of this sort caused the Mexican Commander, Elias Gonzales, called 'General Elias' with affection, to denounce the inhuman Salezar and to put him under arrest. He deserved a worse fate, but I do not know whether he ever received it at the hands of the Mexican authorities. As for the traitor Lewis, he was rewarded with part of the goods taken from the Texans, but he was so despised by both Americans and Mexicans that he finally left for South America and lived there under an assumed name. Everybody hates a traitor.

"The treatment accorded the Texans by General Elias and his aides was in sharp contrast from that they had suffered at the hands of Armijo and Salezar. Mr. Kendall tells how Captain Ochoa, one of the fine young officers under General Elias, 'expressed his abhorrence' of Salezar and his herd of *ladrones* and *picaros,* as he called Salezar's soldiers. He also relates that General Elias invited him and other Texans to his home, and while they were there enjoying the hospitality, the commander of the Texan expedition, General MacLeod, and Mr. Navarro, who took all their meals with the generous host, arrived. 'We immediately sat down to a sumptuous supper,' wrote Mr. Kendall. 'What a contrast! On that very morning . . . Falconer, Van Ness and myself had hastily swallowed a meal of badly-made mush, upon the ground, our minds full of misgivings as to the treatment we might receive on getting out of the hands of Salezar . . . now we were seated at a table covered with luxuries, the guests of a gentleman attentive to our every want. Even the fact that we were still prisoners was forgotten.'

"If General Elias had been given the authority, he doubtless would have been glad to release all the men that had fallen under his charge. This he could not do, however, so he sent them on with Captain Ochoa, who, as Mr. Kendall records, in traveling with them 'for five or six hundred miles, ever proved himself a friend and a gentleman.'

"From El Paso to Chihuahua was a barren region, but thanks to the good people of El Paso the men did not suffer. At Chihuahua there was great excitement, the people all running about shouting, 'Mira! Mira! Los Tejanos, los Tejanos!' The Mexican women were especially compassionate. If they could have had their way the prisoners would have all been set free. In Chihuahua my grandfather secured a number of comforts, and all the men were given shoes and blankets. Here sympathy and bet-

ter treatment, however, did not take away their
longing for liberty and home. The men wanted to
escape, and when they reached a place called San
Pablo, they were about to risk an attempt. Grandfather persuaded them not to do so and afterwards
they saw the wisdom of his advice. It was at this
time he predicted that he would be the last man set
free.

"At Durango they were taken in charge by another officer, Captain Velasco. He took compassion
on his footsore prisoners and mounted each of them
on a burro. On the way, grandfather was placed
under an extra guard; the Mexican leader had evidently singled him out for special treatment and
put him in irons. The common people were filled
with compassion for the unfortunate men, but
there was little they could do except give them
food.

"It was a grueling experience from first to last.
The Texans, with their number cut down by death
from disease and exposure, finally reached the capital of Mexico. A ragged, haggard-looking lot they
were when they reached this journey's end. Even
the prisoners themselves, with a grim sense of
humor, joked about their own tattered and forlorn
appearance. Once in Mexico City, they were consigned to federal dungeons to endure the criminals
there and the vermin that infested them. What a

fate, I often have thought, for the 'White Dove' to languish as he did there for years in the filthy Acordada.

"Mr. Kendall writes of visiting him in prison. He says that he went through many iron doors and at last found Don Antonio Navarro in his cell, pale, ragged and haggard. His only companions were criminals. He had been fed on frijoles until he was ill. The filth of his surroundings annoyed him most. Mr. Kendall who, after months of effort on the part of his friends in the United States, had been given his freedom, carried messages and love to this proud prisoner's friends and loved ones, but grandfather admonished him to tell his wife and family to make no efforts on his behalf in money or petitions.

"Before this time the Señora Navarro had ridden on horseback from the ranch near Seguin to San Antonio. The country was full of Comanches, and her young son was her only companion. The purpose of making this hazardous trip was to secure the services of a lawyer to write in legal terms a petition to Santa Anna pleading for the release of her husband. This was signed by the Señora, and her children, one of the brood being my father. Santa Anna on receiving this document sent it to the prisoner with the message that the petition would be granted if Don Jose Antonio Navarro would also sign it. He refused, and told the messenger that he would never sign. To do so he felt would put him under obligation to Santa Anna. He would have no compromise with the Dictator. Don Antonio was a mild, unaggressive man, yet he had a will of iron. He stood for the principles of liberty, and Santa Anna stood for everything that Don Antonio Navarro loathed.

"Santa Anna even tried indirect bribery on my grandfather about this time. A position in the Mexican army with a money settlement was held out to the patriot. He would not be tempted. In 1842 the United States and the European powers secured the release of all the men of the Santa Fe expedition except one. That one was my grandfather. It was not until 1845 that he finally was given his freedom. That was when the party dominated by Santa Anna lost some of its power.

"Though his liberty was granted in a legal way, his friends feared his life might be taken by friends of Santa Anna. To prevent any such tragedy, the prison commander at Vera Cruz, who had sympathy for Don Antonio, helped him to get out of Mexico in disguise and under an assumed name. He finally reached New Orleans, where he was shown much attention by admiring friends. It was a memorable day of rejoicing when he returned to his old home in San Antonio. The welcome recalled

that given to his good friend Stephen Austin years
before.

"One of the first things Don Antonio did on getting back to the Navarro ranch near Seguin was to
gather his children round him and give them an
examination. He was rather disheartened over the
results of the test. His stalwart sons could break
the wildest mustang, and rope and ride any long-
horn cow, but they were behind in their book education. His own ideals were for a classical education for his children. They had barely learned the
'Three R's' in the limited school training of those
pioneer days. This was hardly a good start towards
the old classics he would have them study in Latin
and Greek; but it was now too late for them to go
that long road. It was a great sorrow to Don
Antonio.

"My grandmother was of a somewhat more
practical turn of mind. She felt that book learning, though of great value, might be carried somewhat too far. She was inclined to feel that her
husband's serious troubles were due in a measure
to his reading and thinking too much. When told
that the names of Zavala, Ruiz, and Navarro would
ring down the ages, she would answer, 'I am proud
of my husband and his good name. I am proud of
this thing called liberty; but the Spanish-speaking
people in Texas are too few to survive in justice

and prosperity among the Americans. We have given all to Texas and my children will have to survive below their blood and station in money, in education, and in society.'

"Perhaps, this to an extent has been true. Yet we of Spanish blood who have descended from the founders of our great Lone Star State have a pardonable pride in our rich heritage; and the day we feel is near when the American people will understand and appreciate the spirit of our sires who rose above race and language to fight side by side with the heroes who gave to Texas its Declaration of Independence, its freedom, and its constitution which guarantees liberty for all its citizens.

"The unswerving loyalty of my grandfather to the cause of freedom came from no passing enthusiasm. Probably his classical education had helped him to catch the spirit in the old Greeks. He had renewed it by his study of English and American history. It was a living part of him. This is shown very clearly in the address he prepared but never had a chance to deliver to the people of New Mexico. I treasure the document in Don Antonio's neat penmanship. It was kept by him through all his torturing imprisonment. It was passed on to me by my father with many admonitions to translate and preserve. The following excerpts from this priceless paper breathe for me the spirit of my revered grandsire; and voice some of his high ideals.

"The manuscript is marked by my grandfather: 'Col Jose Antonio Navarro. To be delivered at Santa Fe, New Mexico. To the inhabitants of Santa Fe and other towns of New Mexico east of the Rio Grande.'

Fellow Citizens:

The flag of the Republic of Texas government claims jurisdiction over the lands you inhabit, is displayed before you, and offers protection and other advantages that Mexico cannot extend to you.

Undoubtedly Mexico has never had the power of self government or if it had, it has lost it entirely. Does its history correspond to their expectations? O! what vain deluding hopes!

The continuing rebellions in Mexico have not permitted the industrious inhabitants to better their conditions in the short intervals of peace they have enjoyed.

The leaders of Mexico make haste to lay exorbitant taxes, they neglect all laws, and administration of justice and the protection of the people. When a nation is in such a deplorable condition the law of Nature which governs us is the preservation of life and the pursuit of happiness.

This Republic of Texas rises like Hercules, invincible from its cradle, suppressing evil, and banishing danger.

The day is not distant either when you will see the Texas nation rolling in wealth and large cities flourishing on the very lands now overrun by the wild savage.

"You see," concluded the Spanish teacher, "my grandfather, Don Antonio Navarro, had a dream and a vision. All has come true."

CHAPTER XVII

SOME ADVENTURES OF "BIG FOOT" WALLACE

THE picturesque frontiersman, 'Big Foot' Wallace, was a native son of Virginia," said Mrs. Neeley, a gray-haired daughter of old Texas. "He was one of the most courageous men among the brave ones that helped to make the conquest of our state—and no wonder, for he had the blood of the great Scottish heroes, William Wallace and Robert Bruce, in his veins. In spirit he was a good deal like Davy Crockett, full of good humor, and ready always to fight for the right.

"The thing that impelled him to cast his lot with the Texans, was the tragedy of the Goliad. His brother, Samuel Wallace, and a cousin, William Wallace, had been shot down with the other brave fellows of Fannin's company who were slain there after they had surrendered. 'Big Foot' Wallace was not out of his teens when the word of this foul killing of these two close relatives came to him. He vowed he would avenge their death.

"The Revolution was over when he reached Texas, but there was much yet to be done in that borderland. Stalwart young men like Wallace were badly needed. Roving tribes of Indians were a constant source of danger. Outlawry was to be held in check, and there was real danger—it was soon to be proved—from raiding bands of Mexicans. Here was one chance for Wallace to even the score against those who had stirred his righteous wrath.

"Of course we mustn't think that this determined young man was always going about with a grim face," continued the pioneer mother who was telling the story; "on the contrary, 'Big Foot' Wallace was as jovial a man as ever played the heroic part. He was ever ready for a good joke. When he first landed at Galveston, an ambitious real estate dealer tried to get him to purchase some lowland in the projected city. Observing that water had lately covered the lots he was offered, he said dryly, 'Wal, I wouldn't mind making a purchase if you'll throw in a boat with the bargain.'

"Wallace soon got all the land he wanted and more without paying for it. Every man who fought for independence was given six hundred and forty acres. That is equal to a square mile of land. He was assigned the portion that would have gone to his brother, Samuel, who was killed at the Goliad. The land was situated near La Grange, not so very far from San Antonio.

"His first venture in Texas was farming. Wallace soon tired of this occupation, not because he wasn't a hard worker, but because he liked hunting and fighting better than following the plow. As a boy in Virginia he, like Davy Crockett, had spent a good deal of his time in the woods with his gun. Texas in those pioneer days was a 'Happy Hunting Ground.' Buffalo, bear, deer and other kinds of game were plentiful. For one who had a daring spirit and a steady aim, hunting offered an easy and an exciting way of making a living, so this natural-born frontiersman quit farming for the more venturesome occupation.

"The years that followed brought 'Big Foot' adventures a-plenty. As a big game hunter, Indian fighter and stage-driver, he was always in the thick of things in that borderland. It took men of just the type of Wallace to tame the frontier. Some one had to protect the settlers from Indian raiders and outlaws just as Daniel Boone and his kind had done in the years before. There could have been no permanent building of homes and towns without such courageous men.

"Wallace had hardly reached La Grange before he had his first Indian fight. A band of Apaches slipped into the settlement one night and stole all the stock round about. 'Big Foot,' Charles King, who was then sheriff of the county, Frank Black and four others followed the trail of the redskins and finally ran into fifteen well-mounted Indians traveling down the valley of the Colorado River. Seeing the whites after them the redskins scattered, but they didn't get out of reach before Black brought one of the thieving band down, while Wallace killed another.

"The fleeing Apaches chanced to run upon some emigrants. One of the braves, in a bear skin, was attempting to spy upon the camp when he was seen by a negro. The negro, taking a shot at the supposed animal, nearly jumped out of his own skin when he saw an Indian leap out of the bear hide. 'Bears! Injuns!' he yelled, dashing towards camp. About that time Black and Wallace rode into the confused crowd of whites.

"A moment later they dashed away after the Indians. Suddenly they came upon a wounded one lying on a bear skin. The negro's bullet evidently had struck its mark. This wasn't enough for Black, however. Not long before this he had lost his whole family in an Indian massacre. His life was given to the avenging of that deed. Off he leaped from his horse to shoot and scalp the redskin. The sight made Wallace ill. He lived to kill a good many Indians himself, but he never would scalp one.

"At one time Wallace while hunting stopped at a clear stream to fill the gourd he carried as a canteen. In pioneer times these gourds served as cups and dippers and bottles and buckets. Wallace had found an ingenious way to get them cleaned out perfectly. He would pour some molasses into the gourd, and let the busy ants do the work of cleaning out the fibers, seeds and molasses. Well, he was stooping to fill his gourd, when he saw the reflection of some Indians in the clear, quiet water. The frontiersman whirled and aimed his gun, but the chief motioned to him not to shoot. Seeing that he was trapped, Wallace decided it best to obey orders.

"The band took him about ten miles to their encampment. There a council was held. He thought that it meant his death; but after a while an old Indian woman came out of a tepee carrying some food to him. These Indians kept him prisoner for several weeks. They were Lipans, a sub-tribe of the great Comanche nation. Finally, he found a chance, as Daniel Boone once did, to escape from his red captors, and he made his way back home.

"Wallace once told me," continued Mrs. Neeley, "of his first visit to San Antonio. It was still an old Spanish town with the river winding through it. A fallen tree served as a foot bridge across the stream. The streets were built crooked, it was said, for protection. Buffalo skins were often hung at the ends of the narrow ways to keep out Indian arrows. In those days children were often kidnapped by the Indians who would sometimes raid the towns in daylight. There were so many of them that the white folk had hard work to protect themselves against the raiding reds.

" 'The first thing I did, when I reached San Antonio,' Wallace said, 'was to go straight to the old Alamo. On every side there were evidences of the terrible fight there. Charred bones of the heroes whose bodies had been burned were lying about; and the walls were marked with bullets. It was all too much for me. I just leaned against those old gray walls and cried like a baby.' This, brave, tender-hearted man, you remember, had lost a brother and a cousin at the Goliad.

"While he stayed in San Antonio, Wallace lived in the old Veremendi house where James Bowie had won his bride, and where Milam had been killed. He paid for his board by supplying the landlady there with wild game. Every day he would go hunting in the nearby woods and hills and come back with a load of venison, which he sold from house to house. Deer was plentiful in those days.

"There were Indians in great numbers too. Despite the fact that old missions were in and around San Antonio, they seemed to have left little lasting effect on the redmen. Most of them were still untamed. There were so many wild ones, in fact, that the people kept a watchman in the tower of San Fernando Cathedral to ring the big bell there if any warlike Indians should appear.

"One day while Wallace was out hunting near the Alamo, he heard the old bell clanging, but paid little heed to it. Suddenly a Mexican woman ran by shouting to him, 'Correr! Los Indies!' Wallace didn't 'savvy' so he just kept on quietly walking with his game into San Antonio. When he reached there, he found the town full of excitement. A band of Comanches had dashed into the place, carried off two Mexican women and killed a boy.

"Most of the men were away at the time on their farms or ranches, or like Wallace, hunting. There were not many Americans living in San Antonio at this time. A few Spanish families still made this historic town their home; and there were some Americans—Maverick, Jacques, Riddle, Smith and others. The rest of the populace was largely Mexican with a sprinkling of tame Indians. Had all the men been there it would have been difficult for them to ward off these surprise attacks. The Indians were wily and numerous.

"The moment the alarm had been spread there was 'mounting in hot haste.' The sheriff, Charles King, with Sam Maverick, Wallace, Jacques, Señor Menchaca, Señor Flores, and others were soon on the heels of the marauders. No Indians, however, did the posse find. It was just another of the murderous scares that kept the people at tension through those earlier years in that borderland.

"Wallace's next move was to the newly established capital, Austin. He was fond enough of San Antonio, but with the seat of government being moved to this other site on the Colorado, there was more activity; and thither 'Big Foot' went to do his bit in the building. Logging was his first work. There were houses to be erected; so up the stream he went into the timber, and soon he had his rafts of logs coming down the river. Another job he undertook was the digging of a well. The price was twelve dollars a foot. He said he hoped he would have to go down fifty feet, but he hadn't dug more than nineteen before there was a rush of clear pure water into the hole. Wallace yelled, 'Haul me up! I'm drowning!' and up he came. The well, which stood for many years on Congress Street, was called 'Wallace's Well.'

"It was about this time that William Alexander

Anderson Wallace—which was our hero's full name —had the nickname, 'Big Foot,' added for good measure. Most folk jump to the conclusion this new name came to him because he had unusually large feet; but this is not so. His feet were not very large for a man who stood six feet two and weighed over two hundred pounds. No, the name came from the fact that he kept trying to capture or kill a prowling chief who left footprints fifteen inches long. This redskin's feet were three inches longer, in fact, than those of King Henry the Eighth, from one of which we got the length of our foot rule.

"The chief who wore such 'heap big' moccasins was such a wily leader and was always up to such mischief that Wallace and Sheriff Charles King determined to put an end to his thieving and murdering. Wallace talked so much about this Indian, 'Big Foot,' and kept so persistently after the troublesome chieftain, that in time folk began to call him 'Big Foot' Wallace, and the nickname clung to him ever after.

"On one of the raids a ranger, Tom Green, wounded the much-hunted Indian. King and Wallace made a rush to capture the chieftain, but were overwhelmed by his warriors and forced to retreat. Some years later while Wallace was driving the overland stage from Austin to El Paso, he chanced

to see the big-footed Indian's moccasin tracks in the
dust of the road. Evidently the chieftain was not
far away, but since Wallace was carrying the U. S.
mail, he could not stop to trail down the Indian.
He passed the word on to a friend by the name of
Westfall to keep his eyes open for 'Big Foot' and
his thieving band.

"A few nights after this the nearby ranches were
robbed of their stock. Westfall with three men and
a boy, Preston Polly, struck out after the marauders. Coming upon the Indian camp, Westfall told
his followers to secrete themselves while he crept
near the camp to investigate. Suddenly he discovered the big-footed chief leading his horse to
water. Westfall fired and the Indian fell. The
band, left leaderless, and thinking perhaps that the
Texas rangers were upon them, fled. When Wallace got back home, there was a pair of huge moccasins. Westfall had sent them on as a souvenir.

"The Indians, blaming Wallace for the death of
their chieftain, plotted to waylay and kill him. On
reaching the Pecos Valley, the watchful stage-
driver, seeing plenty of Indian signs, told his guards
that the stage must be put through with all speed to
get out of reach of the redskins. Within the next
twenty-four hours, they had made ninety miles.
Then thinking themselves safer, they paused for a
little rest in some chapparal.

"About midnight, a blackbird startled from the thicket, lit right on the head of a guard named Hubbard. Feeling he was marked for death, the guard rushed to Wallace. 'Big Foot' drawled, 'Yes, it might mean death, because the Indians are skulkin' 'round, and you stand as good a show of gettin' shot as any of the rest of us. The redskins scared that bird, and it just took you for a stump.'

"At that instant the mules began to blow, and look towards the bushes. Wallace yelled, 'Men, wake up, Injuns!'

"No attack came for an hour or two, so some of the men concluded it was a false alarm, and lay down again to get a few more winks of sleep. One of them—a fellow named Peter—rested his head between the spokes of one of the wheels of the stagecoach. Suddenly the Indians began to shoot, and Peter in his excitement got his head caught fast in the wheel.

" 'Hey, Pete!' yelled Wallace; 'don't run off with that stage!'

"In spite of their excitement and danger, the men all broke out laughing. Their fun, however, did not make them stop their fighting. They were popping away as fast as they could at the Indians. Finally the redskins retreated, carrying away some dead and wounded. There was no further trouble from them for the rest of that trip. They had found out that it was bad medicine for them to fool around 'Big Foot' Wallace. It took cool and daring men of his type to put the mail through in those dangerous days.

"After his stage-driving days were over, Wallace became one of Jack Hays' band of Texas Rangers. The adventures he had under this fine frontier leader would take many hours to tell. These hard-riding, sure-shooting keepers of peace in that borderland were constantly facing danger from Indians, outlaws, and trouble-making Mexicans who carried on their feud with the Texans for some years after the Revolution had been won. There is little doubt that they were aided and abetted in their deviltry by some of the autocratic leaders in Mexico who still refused to acknowledge the independence of Texas.

"The Santa Fe Expedition gave excuse for Santa Anna to back some raids into the Lone Star State. Not that this leader ever hoped to regain dominion over that region; his purpose seems rather to have been to make other countries feel that the war with Texas was not over. If there was open conflict between Mexico and Texas, it would keep down the movement for annexation to the United States—a thing that many Texans and many people in our Country were eager to bring about.

"In 1842 there was a sharp renewal of trouble

between Mexico and Texas. Sam Houston, re-
elected to the presidency, wanted no more war
between the two countries, but events came near
precipitating another such conflict. In early spring
of that year, a Mexican army under General Woll
suddenly appeared before San Antonio and demanded the surrender of the town. Colonel Jack
Hays and his rangers were too few to give the
invaders the worst of an open battle, so they destroyed the military stores in the place and let the
Mexicans march into it with colors flying. Other
troops of Santa Anna also took possession of Refugio
and Goliad. They held these towns for only a few
days, however, and then retreated back to the Rio
Grande. It seemed just a raid made in reprisal for
the Santa Fe expedition, and for the part some of
the Texans had been taking in the revolutionary
movements in Mexico.

"Houston had advised his people to keep clear of
these revolutions. He wanted Texas to steer away
from such trouble and strengthen herself. The
young nation was in no condition to undertake
another war at that time. Some of the Texans did
not agree with this pacific policy; they wanted to
jump in and fight it out with the Mexicans. A bill
was put through the Texas Congress authorizing
the President to sell ten million acres of public

land to get funds to fight the enemy. Houston promptly vetoed it.

"Then came another invasion of Texas. In September 1842, General Woll led about one thousand soldiers across the Rio Grande, attacked and captured San Antonio, and took sixty-seven Texans, a number of them officials, prisoner. The enraged Texans rushed to arms, and under the command of the fighting leaders, Caldwell and Hays, attacked the Mexicans at Salado, repulsing them with heavy loss. The victory was almost annulled, however, when a company under Captain Dawson, hastening to join the Texans, was trapped by the Mexicans and all killed or captured. After this engagement, Woll beat a retreat to the south of the Rio Grande taking with him all the prisoners who could make the trip.

"Houston issued a call for volunteers to carry the war into Mexico. General Sommerwell was given command of the army. The Texans were displeased with this choice, for Sommerwell, they felt, had little sympathy with the proposed invasion. After events seemed to justify this feeling. Their commander led them on to Laredo, and then returned with the main body to San Antonio.

"Two hundred men would not go back. They stayed near the border, elected William Fisher as their Colonel, and crossed the Rio Grande to attack the town of Mier. On Christmas Day the Texans surprised the guard and captured some of the stone buildings. From these vantage points they kept on with the fight until night fell. The next day the Mexican General Ampudia sent a white flag with a messenger who told the Texans that another army was nearing the town. For them to persist in their fighting meant certain death for them. The general offered generous terms of surrender.

"A council of war was held. Many of the Texans wanted to keep on fighting; but Colonel Fisher was seriously wounded and the daring band had lost heavily during their fight. It was deemed best by most of the remaining force to take the proffered terms. They had been assured that an exchange of prisoners would be speedily arranged, so that they might return to Texas. Ampudia's offer was accepted by the majority of the men.

"The Texans were soon to be disillusioned as to what the glittering promises of this Mexican general meant. When it was too late, they found out that Ampudia himself, all but beaten, had played false about the reinforcements about to come to his relief. In the next place, he had no intention of keeping his word. Instead of holding our men as he had promised, near the border, he soon had them marching off to Matamoras, on their way to the prisons of Mexico City.

[305]

" 'Big Foot' Wallace was among the daring band thus lured into capture and tragic suffering. When he used to tell me as a girl of what they had endured during the hard years that followed," said Mrs. Neeley, "I always cried. He protested vigorously against surrendering to Ampudia. The bitter memories of what had happened to his brother and his cousin at the Goliad made him distrust the Mexicans. When the Texans began to give up their arms, Wallace rushed up to Captain Cameron and with him and forty others of like spirit, pleaded for a chance to fight the way out and recross the Rio Grande. He was the very last of the Texans to give up his firearms.

"The prisoners were marched first to Saltillo, then on to Haciedo Salado. Here they charged upon their captors and many of them made their escape. Wallace, riding a dun pacing mule, was among those that got away. By nightfall he and his companions had put a good deal of distance between them and their enemies.

"Unfortunately the escaping Texans headed for the mountains which in this part of Mexico are barren. They were soon suffering severely for want of water and food. Finally they were forced to kill their animals, the pacing mule and the rest. Some of the men in delirium wandered away. Wallace and three companions traveled for five days with not a bite to eat or a drop to drink. In their distress they chewed prickly pears to try to get some moisture, but these, like the green persimmons, were astringent and only added misery to suffering. A few of the poor fellows finally died, and the rest happened to stumble upon a detachment of Mexican cavalry and surrendered.

"General Mexia, the commander, showed a kindly heart by doing all he could to alleviate the wants of the prisoners that had fallen into his hands. When they were able to travel, he returned them to Salado.

"Wallace told me," continued Mrs. Neeley, "that on finding the Mexicans in that desert region, he saw one of the soldiers with a gourd. Rushing up to the cavalryman, he said excitedly, 'Give me my gourd!'

"'Poor fellow, it is my pleasure,' said the Mexican, and Wallace grabbing it began to drink so fast that the soldier finally wrested it away from him, and held it back for a time. He was afraid the thirst-crazed man would kill himself by drinking too much.

"Within a few days the Mexican cavalry had brought in one hundred and sixty men. The Texans were now in such a condition that they could put up no further resistance, so they had to march painfully on under their guard towards Mexico

City. Orders then came from Santa Anna that would have made of Mier a second Goliad; it was his wish that the prisoners should all be shot. General Mexia refused to obey the cruel order; so the Dictator changed it. Every tenth one among the Texans, he finally decreed must die, and the rest should be imprisoned.

"Knowing it would be useless to try to get better terms for his captives, the Mexican general directed

the Texans to prepare for the fate that awaited them. To settle the question as to which ones should suffer the death penalty, a lottery was arranged. As many beans as there were Texan prisoners were placed in a jar. One tenth of the beans were black; the others white. Each of the captives was brought blindfolded up to this jar of fate, and given his chance of life or death.

" 'Big Foot' Wallace used to tell this part of his life story over and over," Mrs. Neeley remarked. "It seemed never to be off his mind—one hundred and fifty-nine white beans and seventeen black ones. It was a cruel ordeal, but the Texans never flinched. They even joked grimly in the face of Fate.

" 'Let us be at it,' said Captain Cameron. He drew a white bean. Captain Eastland was the first to draw a black one. 'They will rob me of just forty years,' said Major Cocke nonchalantly as he thrust in his hand to decide his own fate. 'Big Foot' Wallace joked about his big hand as he put it into the jar and got two beans. Fingering these a moment, he finally let one drop and was saved. Major Dunham was not so fortunate. 'I am ready to die,' he said when the black bean appeared; 'I only wish I could repeat the sacrifice for Texas.'

"Hanging on the walls of the old Alamo today may be seen the copy of the letter that this patriotic Texan wrote to his mother during that soul-searching experience. It reads:

Dear Mother:

I write you under the most awful feelings that a son ever addressed a mother, for in half an hour my doom will be finished on earth. I am doomed to die by the hands of the Mexicans for our late attempt to escape the orders of Santa Anna, that every tenth man should be shot. We drew lots, I was one of the unfortunates—Alas, I cannot say anything more. I die, I hope in firmness. Farewell, may God bless you, and may he in this my last hour forgive and pardon all my sins. Farewell.

Your affectionate son,
R. H. DUNHAM

"As each of the black beans was drawn its holder was placed in the death line. The men on whom the death sentence had thus fallen stood as calm as if they were on parade. At last the fatal lottery was over, and the rifles rang out. Many of the men who had been spared for continuing punishment wept bitterly when they heard the death shots.

"The murderous work done, the rest of the prisoners, chained in pairs, were marched on towards Mexico City. Within seven leagues of that place, they were placed in a room so small that they had to stand up all night. Many of them might have died of suffocation had they not cut holes through the door. It was this same night that orders came from Santa Anna that Captain Cameron be executed. The Mexicans led the fine leader away, and began to bandage his eyes; but he coolly told them to desist. He could look Death in the face for liberty and Texas. This brave captain was a native son of Scotland and one of the finest of the men that had cast their lot with the Lone Star Republic.

"After his cruel execution the remaining Texans were taken on to the dungeons of the Mexican Capital where the members of the Santa Fe expedition were incarcerated. The torturing experiences that came to these courageous men who had simply been carrying forward the fight for freedom remind one of the days of the Inquisition. They were heavily ironed—the shackles on 'Big Foot' Wallace being so tight, he used to tell me, that his arms and legs turned black. At San Luis Potisi, the Governor's wife heard of it, and ordered the chains all removed.

"Despite all their sufferings, the men kept their courage and good cheer. The life of the party was genial Major Bennet. He was about sixty years of age, had fought in the War of 1812, and he knew from experience that a little fun is the best kind of help in trouble. Being a good Christian and knowing his Bible about by heart, he often turned the sayings of Scripture to a good purpose. When they were riding on their burros into one of the Mexican towns, he raised his hands and said, 'Weep not, ye daughters of Mexico; your rulers are coming seated on white asses.' This was to the peons who were uttering their cries of pity as the Texans were marched through the streets.

"At another time when an unsavory meal was

being served, he quoted from Job, 'The things that my soul refused to touch are as my sorrowful meat.' 'My flesh is clothed with worms and clods of dust.' Sometimes he led the prisoners in chanting the Shepherd Psalm, and other comforting parts of Holy Writ. Everybody loved the courageous, cheerful leader. He was one of the quieter heroes of our country.

"Near Mexico City the captives were again put in irons. Once there they were kept in a dungeon by night and then under armed guards were forced to work on the roads by day carrying sacks of sand and heavy stones. 'Big Foot' Wallace grew fairly strong on the hard labor and the hard fare. After a time, however, he and some of the other prisoners were sent to Perote, about one hundred and fifty miles away. Many of them died from the hardships and the filthy dungeon and bad fare. Wallace suffered so much he lost his reason for a time.

"A daring few of them managed to escape. Among these was a man by the name of Twohig who lived in San Antonio. He had been a sailor in his youth, and he built his Texas home in remembrance of his ship. The place looked somewhat like an ordinary Mexican house on the outside, but inside it was suggestive of the schooner in which he used to sail the seas. Mrs. Twohig had difficulty in keeping servants because of the many winding stairs. My grandmother used to visit her, and as a girl I often heard of the adventures of Twohig.

"He had been captured with others when General Woll made his second raid on San Antonio. These prisoners for the most part were confined in the formidable old Castle of Perote. It had dungeons that dated from the days of the Inquisition. A terrible place it was with its walls of volcanic rock—the main wall being eight hundred feet square and sixty feet high. Around this wall was a moat twenty feet deep and two hundred feet wide. Bastions stood at each corner of the great wall. The cells in which the Texans were kept were twenty by seventy feet with only a loop-hole high up to let in a little air. It is little wonder that men shut in this Mexican 'Bastile' would pine away and die, or else lose their minds, especially those who like Wallace had been brought up in the woods and on the open plains, or had been used to life on the farm, or in the office.

"Well, here they were—not only the prisoners Woll had taken, but some from the Santa Fe and the Mier expeditions. There was comfort in the fact that they were together in their hardships. One thing that was in every heart was an intense longing to get back to their homeland and loved ones. Finally, a group of them determined to make

[313]

their escape or die in the attempt. Twohig was one of these. Wallace would certainly have joined in the effort with all his force, but the poor fellow was just then so ill of mind he did not sense what was happening.

"Happily the dungeons were so thick-walled that the plot could be kept a secret. From six at night until six in the morning the prisoners were

kept locked in. During the daytime they were kept at hard labor on the road. Somehow they managed to get possession of a map of Mexico, and stealthily one by one they brought into their cells small tools and bits of rope which they spliced together. These were kept hidden from the guards. Night after night they worked to get a hole through the thick walls. The men would dance and sing to drown the noise of the hammer and chisel. The bits of stone and dirt they carried in their pockets. It was a tedious job, but the time finally came when the hole was drilled through.

"Twohig, being the smallest of the band that had planned to escape, was the first to crawl out one night. The others had harder work to squeeze through, but finally all of them were in the open. They greased their bodies to help them slip away. Down the rope they had woven during the hours of patient toil they went one after another until sixteen of them were at the moat. Making their way noiselessly across this, they struck out into the darkness each man for himself. Twohig used to tell grandmother how he climbed over high mountains and made his way through valleys with bleeding feet. He finally found a bandit whom he hired to guide him part of the way on towards Vera Cruz.

"After two weeks of traveling by night and hiding by day he happened upon two others of the band, Reese and Green. They met in Jalapa, and here they were befriended by a Mexican Don who hated Santa Anna. He provided a trusty guide who took them on to Vera Cruz. After hiding there awhile, and escaping yellow fever, Twohig managed to get aboard a vessel bound for Texas. At last he reached his home and loved ones in San Antonio, where he spent the rest of his years. Some of the close friends of the Twohig family, like my grandmother, used to hear of his exciting adventures and the stories were often told round our fireside.

"Most of the others who escaped with Twohig managed also to get back to Texas. When the tyrant Santa Anna was finally shorn of his autocratic power, all of the remaining prisoners taken in the Santa Fe and Mier expeditions and those seized by Woll were liberated. Their sufferings and adventures would fill a good many books with thrilling tales."

"But what became of 'Big Foot' Wallace?" Mrs. Neeley was asked by one of the eager listeners.

"He was finally released from prison through the influence of the Governor of his old home state, Virginia. Having no money, he walked to Vera Cruz. The Mexicans along the way gave him shelter and food. At Vera Cruz a kindly French Captain of a vessel offered to take him on to New Orleans. On board, the poor fellow contracted yellow fever and all but died. He survived, however, and finally made his way back to Texas where he began all over again by farming—this time near the Medina River. But 'Big Foot' again gave up a job for which he was never cut out and turned once more to hunting.

[316]

"After Texas had become one of the states in our Union, and the war between our Country and Mexico broke out, Wallace joined Colonel Jack Hays and his rangers. It was a good chance to even up an old score. The rifle of the Virginia-Texas hunter did good service in the battle of Monterey. Then 'Big Foot' having acquitted himself in the fight with honors, and having squared accounts, as he felt, with Santa Anna, came back to his old cabin on the Medina. He wasn't there long before there was trouble with the Indians, and he volunteered to help settle this affair.

An outbreak of cholera brought him again into service as a helper of Dr. Cupples of San Antonio. His whole life was one of usefulness and generous deeds. The main reward he received for all he did was found in the satisfaction he took in being helpful.

"In 1859 Wallace went back to his old home in Virginia for a visit. His cultured relatives and friends were doubtless shocked by the manners he had picked up in the school of the wilds. They never had opportunity, however, to entertain a more upstanding American gentleman. His own reaction to what he saw and experienced on that trip which took him not only to Virginia, but to New York and other states, was summed up in the quaint comment he made on his return, 'I wouldn't give Texas for the whole shootin' match.'

"Today the splendid frontiersman lies buried in the land he had learned to love."

CHAPTER XVIII

A YOUNG HERO OF THE MIER

SOME years ago an Old Timers' Reunion brought back to the Lone Star State an upstanding veteran whose life in a strange way linked two nations. This man was Dr. John Christopher Columbus Hill, then an engineer of Mexico. His boyhood days had been spent joyously with his parents in pioneer Texas; but a sudden turn of the wheel of fate gave him another home in a strange land with the president of that country as his foster father.

Dr. Hill, on the solicitation of the principal, visited the Bowie School in San Antonio one day to tell the boys and girls and the teachers there something of his intriguing life story. A remarkably fine looking old gentleman he was, well-dressed, and with snow white beard and hair, and pink-tinted cheeks. There was a free American spirit with a touch of the formality of old Spain in his cordial and courteous greeting to the eager-eyed young Texans.

"We are honored today with the presence of the youngest of the boy heroes of the Mier," said the principal. "I am happy to introduce Dr. Hill, a loyal son of two nations. We all want to hear what he will tell us of the story of his life."

"It is a pleasure for me to respond to your principal's request, my young fellow Americans," began the veteran; "not because I feel there is much in my life of great importance, but for another reason. Some of the experiences I have had may help to bring you closer to the real history of this great state. There are not many of us old timers left to tell that story as we have lived through it. If boys and girls can have a true and living knowledge of what it has cost to win our liberty, they will be readier not only to die for our country when need calls, but also to live for it. And this we must do if our priceless heritage of freedom is to be preserved.

"A man who is disloyal in spirit, or who breaks our laws, is not a true American. The proudest part of my message to you today is that I stood by my country. And here I must pay tribute to the Mexicans; they honored me for my honesty and loyalty. I volunteered as a boy to fight by the side of my father and my brother for Texas; and then in an hour of peril and need, I was given the opportunity to save their lives, and still to live on with love in my heart for my Lone Star Land, yet true to the pledge I had made with those who had set my father and brother free. The precepts of my parents and my faith in God and country gave me strength to keep loyal under the unusual circumstances that life brought to me.

"I was born an American—a native son of Georgia—in the year 1829. When I was seven years of age my parents moved with their children to Texas. That was in 1836, the year of the Revolution. We were encamped on the Sabine River during the battle of San Jacinto. One of my brothers was in that fight. After the great victory, we moved on to La Grange where my father settled upon a farm he purchased. He had previously taken a trip to Texas with his brothers, Jackson and James Hill. Being pleased with the new country, he had returned to Georgia to sell out, pack up his belongings and take mother and us children to this borderland.

"In Georgia we lived on a fine plantation and had many slaves. I recall that on our trip westward mother rode in a carriage drawn by two good horses. I occupied this vehicle with her and my black mammy. My father and my brothers were outriders. Some of our slaves came along comfortably in a prairie schooner pulled by several yoke of oxen. Our household belongings—and we had some good ones—were brought along in ox-carts driven by other negroes. We were a typical pioneer caravan as we followed the old Spanish trail into the frontier realm. I well remember that interesting journey. We made, so mother used to say, about fifteen miles a day—not very swift traveling now.

"There was a good deal of excitement still about the war that had brought freedom. It was fireside talk in our home. Our part now was to help build up and protect our free Republic. The hearts of all our family were with Texas in all her struggles. The years ahead gave us plenty of chances to show our loyalty for the young nation we had chosen for our new homeland.

"When I was about nine years old I went all alone on horseback from La Grange to Austin. That was nearly forty-five miles through an Indian-infested country, but I enjoyed the trip in spite of the dangers. I took pride in helping my father and brothers. They could not leave the crops, and some valuable deeds had to be recorded in the Capital City. I'll not deny that I got pretty lonely and at times was a bit scared on that journey. Luckily I didn't see any Indians, but the wild animals so frightened me I did not sleep much. At last I reached Austin, which seemed a big city to me.

After filing the deeds, I returned to my home, reaching there after about a week's absence. It was a great relief to mother and father when I got back safe and sound.

"My father, Asa Hill, was a sincere and quiet man. Mother was more talkative, and very pious. She impressed her faith on all her children. We had implicit confidence in her helpful counsel. She and father taught us obedience, and we liked to obey them. We lived in fear of God, and tried to be kind and considerate of others. We were a happy and contented family.

"Our home was a plain, one-story dwelling with a long hallway and two rooms on each side. The negroes had their cabins not far away. Because we were in constant fear that Indians would steal our cattle, we built the corral near the house. Every one of us men learned how to use a gun. We did a great deal of hunting to help us with our food supply. Game was plentiful all around us.

"There was a one-room cabin school in the neighborhood. To this I went on horseback for about three years. The 'Three R's' were about all we were taught, but I learned to read, and was fond of books. From Georgia we had brought our family Bible, Plutarch's Lives, Pope's Iliad, one English History, War of the Colonies, Addison, Spenser, Dryden, Pope, and other classics. These may seem rather heavy reading for young folk today, but we learned to enjoy them.

"It was our family custom to sit around the fireplace of an evening to hear father read the Bible. The negroes would gather in the big hall and listen to the stories and the explanations of the Scriptures. Verses from the Bible were given to the various members of the family to memorize and explain. The melodious 'amens' from the negroes sometimes made it all seem like a Georgia camp meeting.

"The Bible readings over, we dismissed the negroes and read some of the classics. Often when a newspaper fell into our hands, though it might be a month old, we would share the news of the outside world with one another. We discussed politics, and felt that the weight of Texas and of the United States was upon our shoulders. I recall that we all grew very much excited when our weekly Texas paper suggested that there was danger of Texas being annexed to England. We were all in favor of joining the United States, but since Texas was still menaced by Mexico and was becoming a slave state, the United States was slow to accept Texas into the Union.

"Mexico might have been more of a menace if she had not at this time had troubles of her own. Revolutions were constantly springing up, some of them doubtless aided and abetted by outside peoples.

Many Mexicans wanted to unseat Santa Anna, who was ruling the country in dictatorial fashion. The idea spread that New Mexico was ready to join with Texas. This and the thought of opening up trade with that neighboring province, brought about the ill-fated Santa Fe Expedition. Everybody in Texas was excited over that move, some violently opposing it, while others, including President Lamar, were giving it their approval and support.

"I was twelve years old at this time. In those days that meant I was ready to do a man's part; at least I thought so. The fireside talk on the Texan and Mexican situation interested me greatly. I knew more then about affairs in Texas than I do now. We were all eagerly awaiting the outcome of that expedition to Santa Fe. The word of its tragic ending was slow in coming, but when it came it stirred up bitter feelings between the Texans and Mexicans.

"One evening in September, 1842, we were almost ready for supper when we heard hoofbeats of a galloping horse and then its rider calling, 'Mr. Hill! Mr. Hill!'

"All of us rushed from the house as father came running out of the corral.

" 'Get your rifles, boys!' he shouted as he ran to meet the courier. We jumped to the conclusion that it was an Indian raid.

" 'No, it's not redskins this time,' the messenger replied to our excited questions; 'it's Mexicans. They have invaded our country again under that French leader, Woll. Captain Jack Hays didn't have enough rangers to hold San Antonio, so he is rallying his forces at Seguin, and sent me to rouse the men round Bastrop and La Grange.'

" 'You can count on us for help,' returned father.

"It was one of Captain Hays' messengers that had ridden, like Paul Revere, to gather the Texas 'Minute Men.' Mother urged him to stay for supper, but he said he hadn't time just then to eat, and away he went like the wind.

"After he had gone, we ate our supper rather seriously. There wasn't anything pleasant in the prospect of a renewal of war between Texas and Mexico. I could see that it was a hard blow to father. He had just got his family started towards the making of another good home. What we needed was more peace, not conflict. But we ate a good meal of venison and hominy and hot corn bread in spite of the bad news. The hard day's work had sharpened our good appetites. The candles flickered on our guns that hung upon the wall.

"At last I said, 'We will go early in the morning, won't we, father?'

" 'We!' echoed my mother. 'You are not going, John; you are too young.'

" 'I went to Austin all alone three years ago,' I protested; 'and Indians are as bad as Mexicans. Father promised me I could take part in the next war. James fought at San Jacinto. He is not well, so he must stay with you. I'll go and take care of brother and father.'

"My sister laughed aloud at this suggestion, but I insisted that I could take care of father and my brother Jeff.

"Mother looked serious and turned to father saying, 'Asa, you're not going to encourage that child?'

" 'He doesn't seem to need any encouragement,' answered father. 'John Christopher Columbus Hill has a mind of his own. I leave the matter to you.'

" 'Do let me go, mother,' I pleaded.

"Tears were running down her face. 'I am willing to help Texas!' she said; 'but I don't know, son, about letting you go. Don't you think that if I give up two it is enough? Let me take it to the Lord in prayer.'

"I did not sleep much that night, and in the morning I crept to my mother's bed and asked in all faith and reverence, 'What did God say, mother?'

"She put her arms around me and cried. I knew that my prayer was answered, and though I was happy to go, I cried too for mother. A strange notion was in my mind that I was going to take care of my father and my brother. I ran out to the corral, threw my saddle on my pony, and then joined the family at breakfast. After that all was hurry until we left.

"Just before we rode away, mother gave me a small Bible that had been her mother's. My brother, James Monroe, was cleaning his best rifle. Calling me aside, he said solemnly, 'John, little brother, I carried this gun at San Jacinto. Since I cannot go, I'll give it to you. Don't you ever surrender it to a Mexican.'

"I looked my thanks for the gift and said with determination, 'No enemy shall ever shoot this rifle.'

"'That's the spirit of a true Texan,' he replied. 'You will do.'

"My mother smiled and kissed me good-by; and I rode away with brother Jeffrey and my father, little dreaming of what the future held in store for them and me.

"At La Grange we found a band of about fifty recruits under Captain Dawson. Colonel Caldwell with another group of men was ahead of us. We hastened on to join Captain Hays at Seguin. When we reached this rendezvous, I found five other boys under sixteen years of age. These were Orlando Phelps and Billie Reese from Brazoria, Gilbert Bush from Fort Bend County, Harvey Sellers from Fayette County, and Chris Yocum from Liberty. It happened that I was the youngest of all the band. We were all proud to be followers of such brave frontier leaders as Colonel Caldwell, Captain Jack Hays and 'Big Foot' Wallace.

"Not many days had passed before we were in a fierce fight at Salado, with the Mexican army under General Woll. The enemy lost heavily in that battle; but we suffered severely too when Captain Dawson through some mistake led his company of men into a trap. Practically all of these brave boys were slain. Woll slipped away in the night carrying off a good many Texans as prisoners. Couriers were sent in every direction for more men to follow and punish the invader.

"President Houston, who had tried to keep out of war, now issued a call for troops. Our camp was made on the Medina River while the army was being gathered. We fairly feasted there on venison, so plentiful were the deer. We had plenty of corn bread, too. The outdoor life agreed with us boys. We felt that we were as big soldiers as the men.

"At length we marched on to Laredo under General Sommerwell. There was dissatisfaction over the choice of this leader, many of the men feeling that he did not want to go into Mexico. Finally he gave proof that they were not far wrong by returning with many of the volunteers to San Antonio. About three hundred, including father, brother and I, refused to go back. Colonel Fisher was elected our commander. It was determined that we would invade Mexico. About this time father said to me, 'John, don't coax the other boys to go across the border line; it is a matter of life or death.' I obeyed him, but some of the boys went just the same.

"Tom Green of Austin took charge of our barges at Guerrero, and down the river we floated on them. This was our navy. We also had a land force. The river was beautiful with its high bluffs covered with chaparral. At last we reached Mier, a small Mexican town about midway between Laredo and Matamoras.

"One evening after supper, Captain Green invited all us boys to a conference with the officers. We were ready to pitch right into the Mexicans and annihilate them. The older men, much amused at our plans and spirit, called us 'the fire-eaters.' Led on by them we expressed our opinions very freely, and boasted a great deal about our skill at riding and shooting. We really could ride and shoot, for we had been born, almost, on horseback, and had learned very early how to use firearms. The Mexicans, according to our notions, would stand little show once we got at them.

A YOUNG HERO OF THE MIER

"It was not long before our mettle was to be put to a severe test. One dark and rainy night, after a good deal of difficulty, our band all got across the river and made a surprise attack on Mier. Very soon we had taken possession of a number of adobe buildings there, and were entrenched for further fighting. During the next day, which was Christmas, we fought on through the houses and over the flat roofs to the main plaza. Colonel Fisher was badly wounded during the battle.

"Some time late in that day a Mexican bearing a white flag appeared. The firing ceased while our men held parley with him. He came from the Mexican General Ampudia with word that a large force of Mexican troops were nearing the town. When they came it would mean certain death to all the Texans. The General, to spare us that fate, proposed that we surrender on generous terms to him. There was angry protest from many of our men, but Colonel Fisher, suffering from his dangerous wound, decided it was best to accept the offer. He and General Ampudia had known each other in the United States, and the Mexican leader seemed to be acting fairly, so the surrender was arranged.

"Our men were in a rage. They wanted to fight it out with the enemy. Denied this opportunity, most of us were ready to take the one chance in ten to cut our way through and get back to Texas. Captains Green, Cameron, Reese and 'Big Foot' Wallace were all against surrender. Wallace was the last to give up his gun. It was a bitter ending to all our sacrifice and struggle. Few had any confidence in the Mexican General's promise that we should be treated with consideration as prisoners of war.

"We were soon to learn that we had been deceived by Ampudia. There was really no force of Mexicans near to reinforce him, and the chances are we might have gained a victory with further fighting. But it was now too late. Our forces were badly divided as to the surrender; it seemed useless for those opposed to it to try to carry on.

"The Mexican leader was not without his troubles. His own son, a fine young man, had fallen mortally wounded in the battle. When the surrender was in progress, the general with one of the Texan leaders came upon the young man dying, and Ampudia, with tears streaming down his face, said, 'See, this is war.'

"The scenes of that surrender are vividly impressed on my memory. Some of our men were sullen, some cursing, and some followed their leaders in silent obedience. Tom Green, afterwards known as General Green, marched up to Ampudia and said, 'I am against this surrender; but here I am to be shot or put in prison. This is my sword belt. I broke my rifle and my sword on purpose ten minutes ago.'

" 'Keep your belt,' replied Ampudia; 'I am sorry for you, and I will do all in my power to help you.' Green only shrugged his shoulders and walked away.

"As the Mexicans came for our arms, I threw my rifle down and broke it.

" 'Why did you do that?' asked a Mexican captain in English.

" 'Because I promised my brother I would never surrender that gun,' I answered angrily. 'It was used at San Jacinto.'

" 'Are you not afraid?' the captain continued.

" 'Of what? I came to fight and to take care of my brother and my father.'

" 'What is your name?' he persisted.

" 'John Christopher Columbus Hill, sir,' I said proudly.

" 'May the saints protect you,' was his final remark as he walked away.

"Since I was a small fellow, the Mexicans let me go about much as I pleased. It happened that we had left some of our men on the other side of the Rio Grande. A number of Mexicans were sent over with a man named Lyons to tell these Texans to surrender, and I rode behind Lyons on his horse.

When he reached our men across the river, instead of telling them to surrender, he yelled, 'Boys, we are prisoners. Take the good horses and git!' They obeyed. About one hundred and twenty of them escaped. The pursuing Mexicans never caught up with them. I told all this in great glee to Billie Reese when I got back.

"My father was kept a prisoner in an adobe house. My brother Jeffrey, who had been wounded, was in a hospital. He, with the rest of the wounded men, kept up their cheer, joking about everything. I was allowed to be an errand boy for them and other prisoners, buying food and other little articles for such as had money. All my own allowance I had spent in Laredo, thinking that I should soon be back home.

"One day while I was with father and brother, a messenger came to me and said, 'Report at once at General Ampudia's headquarters.'

"Father and Jeffrey groaned. They thought it meant my death sentence. I was angry. The guards took me to the Mexican General. He was surrounded by officers and soldiers. I was ragged and not very clean. Being rather small for my age, and thin from want of food, I must have looked rather small to those big officers.

"The General looked at me with tears in his eyes

as he said, 'Mi Hijito (my little son). Do not fear. I shall not harm you.'

"I was tired and dazed and failed to understand. I just looked earnestly at the group.

" 'Queridito,' (dear one) 'come here,' the General went on, putting his arm around me. Then he asked, 'Why do the Texans send little ones to fight? Are men so few?'

" 'I am no little one,' I answered.

" 'I beg your pardon, Señor,' returned General Ampudia. 'Now, Señor Juan Christobal Colon Gil, why did you come to Mexico?'

" 'I came to fight Mexicans. You must leave Texas alone.'

" 'Have you no father or brothers to fight for you?'

" 'Yes, my father is here and my brother too. My brother is wounded.'

" 'And your mother let you come?'

" 'Yes, to take care of my father and brother.'

" 'Well, Señor Gil, tell me why you broke your rifle.'

" 'Because my brother told me never to surrender it, and I kept my promise.'

"One of the officers standing near said, 'Were you one of the boys who killed so many of Captain Castro's men?'

" 'Yes, sir, I think we shot about fifteen of your men near the cannon.'

" 'Who were the other boys?' asked General Ampudia.

" 'Harvey Sellers, Billie Reese, Orlando Phelps and Gilbert Bush were with me. We lost poor Chris Yocum, who was accidentally shot before we reached Mier.'

"The general wrote the names of my companions, and then said to an officer, 'See that this boy gets food and rest.'

"Overcome by this gentle treatment, I said with trembling voice, 'My father, sir, thinks I am going to be shot. Please tell him of your kindness.'

" 'I'll obey your orders,' said the general smiling, as the orderly led me away to an apartment. Here I found the other boys. We were sent a fine supper and told to sleep on some cots in the room. All we wished was that we could share these comforts with the rest of our men.

"I dreamed that night that mother came to me and said, 'Take care of your father and brother.' When I awoke the next morning the other boys were not with me, but a Mexican servant was standing by my cot with an elegant suit of clothes.

" 'It is the will of General Ampudia,' he said, 'that you wear this suit.'

" 'I don't want a Mexican suit,' I replied. 'That

is velvet, and too fine.' I looked about for my old clothes, but they were gone. There was nothing for for me to do but to put on the finery. An orderly soon came and led me again to the general, who was having breakfast. He bade me sit down with him, and I did, but I could not eat for thought of my father and brother.

" 'Dear child, you must eat,' said the general.

" 'I can't,' I said, 'my father and brother are hungry and my comrades sad.'

" 'Well,' he returned, 'I can't do for all, but I'll send breakfast to your father and brother.'

"A servant was called. He filled a silver tray with good food, and I was permitted to go with him. Just outside the room I found my father, and cried like a baby. We hurried with the food to Jeffrey, and I told them all about General Ampudia's kindness.

" 'Your mother's prayers are answered,' said father.

" 'I dreamed of her last night,' I said.

" 'She must have been with us in spirit,' said Jeffrey.

" 'But I don't want to wear these silly clothes,' I complained.

" 'I wish they would give us some clean finery for our old rags,' laughed my brother.

"Just then they brought in the other boys all

dressed up, but not in silk and velvet. Soon 'Big Foot' Wallace came along. I felt very humble and turned red when he said, 'Señor Juan, you seem to be in luck.'

" 'He doesn't call it luck,' said father. 'He feels sad about us.'

" 'Take my advice and hug your good fortune, boy,' said Wallace. 'Don't be a fool about it. Just send us some good clothes as soon as possible.'

" 'Yes, I need trousers badly,' said Jeff.

"Father said sternly, 'John, we are all prisoners. You must obey and show General Ampudia you appreciate his kindness. We feared you would be killed. Because of the sorrow over the death of his own son, and in admiration for the bravery you have shown, the general is treating you with all kindness. Clothes do not make a man. Show your benefactor that a Texan has not only courage but courtesy and good manners.'

"I acted on father's good advice. After this, I saw him and brother each day and brought them many comforts. General Ampudia treated me as his own son.

"On New Year's Day, the able-bodied prisoners were all started towards Matamoras, one hundred and sixty miles away. Our wounded men, Jeffrey among them, were left behind in Mier. We boys rode between General Ampudia and Captain Castro, and were given every consideration by them. Most of the men were on foot, but the general provided a horse for my father, otherwise I should have died of shame.

"At Camargo there was a fiesta to celebrate the Mexican victory. Crowds were gambling, dancing and yelling as we were marched through the town, but they offered no direct insults. When we finally reached Matamoras, a ball was given in honor of General Ampudia. The Texans were quartered in several prisons. Then came orders from Santa Anna that all prisoners were to be sent on to Mexico City. The hope that our men might be exchanged and returned home was dashed.

"Two days later my father, with Billie, Harvey, Orlando, and the rest of my friends were marched away. I was put in school in Matamoras. One comfort that came to mother and me during these lonely days was the letters that passed between us. I tried also to forget my troubles by studying hard, and I succeeded in learning a good deal of the Spanish language.

"Not many months had passed before an order came from Santa Anna directing that I be taken under safe escort to Mexico City. Somehow I felt happy over this, even though I was still in the dark as to what it all meant. A captain, a lieutenant, two orderlies, and twenty men were given me as an escort. General Ampudia seemed sad over my leaving him. He kept saying 'Mi Hijito,' (my son) over and over as he bade me good-by. It is probable he had found in me some consolation for the loss of his own son. He did not want me to go, but he said that Santa Anna demanded obedience.

"It was a long and lonely journey. I cried many times in secret. At last we came to the Mexican capital. Santa Anna was ill at the time, so I was sent to the Archbishop. He treated me with all kindness, but my greatest joy was in a letter that came from mother. General Ampudia had forwarded it by special couriers. I felt like a king that day.

"In a few days I was waited upon by a Mexican officer who said, 'Santa Anna wants to see the little Texan.'

"I followed him with misgivings, thinking that I was to be killed. But I was determined to plead for my father and my brother. The officer led me to the National Palace—a very fine place. In the reception room sat Santa Anna."

"Won't you tell us how he looked?" asked one of the listeners.

"He was a rather handsome man and wore fine clothes and many medals. He was not tall, being

[340]

only five feet five inches in height. Nor was he very dark. His eyes were clear and bright. He wore his hair combed forward One would hardly take him for a dictator or tyrant.

"As I was brought up to him, he reached out his hand and said in Spanish, 'I am glad to meet you. I have heard a great deal about you.'

"Just then General Tornel came up. He had been a minister to the United States and spoke to me in English. Another general named Farias stood near us. Santa Anna told us all to be seated.

" 'Now we will settle about young Gil,' began the President. 'I want to adopt this boy and make a soldier of him.' He looked straight at me.

"I was almost breathless, but I answered, 'Your Excellency, I can't be your son I have a good father, and I can't be a soldier in your country, because I am a Texan.'

"Santa Anna seemed astonished and angered for a moment, but finally he smiled and said to his generals, 'Our prisoner dictates terms.' Then to me he said, 'Pray, what is your pleasure?'

" 'I don't know,' I answered frankly. 'I am too anxious about my father and brother to decide.' Then I told him of Mier and the promise I had made to my mother to take care of them.

" 'My son, don't grieve,' said Santa Anna, 'we

[341]

will attend to that; but you must come to my home.'

" 'Will you send my father and brother back to mother if I stay?' I asked.

"Santa Anna was silent a moment. I was too much in earnest to feel self-conscious in his presence, or realize my position. Finally he said, 'You killed many of my men. If I give you your liberty will you come back again?'

" 'Yes, sir,' I answered.

"Generals Tornel and Farias looked troubled. I gazed at Santa Anna and begged him in my mother's name for the freedom of my father and my brother. At last he said, 'I accept your terms, Juan. You stay in Mexico and your father and brother go home.'

"I laughed and cried and thanked him with all my heart.

" 'What about a school?' he asked. 'Would you like the Mineria?'

" 'Yes, yes,' I answered, overjoyed at the prospect of it all.

" 'Let the boy come into my family,' said General Tornel.

"Santa Anna agreed that I might spend part of my time at the home of the general who had a son about my age.

" 'You are all so good to me,' I responded; 'but no

place can be a real home to me until my father and brother are safe in Texas.'

"From that day Santa Anna treated me as a son. I did not see very much of him, however. He was a very hard man to meet, being ever surrounded with officers. Doña Dolores, his wife, was closer to me. She was a beautiful woman, and so good to me that I learned to love her next to my own mother. Santa Anna himself was devoted to her all his life.

"The promise to set my father and brother free was kept. As for the other prisoners, they were held for many months and even years. Meanwhile I made my home for the most part with General Tornel and his family, spending only the week ends with Santa Anna and his good wife. The son of General Tornel and I grew to be fast friends. Often I would have arguments with him and other members of the family over Texas and the United States, but these did not disturb our friendship. They did not try to influence me as to my political and religious views, but treated me with every consideration and courtesy, and I tried to do likewise with them.

"Often General Santa Anna and his wife would take me for long drives around Mexico City. It was all most inspiring. From high points one can get unforgettable views of that city set in its mountain land. To the southeast is the monarch Popo-catepetl and the White Woman, Ixtaccihuatl, robed in eternal snows, yet with smoke ever issuing from the volcanic fires that are burning within them. Each of these mountains is over seventeen thousand feet high. They supply both ice and sul-phur for the people that live near them. Scenes like this and other impressive sights made it all a wonderland for me. Since those days I have traveled far and wide over the world, but have never found more beautiful scenery than that of Mexico."

"When you were given such freedom, why did you not run away from Mexico?" asked one of the eager listeners.

"The thought of running away was never in my mind after I had given my word of honor," re-turned Dr. Hill.

"But you owed Mexico nothing. They had captured you," argued the listener.

"I was indebted to the leaders of that nation for my life and the life of my father and brother, and for liberty and education. I was not asked to give up my precious American citizenship, nor to change my religion. Mexico has been very good to me. I would give my life for that country at any time if it did not involve my native land and my own people."

"When did you first return to Texas?" asked one of the teachers.

"In 1855, some thirteen years after I went on the Mier expedition. At this time I came back home to ask consent of my parents to marry. My request was granted, and I returned to Mexico. Soon after this my sweetheart, who was a sister of Segrada, a noted Mexican artist, and I were married. We were very happy."

"What finally became of Santa Anna?" came another question.

"He lost his power and died a poor man. Today he lies buried on the hill of Guadalupe in Mexico City."

"Tell us what became of the other boys of the Mier expedition," some one requested. "How were they treated?"

"They were treated kindly by Santa Anna. One of them, Orlando Phelps, he released because after the battle of San Jacinto, Orlando's father had been kind to the captured Presidente. The boy returned to Texas and married. Several of his children, I understand, are still living in the Lone Star State. Harvey Sellers also gained his freedom through the pleadings of the Señora Santa Anna. He lived for many years in Galveston where he reared some fine boys of his own. Gilbert Bush and Billie Reese likewise gained their liberty, and a few years later they came back with the United States army to fight at Monterey. Billie afterwards went to California where he died rather young. I am not sure what became of Gilbert after the Mexican War.

"That conflict was a somewhat trying time for me. The feeling ran high in Mexico against the 'Gringos,' as the Americans were called. This was natural because the direct cause of the war was the annexation of Texas by the United States. My Mexican boy companions, however, never let this make any difference between them and me. They were always considerate of my feelings. At the battle of Chapultepec, many of my friends, young Mexican cadets, lost their lives. They were patriots and loved their country, and I wept over their fall. At the same time I showed my joyous feelings so plainly when the American flag went up over Mexico City that one of my teachers in the Mineria, our mining school, took me aside and requested me to be more cautious. I went to school every day during the war. And I continued for some years afterwards in that fine school, taking courses in medicine and in engineering; so today I am both a mining engineer and a doctor.

"During the war, the Americans camped at my beloved 'Mineria' and destroyed the building. But I went to the headquarters of General Scott and had the troops removed. I was ashamed of their vandalism. It always seems to me dreadful to destroy public property unnecessarily, and very silly and ill-bred for people to write their names over walls and furniture.

"While the Americans were in Mexico City, I visited the encampments when I had spare time. Since about eight thousand Texans took part in that war, I found among the soldiers many old friends and acquaintances. The struggle was not of long duration. Mexico, weakened by internal dissensions, could not put up a very strong fight. The battle of Monterey and the fall of Mexico City put an end to the conflict. Then came the treaty of Guadalupe Hidalgo. I was called upon to help with the translation of this international document, so I proudly served my country after all. That treaty not only settled the boundary dispute between Texas and Mexico, but also added to the domain of the United States the vast region of what is now California, Nevada, Utah, parts of Colorado, Wyoming, New Mexico and Arizona; and all this came as an aftermath of the Texas Revolution.

"And now I must close my story with an incident that concerns my good friend, Ampudia. Through this I was enabled to repay in some measure the debt I owed to the General for his kindness to me at Mier. The happening grew out of the political intrigue on the part of Louis Napoleon to set up Maximilian as Emperor of Mexico. The unfortunate affair was carried through to the extent of bringing this Austrian prince over to Mexico City with his Belgian princess, Carlotta, and crowning them there with pomp and ceremony. Then France, warned by the United States that this was in violation of the Monroe Doctrine, withdrew and left Maximilian to his fate.

"I saw the two at the height of their power. He was a handsome, amiable but impractical man; she was a pretty blonde woman who greatly loved her husband and was ambitious for him to be a ruler in his own right. It all ended tragically, Maximilian being shot, and his wife losing her mind. Happily it would seem, time stopped for her. She just lived on through many years still believing she was ruling as Empress of Mexico.

"It was during the brief reign of the Maximilians that Captain Ampudia, a brother of the General who had befriended me, was thrown into prison. He with many others had resented the usurpation of the Maximilians, and because of this was charged with treason. The sentence was death. I heard of it, and decided to take a daring step to free him.

"Securing permission, I took Captain Ampudia's

sweetheart into the prison to visit him. We managed to get a reboso and a dress into his cell and quickly costumed him as a woman. He walked out with me past the unsuspecting guards, hiding his face in the reboso as if overcome with grief. His sweetheart meanwhile remained in the cell. We had no fears for her safety as her brother was on the side of the enemy. Though he could not save Ampudia we knew he would help his sister. For some time after this I had to keep myself hidden. It was a relief when the French finally left Mexico, and the republic was again set up under the patriot Juarez."

"Did Captain Ampudia and his sweetheart get married?" asked some one.

"Yes, indeed; and I danced at their wedding."

"Have you lived in Mexico ever since that time?" came another question.

"It has been my home since I went into it first as a fighting young Texan. I have made my living there as a mining expert and as a physician. At one time I taught in college. My dear wife passed away some years ago. We had lived happily together for years. Our grandchildren have been educated in the University at Austin, Texas.

"Mine has been a busy life. It has not brought me great fame, but I have tried to be honest, earnest, and sincere. I thank God for my good father and mother. They taught me to be true to myself and others."

TEXAS COMES INTO THE UNION

CHAPTER XIX

A MOTHER'S MEMORIES OF OLD TEXAS

AMONG the treasured possessions of one of the
daughters of two Texas pioneers is an old letter which gives revealing glimpses of the Lone Star
Land in days of long ago. It reads:

Austin, Texas
June 2, 1840

Dear Brother:

*It is with pleasure this day I received a letter from you of
April 17 in answer to mine of December 1838.*

*I intended to visit you this summer but gave up the idea
on account of the state of currency which is very bad at
this time. There is no good money in the country and ours
is not worth more than 20c on the dollar. The Republic of
Texas is having a hard time and I hope we will go into the*

Union before I die. Many favor the idea of joining. However, you may hope to see me in the course of another year.

I am now in Austin. I left San Antonio last August and came here at the first sale of town lots. I bought one and built a house on it.

We keep busy chasing Indians and every man has to do his share. You ask for an account of myself since I arrived in this country. I will give you a short detail. I arrived in Matagorda in January 1836. I spent some time hunting, for there was game in abundance. It was needed by many families who were suffering from illness and poverty.

During the end of 1835, there was great confusion in Texas in spite of the fact that they drove Cos from the country. We did not expect the Mexicans until after March, but they came in February. On March 2, I started to join Col. Fannin but was taken very ill on the way and missed the fate of Fannin and his men by a few hours. I was ill for some time and hardly able to move in advance of the enemy. It was a terrible time for all.

I was detailed with others to watch the sick and wounded near San Jacinto—a dangerous position. I was in volunteer service but I helped in pursuit of the Mexicans. Then I joined the army and was kept on the frontier for some time. Before this all service was as a volunteer and without pay. As a regular ranger I received small wages. My bed was a blanket upon the earth, and my board dried beef and corn cakes. It's a healthy life if the Indians don't get you.

When I got my discharge, I returned to Matagorda where I had left a lot of good clothes. I was now nearly naked but the enemy had been there and destroyed everything. I had been there a week when I was taken very ill with typhoid and was laid up for four months. I had every attention paid me that one could expect from strangers who did not know that they would get anything for their trouble. I could write more but have not room.

There was an order issued today by the Secretary of War ordering out three thousand of the militia which is believed are intended for invading Mexico and forcing them to acknowledge our independence. If such should be the case I shall go but will write soon again.

Give my regards to Van Ranselear and tell him things remain about the same as when he left Bexar. The Indians are very troublesome and the Mexicans are no better. I have been in some exciting skirmishes but still have my scalp. The Americans remain about the same as when Van Ranselear left with the exception of a few killed by Indians, for I believe no one dies a natural death in Texas.

With kindest regards,
Yours,
C. F. KING

To Lucian King, Attorney
Rochester, New York.

The writer of this letter was born in New Hampshire. Lured, like a good many other young New Englanders, by prospects of adventure and better fortune in Texas, he had gone into that borderland while the fight for freedom was being waged. That conflict and its aftermath of pioneer and frontier difficulties brought the son of New Hampshire adventures aplenty—and the joy of romance too.

About five years after the above letter was written, a bright-eyed girl, Emily Brackett, came with her parents, native New Yorkers, of New England lineage, to make their home in old San Antonio. She had not been in Texas many years before she met the fine frontiersman, Charles F. King, and very soon they were married. Their home in this historic town became one that echoed the prattle of children, that radiated the spirit of the true American pioneer. Theirs was a hearthside where friends loved to gather, where young and old would come to sing songs and to share the stories of America's making.

In the after years, when her stalwart husband had passed away, Emily Brackett King still carried forward with courage and cheer. She was a true Daughter of the American Revolution, as he was a Son. What they did in helping to build the Lone Star State enriched and strengthened that precious heritage.

Out of her treasure trove of mother memories Mrs. King would often bring stories and bits of description that make history come to life. Her own children and her many friends were privileged many times to share with her the intimate word pictures she could sketch, and the true stories she could tell not only of Texas but of other parts of our country. Once when a group had gathered about her genial fireside, some one touched off a train of choice reminiscences by saying, "Please,

Mrs. King, tell us of your life—right from the beginning."

The little gray-haired mother smiled as she responded, "That is rather a long story. You see, I come from a lineage that goes back in America to the Puritans. My first colonial ancestor in this country was Governor Winthrop. My forebears fought in many of the battles of the Revolution, so the blood of freedom is in me. One of our family line was a secretary and treasurer of Harvard College. In an old letter written by another member of the family, is this sentence, 'The schoolhouse is the sentinel-box of liberty.' It is evident that some of those from whom I came believed in education.

"All this, however, goes back too far for any personal memories. It is only when I get to the stories my own grandmother used to tell me as a little girl, that I feel I am close to history. Her grandfather, so I learned from her, was captain of a Massachusetts company in the Revolutionary War. He lost most of his possessions during that struggle, but nothing daunted, moved on to New York State to rebuild his fortunes. Settling where Syracuse now stands, he erected a new home and began to mine salt.

"A few years later he was appointed as government agent of the Onondaga Indians. Later this same honor was bestowed on his son-in-law. It was while great-grandfather was serving as agent in 1824, that Lafayette visited the reservation. The French leader was entertained there by my great-grandparents. A grand ball and also a banquet were given in honor of the famous guest. Some of the Indians were invited to the sumptuous repast.

"In return, the head chief of the Onondagas spread a feast for the white folk. It consisted mainly of succotash—an Indian dish made of corn and beans. This was cooked in a great kettle, two Indian women proudly stirring the mass of food. All the guests sat with the Indian chieftains round the fire. When the meal was ready, the big chief said, 'Lafayette, you like succotash?'

"The Indian women filled plates and cups they had borrowed from my grandmother. Aunt Dinah, a good old Indian mother who helped to raise my mother, was one who assisted at the serving. As the dishes were emptied, the chief would call, 'More succotash!' and again the plates and saucers would be filled. My mother, a little girl of twelve at the time, said that she had four helpings. For politeness sake she did not dare refuse, so she had corn and beans enough once for all to last her for life. Never again would she touch these foods in succotash or in any other form.

"A few years after the visit of Lafayette, my

father and mother were married. Three little girls
—myself among them—were born to them in our
New York home. We all might have remained
there in comfort among relatives, but father's
health failed, and the doctor advised a warmer
climate for him. At this time there was a great deal
of talk about opportunities in the new Republic of
Texas, so my parents decided to move to that borderland. Father went on ahead to prepare the way
for us.

"All was now hustle and bustle getting ready for
the long journey. Old furniture, books, silver,
clothing and other articles were packed in a covered
wagon and sent on to Lafayette, Indiana, by a
trusted teamster. Mother and we three children
took a coach from Syracuse. Grandfather, who
had been an officer in the War of 1812, rode with
us on his horse for about fifty miles before he bade
us good-by. I was only ten years old at the time
but I recall thinking how fine we looked as we
journeyed along. I remember too the many small
rivers we had to cross, and the woods through
which we passed on our way.

"In Lafayette we stayed with an aunt and uncle.
Finally mother thought she would give father a surprise by joining him in Texas. Leaving us three little girls in the good care of our relatives, she took a
boat down the Mississippi to New Orleans. When

she reached that town, she dreamed one night that my little sister was very ill. It was all so vivid that she came right back to Indiana as fast as she could; and she did find sister at death's door. She nursed her through months back to health. We always felt that God had sent that dream.

"A subdued family then took up the long journey southward. The steamer was filled with other folk—mainly southern planters and their families bound for New Orleans. All was gay, and we partook of the cheery spirit until we learned that the flat boat on which our furniture and other goods were loaded, had struck a snag and upset them all into the muddy waters of the Mississippi. We went right on, however, to join father in Texas.

"At Decrow's point on Matagorda Bay we first set foot on the Lone Star Land. Here we were overjoyed to find our dear father. He had come to take us on to our new home in San Antonio. Our next stop was at Lavaca, and here we stayed for a short time with a woman that had once been a captive among the Indians. Her story fascinated me.

"While we were at Lavaca a ball was given by the citizens. Mr. 'Limpy' Brown, who had a hotel and a livery stable at Victoria, came with his charming wife. They traveled in a two-seated carryall. Father arranged with him to drive us on to San Antonio, so after taking Mrs. Brown home, he returned for the journey. Away we went in state in the carryall with father and Peter Gallagher acting as outriders. Every once in a while Brown, to tease us, would yell, 'Indians! Indians! Here they come.' This so frightened us children that father finally requested him to stop his rough joking. We were used to tame Indians but the tales we had heard of the wild Comanches had set our nerves on edge.

"San Antonio was still dominantly a Mexican town when we went there to live. Only a few Americans then had made it their permanent home. Some of these had married Spanish señoritas. It was Spanish speech we heard on every side. This with the strange costumes, and the strange-looking houses, made it seem as if we were in a foreign land.

"We saw Indians every day upon the Plaza. Ox-teams drawing covered wagons and stage coaches came and went. Cowboys, vaqueros as the Spanish called them, were always about. Mexicans with their great wheeled carts or with burros were a common sight. It was all colorful, and so new and strange to us wonder-eyed little girls from down east.

"Heroes who had fought through the war for the freedom of Texas were all about us. People were too busy with the problems of the present to talk much about the past; yet sometimes we might hear a person remark, 'There goes Señor Navarro—there is Señor Ruiz—there is Señor Maverick. They signed our Texas Declaration of Independence.' Or, 'There is Sam Houston who led the Texas army'—or, 'Here comes Jack Hays, Captain of the Texas Rangers.' It was more or less everyday talk with us. I was fully grownup before I realized that I started life in Texas during its romantic and heroic days. Nor did I appreciate until later how my father and mother were among the struggling pioneers who carried forward the work of the founders of our state. What stout hearts they did have to make their home in this strange environment, and to go bravely on despite homesickness and other trials that must have come to them. To us children, free then from the responsibilities they bore so cheerfully, it was all a picturesque and generally joyous life.

"Our first home was in part of the old Trevino house. This was much like the other dwellings—an adobe structure built round a patio. It fronted on the Main Plaza. All the doors opened on this patio; there were no connecting openings between the rooms; one had to go outside to get inside. Later mother persuaded Mrs. Trevino to make a doorway between two of the rooms. The windows were iron barred. The floor of the kitchen was of adobe clay kept hard and cool by sprinkling. Many

of the houses had nothing but dirt floors throughout, but in our other rooms we had pine flooring.

"We made our own candles and soap, but did not
do any spinning and weaving. Mother had never
learned this art, for in New York during her girlhood, the Onondaga Indians did all the spinning
and weaving for her people. We still have some of
the covers woven by 'Aunt Dinah' for our family
back in the 'eighteen-twenties.' We loved this kind
old Indian woman as some of the Southern children
we knew loved their 'black mammies.'

"The patio was our playground, and the big
arroyo, or canal, in front of our house was a joy.
This arroyo had been built in the long-ago days by
the mission fathers, for irrigation. It carried a
clear stream of good water, and was walled on each
side within the village. How we loved, like all children, to play in and around this cool, life-giving
stream, or acequia, as the Spanish called this main
canal.

"One day mother was given a pleasant surprise
while getting water from the acequia. 'Why Emily
Wood!' a voice called, 'Are *you* here?' It was Olive
Van Secraig, a roommate of hers at the Emma Wil-
liard School of Troy, New York. She had married
Enoch Jones, a highly respected citizen of San Antonio, and had come to live there. How this meeting did help to cure the homesickness both these

pioneer women must have felt at times in that land.

"We children had far less difficulty adjusting ourselves to the new life. It was not long before we were speaking Spanish almost like the natives. The Garza and the Menchaca girls, whose fathers had fought in the Revolution for Texas, were some of our best friends. We mingled among these good people and enjoyed our pastimes with them. One thing though that I never could enjoy was the Mexican food; some folk however seem to take to it 'like ducks to water.' The tamales, frijoles, chili-con-carne, and pumpkin meat were no temptation to me, yet these dishes of Indian-Mexican origin are often done with rare perfection by these people.

"One thing I did like, however, was some of their good candies. They had about thirty varieties of such sweets. Mexican taffy, cream candy, pecan candy, candied fruit, candied pumpkin, cactus, and even candied potatoes were among some of their creations. The candy man would come around and yell, 'Carmencillo—de-lecke! Dulce! Dulce!' and out we would go with our centavos, or pennies. Vendors also came with hot tamales. The milk man too would come driving his cow right up to the door and milk her before our eyes. There were not so many temptations as we have now with not only candy, but soda pop, ice cream and a thousand other dainties; yet we had enough to tease away our small allowances.

"When we came to Texas there were no public schools, nor were there any of these for some time. We children went to the convent school for three years. Then several of the American families employed teachers for their children—usually one of the lawyers or ministers. There were a goodly number of cultivated men and women in San Antonio who were willing to teach. Education was a hobby with my father and mother. There was no plan to make our work easy; we had to study, or we were punished. The teachers were kind but firm with us.

"Our recreation was what we made for ourselves. We learned to dance and to swim. The river was used for bathing. Of an evening we would walk around the Plaza, but we never went alone. Another favorite pastime was horseback riding. We did not dare to go far because we were afraid of Indians.

"I was never harmed by any of the redmen, but once I did get really frightened by them. It happened that I went to the Plaza one day wearing a bright blue dress. Suddenly I found myself surrounded by Indian women begging me for that dress. It was with difficulty that I freed myself from them and got back home. Afterwards I learned that blue was an almost sacred color with them. It was all linked in some mysterious way with a legend of the Woman in Blue, which persisted as a spiritual influence with these children of nature.

"Our clothes were of the best materials. We copied the styles from Godey's Lady's Book. I learned to sew, but a Mexican seamstress was often employed to help us with our dressmaking. These

Mexican women were experts at sewing and could copy almost any printed design.

"Father had been a merchant in New York State. When he came to Texas he naturally turned again to merchandising. He made many trips for goods along the old Spanish Trail from San Antonio to New Orleans and also to Mexico. Big caravans of heavy covered wagons drawn by oxen or mules brought the merchandise. Father, riding a big dun horse, usually led the caravan. He had outriders for protection against surprise by the Indians. The wagons were driven by Mexican teamsters in whom he had confidence. None of these men ever betrayed their trust, even though at times they had a fortune within their care.

"At one time father did suffer a great loss. A caravan of his coming from Mexico with a rich load of silk, Spanish shawls and jewelry, was attacked by the Apaches and the drivers killed. The train was looted by the savages. Sixty thousand dollars' worth of goods was taken. For that year the Apache Indian women were decked in silks and white man's jewelry. Father's life was saved only because illness kept him from making this trip.

"I recall how he would always start out with his trains from the Main Plaza. We would wave good-by from our barred windows and then go to our rooms and cry. It was ever a sad parting because there was constant danger from the Indians and outlaws. This was particularly true when he went to Mexico City.

"Captain Hays and his band of rangers often camped on the Main Plaza. Troubles that occasionally broke out in and around San Antonio brought them there. Sometimes Indians would creep into the city and steal children so you may be sure that we kept pretty close to our home. The patios were a protection against such attacks. The red raiders seemed to take delight in shooting their arrows at the poor Mexican wash women working along the San Pedro Creek. One of these faithful women was killed in this way while she was doing our family washing. Those who settled on ranches suffered most from these attacks. At times the marauders would steal their cattle, and keep the white folk so close to their cabin homes they couldn't get out to hunt. It was then a scanty as well as a dangerous life. Captain Hays and his rangers kept down this menace in a splendid way, but the Indians were never completely subdued until after the Civil War. Not only wild Indians but wild white men had to be held in check. It was a rough borderland. San Antonio was on the frontier. Some suggestion of the wildness is found in the laws that were made. There was one that forbade the breaking of wild horses on the Plaza and another against storing gunpowder. Firearms were forbidden in church.

"Those who lived in the towns generally had plenty of good food. Meat was very cheap. We had enough corn meal, but flour was rather scarce. Fruit was high, apples being sometimes twenty-five cents each. These had to be brought from way up north. We had a goodly supply of eggs, but not much butter. This was not because Texas lacked cows; but the Spanish people used little butter and there was no demand for it. We had to ship what we used from the north, and it came high. We had an abundance of vegetables. One of the tame Indian hunters kept our table supplied with a variety of game. Sugar and sorghum from New Orleans gave us our sweets; and with these and such native fruits as we could get we often made preserves. I remember too the fun we used to have making molasses candy and popping corn.

"The irrigated gardens cultivated by the Mexicans were close to the town. In the early morning we could often hear the laborers there singing praise to Marie Santissima, protectress of the fields. This is a translated verse of one of their songs:

> Thou art a shepherdess
> Lovely and fair,
> The sun that surpasseth
> The moon and the stars.

"Such native music brought back memories of the old mission days when the good fathers taught the ancestors of these people the story of the Blessed Mary and the Savior, and helped them also to grow their gardens in this land of the Southwest.

"A great many celebrations in honor of the saints were held in San Antonio. The priests wisely allowed the Indians and Mexicans some expression of their native dramatic talent in what you would now call 'pageants.' I took part many times with my Mexican friends in the festivals except on Sunday. Father and mother held us to a Puritan observance of the Sabbath; though our Mexican neighbors saw no sin in some gayety and pleasure on the Lord's Day after they had attended mass. The natives had their virtues and graces, and we had our Anglo-Saxon ways of life. These differences in our worship did not interfere with our sympathy and friendship.

"I loved the form and color, the stir and activity of every celebration. Even 'All souls and all saints day' brought joy to me. This was a feast of remembrance suggestive of the spirit of our Decoration Day. Candles were burned on all the graves, and from booths erected in the graveyard, fruits, candies and refreshments were sold. I loved to bestow gifts, so this was a shining event for me.

"The Mexicans used to say 'Ah, Emilie!' and then give me everything I wished. I was friendly and full of life, and they appreciated my entering so whole-heartedly into their festivities. I always took part in burning Judas during Holy Week. Once I was allowed as a special honor to apply the torch to the effigy of Judas hanging in the Plaza. Our Mexican friends made it a practice to entertain the players and their friends. The young folk dressed in their best frocks and made real parties after the different pageants on Christmas and Easter. Some of these plays from Spain centuries ago still survive in remote parts of Mexico and our southwest.

"The 'Pastores' may still be seen in certain places. It is really a beautiful miracle and folk lore play, portraying the stories of the Wise Men, the Shepherds and the Christ Child. It was a joyous time for me while the preparations for this drama were on. I joined with our Mexican companions in fixing candles in mud candlesticks on the sides of the adobe walls of the houses. We made gifts to put on the altar where the Christ Child rested. The representation of the manger, the Wise Men and the Shepherds and Mary and Joseph were very realistic. The gifts were often passed out to the poor, and we were encouraged to be generous.

"When the play was over there was feasting. On these Saints Days little tables were placed out on the Plaza. About the tables four poles were set and at the top of these a buffalo skin or a cowhide was stretched for shade. Our Christmas was usually a sunny day in San Antonio. At these tables one could sit and eat chili-con-carne, frijoles, and other foods and Mexican sweets.

"Another Mexican festival that was dear to the hearts of us young folk was the one where the animals were blessed. The peons would gather their ponies, burros, dogs, cats, oxen, and other creatures and wash, brush and decorate them. These were driven or brought in gay procession before the waiting priests for their blessing. It was all most exciting for us to watch this ceremony and to take part in it all.

"When I was about thirteen years old I had a big Newfoundland dog named 'Chulo'—which means beautiful. On the morning of the blessing I was up at five o'clock. I had cut up a red blanket for my pet. I tied his ears with bright red ribbon, and joined the procession. As I crossed the Plaza, the Mission Indians came trotting by with their burros. Their burritos, little ones, were all dressed up with fresh and lacy ferns and with wreaths of bluebonnets round their tubby stomachs. Behind these came peon teamsters with horses, oxen and burros all decorated with branches of yellow huisache. An almost endless array of brightly-costumed men, women and children gathered on the Plaza in front of the Cathedral.

"One little mozo had given his imagination free play. A white puppy had taken about a week's wages from this ranch hand for paint. Around the doggie's fat 'tummy' gleamed red, white and green stripes—the national colors of Mexico; but even this was not enough. The fluffy tail of the puppy was dyed pink, and its ears were blue, while around its neck was a gay red ribbon.

"It was all a squirming, picturesque mass—with barking of dogs, meowing of cats, braying of donkeys, bleating of sheep, crowing of roosters, and lowing of cattle all mingling with the talk and laughter of the populace. Father Santiago and two acolytes stood ready to invoke the blessings on the various creatures of good St. Anthony, the protector of animals. Not even the lowly, squealing pigs were forgotten. After the dogs had been blessed we gathered in groups to compare our pets. My Chulo was the finest and best dog there, of course.

"The old Plaza holds many memories for me. There the community life was centered. We used to like to watch the pony riders dash in and away with the mail and the great freight outfits come and go with their teams of oxen and mules. The latter were driven by a jerk line, one jerk giving the signal, 'Go left'; two jerks, 'Go right!' The intelligent lead mules would obey the jerks. Calls like 'Gee' (right) and 'Haw' (left) were used in guiding the oxen. Sometimes a crack of the big whip emphasized the commands.

"The arrival of the stage was a thrilling event. It brought the heavy mail, and also many interesting people. The stage-drivers always gave an extra flourish to their whips as they came dashing into the Main Plaza putting their fine horses on their mettle for the last lap of the run. The big Concord stages would career like ships in a storm, and the passengers look frightened as they were being whirled up to the station. The high-spirited animals seemed to enjoy this 'grandstand' play for the waiting crowd as much as did their proud driver. All of us were thrilled with the performance and waited with eager anticipation for the letters and news from the outside world.

"During the war with Mexico we had even more exciting days. Our town was filled with young men who had volunteered for that conflict. Many of them came from our old homeland. Father and mother tried to make their stay in San Antonio as pleasant as warfare would allow. We entertained in our parlor almost every evening and my older sisters sang for the company. Carnivals and masquerade parties were frequently given. Although I was young, I was permitted frequently to enjoy some of these good times. Those who came were among the best young men of our country.

"At one time a party of us rode to Seguin, thirty miles from San Antonio, to attend a ball. With us went a small escort of soldiers. Mrs. Albert Sidney Johnston, and several other wives of army officers were in the party. The older women rode in an army ambulance, while all the younger women rode horseback with their male escorts. The men were very handsome in their broadcloth riding suits and the ladies pretty and graceful in their riding habits with a basque effect and skirts that nearly touched the ground. Hats with heavy veils were worn to protect their complexion.

"In my girlhood it was considered uncouth not to be feminine and dainty. The athletic girl was unknown. We took our party dresses on this trip in saddlebags. Mine was of blue tarletan. Each of us wore from three to five petticoats of this thin material. We certainly 'stood out.' I must confess that present styles are generally more sensible.

"At the Seguin ball we were served a big supper. The tables fairly groaned with good things to eat. Then we danced the plain quadrille, the Virginia reel, the Lancers, and the waltz. This ball was talked of for months afterwards. It was an elegant affair, yet one of friendship and sociability, characteristic of the cultured folk who had come to make Texas their home. Many of the first families of America were represented in that pioneer society of the Lone Star State.

"Besides, we had a goodly representation from foreign lands. There were Irish of the old school, and Englishmen with titles. Spanish families of high rank had been in Texas from the first, and

[373]

some French had come into the land. Besides these there was an influential colony of Germans founded by Prince Solm and Baron Von Mensebach and others of the nobility of that nation. All these people joined in the development of the state, discarding their titles and showing the true American spirit.

"Mensebach, to please the Indians, once gave some of the chieftains discarded uniforms of the Germany army. I shall never forget the sight of one chief strutting about on the Plaza decked in paint and feathers and wearing the gaudy coat of some Prussian officer over his breechclout. Oh, we had atmosphere and color in those days; though at times it was far from funny.

"Once Eugene Antonio Navarro was captured at his father's ranch not far from San Antonio. The Indians stripped him of his clothes and gave him a breechclout. They kept him a prisoner and were treating him rather roughly, when one of the Indian boys whispered to the luckless young captive, 'I'll help you because you gave me sugar at San Antonio. When we go for a hunt, you get on my horse behind me.'

"Antonio followed the advice of his red friend. Then when a good chance offered, he slipped off the horse and hid. Sometime later he arrived in San Antonio about as naked as a snail without its shell.

When he knocked at the door of his old home, a cry was raised, 'Indians! Indians!' It was with difficulty that the escaped captive finally obtained recognition from his own family.

"My father was in Castorville once, when 'Big Foot' Wallace came to town with an Indian boy he had captured. Wallace's dogs had treed the young redskin. He was about fifteen years of age, and all painted for warfare. One of the crowd that had gathered to see the captive, asked 'Big Foot' to give him the Indian boy.

" 'No,' replied the frontiersman; 'this is my Indian. If you want one, go and catch him. There are plenty left.' After a time the boy was given his freedom.

"Our Lone Star land is full of true stories of the Indians and the pioneers, of the mission building fathers, of the soldiers and the rangers. The archives of the old San Fernando Cathedral hold records that suggest thrilling and romantic stories. For more than seventy years I have heard its bells; they call back precious memories for me.

"Texas is my all-American state. Here I spent my childhood and my days of romance when I met my brave Ranger. Our home was builded here and to it came our children. You cannot wonder that I love to linger over the days that have been so precious to me. I thank God for my heritage, and

I pray that the children of our land of liberty will ever cherish what has come to them through the courageous men and women who have made not only this great state but our America."

CHAPTER XX

SOME TEXAS INDIAN AND RANGER STORIES

OLD TIMERS had gathered in San Antonio for the annual Old Trail Drivers' reunion. Suddenly there appeared in their midst what seemed to be a real Comanche Indian in all his paint and feathers. Introduced to an audience of the veterans and their friends, this picturesque person soon revealed himself to be no redskin, but a whiteman named Buckelew who had spent several years of his life as a captive of the Lipans. There was eager interest as he told the story in his simple yet intriguing way.

"I was born in Louisana," Buckelew began; "but when I was two years old father moved from there to Cherokee County, Texas. He wanted 'more elbow room,' he said. Well, we certainly got it out in that frontier country. It was a rather thrilling life that came to us in this new land. We were not very well-off in this world's goods, yet we managed to get along somehow, struggling with the rest of the pioneers, and keeping happy in our cabin home.

"Dark days fell upon us, however, when my father and mother both died. We children were left orphans with no relatives near to take care of us. The good neighbors were kind, but we were having a hard time with poverty when Uncle Berry Buckelew heard of our plight and sent for us to come to live with him in Uvalde County—a good deal farther west.

"Hurried preparations were made for the trip. Our neighbors gave us provisions. Finally we started with all our belongings packed in a covered wagon, which was drawn by five yoke of oxen. We had written ahead to Uncle Berry that we were coming, and when we rolled into San Antonio, there he was waving his hat to welcome us. That filled us with joy and hope for the rest of the journey.

"We soon reached my Uncle's home and again were heartily welcomed by good Aunt Mary and our cousins. The place was called 'Cedar Brake Ranch.' There was a cozy cottage nestled between rolling hills. A large fence of cedar pickets was around the place. The kitchen, built apart from the rest of the house, had a huge chimney made of split timber daubed on both sides with clay. Our home overflowed with hearty children, but as Uncle

Berry said, 'We have all outdoors and don't use the house much anyway.'

"It was an exciting life for me. I was about ten years old at the time, but I felt as big as a man. The first thing I helped to do was to brand some calves. Uncle let me ride a pony over the range with him and the other men. Sometimes I went with Uncle to Bandera to get our corn ground. The mill there seemed very big and grand to me.

"The first trip I made brought me a real scare. Uncle Berry had warned me so much about Indians that I was nervous. We lived close to Sabinal Canyon, which was a favorite hunting and hiding place for them. Well, as we crossed Verde Creek we happened to meet Tom Sandy. Uncle Berry was on his horse and I was driving the wagon. He stopped to chat with this neighbor, and told me to drive on. I kept going and going until I finally decided that the Indians had caught my uncle. The very thought of it so scared me that I stopped my oxen and jumping off the wagon, hid in some nearby bushes. After a time I was overjoyed to see Uncle Berry galloping along the trail to catch up with me. We reached Bandera all right, had our corn ground, and were back home in a few days.

"The settlers took turn about going to San Antonio for supplies. All along the Medina River there were great cypress trees which were cut down to make shingles. Those making the trip would stop at the shingle mills and take on a load for San Antonio. The shingles delivered there, they would load up with supplies and goods and return home. This carrying loads both ways made the trip more profitable.

"At one time Uncle Berry made such a trip. He reached San Antonio all right, and then with his wagon laden with meal, flour, calico and other goods for himself and our neighbors, he had made the journey back as far as the Cosgrove ranch about ten miles from home. While having dinner there, he was told by Mr. Cosgrove that Indians were prowling around. The ranchman was sure of this because of the restlessness of the cattle. Both he and a Mr. Gibbons, who was at the ranch, advised against Uncle's going on home alone, but Uncle Barry, anxious for the safety of his family, decided to take the risk. He told his friends that by following a shorter, somewhat rougher road he felt he could dodge the redskins.

"About nightfall he had crossed the little Seco Creek and was driving along a narrow ledge of rock. The trees and grass that bordered this stream made a screen. Evidently Uncle was walking by the side of his oxen, and probably was without his gun. Suddenly two arrows whizzed and struck him in the back. As he fell, the red devils rushed out of their hiding place and beat him to death with rocks. Then they stole everything from his wagon and fled.

"Next Sunday evening Mr. Gibbons came to our house. Finding that Uncle had not reached home, he immediately organized a searching party. I was a rather large boy at this time and joined the men. For two days we searched; and then we came upon my Uncle's body. His faithful dog Cuff had stayed with it fighting back the wolves. It was a time of mourning for Aunt Mary and all us children when Uncle Berry was taken away so cruelly from us. His many friends shared in our deep grief.

"That was not to be the last of the tragic happenings in that part of Texas. Not long after Uncle was killed, a band of murderous Indians came upon three boys, Miller, Rothe, and Weinert. The boys had killed a beef, and Miller was dressing the hide to make a lariat of it when his companions sighted the redskins. They yelled for Miller to run, but he thought they were fooling him. Weinert dashed away on his pony to get help; but the Indians captured him and took him to Mexico. They killed Miller; but Rothe kept them off with his gun until he finally reached the settlement. These happenings made me very much afraid of Indians.

"After Uncle Berry's death my Aunt Mary decided to leave the ranch. I went to live with a Mr.

Davenport. The first job he gave me was the breaking up of a ten-acre field. Morris, a negro boy, was my helper. Three yoke of oxen made our motive power. We took turns 'gee-hawing' them around with the plow. It was heavy work, and we were very happy when Saturday evening came. The cattle were belled and hobbled for their rest over Sunday.

"One Saturday night we were in a hurry, and Morris was careless fastening the bell. Next morning Mr. Davenport, discovering it had fallen off the neck of the ox, told Morris he would have to find that bell or get a whipping. Morris begged me to help him hunt it, and not wanting to see my black comrade punished, I promised I would.

"I had a large shotgun, but Mr. Davenport told me not to take it. Not wishing to disobey him, I left the weapon behind. Morris and I started off, turning handsprings until we reached the glade where we had let the cattle loose the night before. We found all the oxen, but no bell. Suddenly some frightened steers rushed passed us, and I yelled, 'Indians!'

" 'Dem steers got skeered from us ones,' said Morris. 'You'd better come help me find dat bell, or Marse Jim will beat me to death.'

"Well, frightened though I was, I scoured around with Morris until suddenly I saw an Indian in war paint and feathers like these I have on. The negro boy gave a yell and ran for his life. It was the first time he had ever outstripped me in a race. I heard the Indian right behind me, and glancing back saw he was getting ready to put an arrow through me so I stopped short. The Indian lowered his bow and pointing at the fleeing Morris broke into a laugh. Terror had given the negro speed, and had paralyzed me. Finally the Indian caught me by the shoulder and said, 'Vamanos.' By this time other Indians were about me.

"They took me back into the woods where there were more of their band. Here they stripped off all my clothes and danced about me in glee. Then an old Indian got a thorny stick and as they started to march away with me he would hit me every few feet. After some miles of this, we met another Indian who seemed like a chief.

" 'Howdy!' he said. 'You Dutch? You Merican? Me kill Merican.'

" 'I am American,' I answered.

" 'Me kill Merican,' he repeated.

" 'I can't help it,' I said. 'I am American.' I was trembling from head to foot, but I could not deny my nationality.

"That reply saved my life. The Indians were angry at that time with the German settlers, or Dutch as they called them. This chief, who could

speak a broken English, told me that his name was
Custaleta. I pleaded with him for my life and freedom. He seemed willing to let me go, but the rest
of the band angrily refused consent. At last he
said, 'You no go. I make you big Indian.'

"The redskins sat there smoking in silence for
some time. Then they rose and started to march
away in single file. I was placed third in the line.
In time we came to a bluff overlooking my home.
From there we could see the women of the ranch
running about excitedly. The scared negro boy
had dashed into their midst with news of the Indians. Custaleta told me to yell to them, and I
called loudly to my sister. She shouted, 'Frank,
Frank! I'll come!' but the other women held her
back. She could hear but not see me, for the Indians kept me hidden with them behind the bushes.

"We saw Morris jump on his pony and dash
away towards the Thompson ranch for help. The
Indians joked about my dusky playmate, imitating
his big rolling eyes and his panic. Some folks think
that the Indian is always stern, but he has his jokes,
though sometimes they are very cruel ones.

"Suddenly Custaleta gave a warwhoop, and hurried away with me. The rest of the band followed.
Why they did not attack the ranch I do not know.
We passed on down the creek and hid for some
time. Then we filed on for several hours and

finally pitched camp near the top of a mountain. The old savage that had whipped me with the thorny stick, now shared his blanket with me. Worn out, I slept till morning.

"At daybreak we started on the trail again. I was tired and hungry, but the Indians did not eat anything for twenty-four hours. At last they killed a heifer, drank its blood, and cooked some of the meat. It was only half done, but I enjoyed it. That night we had rain and sleet and I nearly froze to death. Next day we had but one meal, but that seemed enough for the Indians.

"When evening came the old Indian took hold of me and plucked out my eyebrows—every one of them. It hurt like blazes, but I had to stand it. Redmen seem to detest eyebrows and beards with all their might.

"Later on Custaleta said, 'Big Indian wants you to turn and turn.' They had watched Morris and me doing handsprings just before they sprang out on us. I had to perform a few more of these to keep on the good side of them. Then they asked me to dance, and much to their delight I gave them a lively jig.

"The next day Custaleta, after directing two of the Indians to take me to his wigwam, left the band. We trailed on and on through country that was strange to me. For the first time in my life

I saw buffalo. The band killed several of the shaggy animals. That night I was tied so tightly that I nearly died while the Indians left me for three hours. If they had been killed I should have starved to death. In the morning we found two horses and for several hours I rode behind one of the band. Then we camped in a bee cave, and had a feast on honey and jerked beef.

"All the while I was hoping to find some way to gain my liberty. One night I planned to escape, but the eagle-eyed old Indian kept too close watch over me. We had now reached the Pecos River in West Texas. There were a good many tepees along the stream. As we neared one of them an old squaw came out and seeing me, dragged me off the pony and whipped me with a rawhide quirt until my skin bled. Then she led me to the Indian village and every boy and girl there gave me a lick with sticks till I was ready to drop. Finally the old squaw led me to an open space. All the others gathered round in a circle while she sat down and pulled my head into her lap. I did not dare resist so I just lay there while she began to chant and draw a big knife across my throat. It seemed that my end had come, but it was just their way of testing my courage. I had been so punished that I didn't care much just then whether I died or not, so at least I kept calm. Finally the chanting ceased and I was led off to a tepee where they gave me a straw bed.

"Next morning almost the whole tribe seemed to be round that tepee. The old squaw jerked me outdoors and painted me. Then I was dressed in Indian style. All this was in the process of making me one of the tribe. In a few days Custaleta returned. I was really glad to see him. Soon I was set to herding horses with a Mexican boy captive and we became fast friends.

"The Lipans and the Kickapoos afterwards made a peace treaty and the chief of the Kickapoos wanted to buy me. This old fellow could write and speak English. The Lipans, however, would not let me go. They put me to breaking their wild horses. Often I would get thrown and hurt seriously, but I finally learned how to master the mustangs. I also learned how to handle big Indian bows and arrows. The quivers they carried were about four feet in length. Another thing I learned was the Lipan language.

"We kept moving back and forth between the Pecos and the Rio Grande. It seemed to me the tribe wandered about without much purpose, but I suppose it was because of getting food supplies. Once we had a feast on wild hogs. At another time we ran into an army of rats. The Lipans caught these and roasted them whole. They would peel off the skin of the rodents and eat their flesh. When one gets hungry, as we often did, any kind of food tastes good.

"It was in old Mexico that we had our worst times. I made bows and arrows there and traded with the Mexican boys for food. One day I happened to meet a Mexican who spoke English, and he told me of a Mr. Hudson who was working on an irrigation canal near San Vicente, but on the Texas side of the river. A short time after this, the Mexican came and told me secretly to get a good horse and come to that town. I followed his advice.

"That night a young Mexican took me across the river. He uttered not a word until we got onto the Texas side, then pointing back at the Rio Grande, he said, 'Injuns!—go to hell!'

"The young Mexican had been as scared as I was while he was helping me to escape from the redskins. Now, however, we felt safe. We hurried on to Mr. Hudson. As we dismounted, he said, 'I will take you home as soon as possible. Now you must go to bed.'

"I was given a pallet in the kitchen. When I awoke in the morning there stood Mrs. Hudson and her two pretty girls. They were very kind to the Indian white boy who had come to them. After breakfast, Mr. Hudson took me down the river to a dense swamp. He told me to stay there all day and

to come to the house at night. It was a great risk
he was taking to rescue me, for if the Indians had
found me at his home, they would have killed him
and his family.

"When I got back to the Hudson home, he said,
'Come now and be a white boy again.' With that
he gave me a tub in which to bathe, and some clean
clothes. My old, lice-ridden Indian suit was burned.
I was very happy until I looked in the glass. What
I saw there was a brown-faced boy with long hair
almost burned red with the sun.

"That night the Mexican who had helped me to
get free came and said, 'The Lipan squaws are weep-
ing. They think that the Kickapoos have stolen
you.'

"The next day Mr. Hudson and the Mexican
started homeward with me. We went by Fort
Clarke and the officers and soldiers kept me up
almost all night answering questions. I told them
that the Indians had watched them all summer on
the Pecos. They were astonished. The commander
at the Fort wanted to send me home with an escort,
but Mr. Hudson refused, saying he was a frontiersman and never off his guard.

"When we reached the Neuces we rested at the
home of Bill Adams, a brother-in-law of Mr. Hudson. From there we went on to the home of Judge
Patterson. He told me that my relatives were all

alive and well. This was a great relief, for Custaleta had said that my sister had been killed. Mr.
Hudson was worried over his own family, so he
hurried on with me to the ranch. The Davenports
made a great fuss over me and thanked Mr. Hudson
over and over. My sisters, Mrs. Finley and Martha
Buckelew, were sent for. When they arrived
everybody had a good cry for joy."

"What became of the Hudson family?" asked
one of the eager listeners.

At this Eddie Hudson, a youth in the audience,
exclaimed, "I know! I know!"

Mr. Buckelew, growing as excited as the boy,
called, "Come here, come here, lad, and tell us the
story."

"You are talking about my grandfather," said
Eddie. "Well, when he got back to Fort Clarke
he heard that the Lipans were going to murder him
and his family, so the soldiers hurried with him to
his home and helped him move grandmother and
their children to the fort for protection. The Indians had learned that he had helped you to escape
and they were lying for him along the trail. He
had to give up his home on the Rio Grande, but
he and grandmother never talked about that. They
were only happy they had rescued you from the
Indians."

"They were the salt of the earth," said Mr. Buckelew. "I thank God they were saved. If they had been killed, I should have felt I was the cause."

Just as the story-teller made this concluding remark, a warwhoop resounded through the room. Buckelew and the rest turned with half startled looks towards the doorway, and there stood another Indian. After a moment of suspense, all broke into laughter, and then the new redskin was introduced by his fellow Indian.

"This is my friend Herman Lehmann," began Buckelew. "He has come to hurry me to the Old Trail Drivers' Barbecue. But before we go, I think you will want to hear how he was captured by the redskins and how he became an Indian boy like me."

A burst of approving applause greeted the suggestion.

"Yes, I was stolen away," responded Lehmann, "but it was some years after my friend Buckelew had his experience. You see he belongs to the grandfather class, while I am still only a middle-aged fellow. It was not the Lipans but the Apaches that got me. Still we had pretty much the same sort of experiences with the roving redskins.

"I was living in Mason County, Texas, when I was stolen. I was eleven years old at the time. One day I was out in the pasture looking for my horse when suddenly a band of Apaches surrounded me. It seemed as if a thousand of them had sprung out of nowhere, but I learned afterwards that only about a dozen were in the raiding party. It was father's horses they were after when they ran on to me.

"Well, a strong young Apache swung me upon his horse and away we rode like mad. We did not stop to eat. The Indian never worries about regular meals. This band was afraid of pursuit by the ranchers or rangers and there was no stopping for twenty-four hours. Then they paused long enough to kill a calf, drink its blood, and eat its meat raw. I refused at first, but they wrapped the bloody skin around me and forced the meat down my throat. Afterwards I grew to like raw meat. This taste I think made me half savage. I was what you would call a mess after that experience. They took off the calf skin and threw me into the creek. I could swim but they kept ducking me until I was nearly drowned.

"The water felt so much better than that bloody calf skin that I laughed when they pulled me out of the stream. I was a well-washed boy, and that is the last time I really was clean for eight years. In living with the Indians I got used to dirt and to the peculiar Indian smell that comes from the dirt. Cattle and horses, scenting this odor, grow restless and give warning of Indians.

SOME INDIAN AND RANGER STORIES

"The Apaches were not unkind to me so I soon became one of them. I liked the wild, free life of the plains and mountains. In time I practically forgot my own speech and became in thought and deeds a true Indian boy. After a little while whatever homesickness I may have had all left me and it never came back. I became an Indian under the skin and felt the white man as my enemy.

"The Apaches took me with them on many of their raids. It gave me a pleasurable thrill to join them in their deviltry which often included stealing and murder. They felt no sorrow for such misdeeds for the whites had fought their forefathers and were forever taking their land. Somehow my own sympathies and loyalties belonged among the Indians.

"For four years I lived with the Apaches. The old squaws made me fine clothes like these I have on. I looked like a real Indian and was one. My sense of obligation to my own blood seemed for some reason to be lost during the wild roving years I spent with the redmen. My Indian name was Montacena.

"Once while I was with the Apaches I joined them in such a mean and bloody raid that the rangers under Captain Roberts determined to put an end to our deviltry. For days they trailed us. Finally on the Conco Plains they caught up with our band. We had a running fight with them, and I enjoyed the excitement of it all. An old Indian with us lost his horse, and I raced back and took him on behind me. One of the rangers named Jim Gillett overtook us and blazed away with his rifle breaking the neck of my horse. My Apache friend was thrown free of the falling animal, and started to run like a streak of lightning. I was caught under the horse. Gillett and another ranger who had come up were about to shoot me, when they saw to their surprise that I had red hair and blue eyes.

"With that they turned attention to my fleeing Apache friend and brought him down with a well-aimed shot. While this was happening I had got free from my dead horse and was off like a shot into a hiding place among the mesquite. The rangers could not find me. It was a puzzle to them why a white boy would slip away to the Indians. They did capture a Mexican boy, however, during that fight, and restored him to his friends living near Fort Clarke.

"As for me, I continued to live on among the Indians. It was not long after this battle with the rangers, however, that I had a quarrel with one of the Apache medicine men and in the heat of it killed him. I had to flee for my life. Even then I did not want to go home, but hid in the mountains. For a year I lived as a solitary Indian keeping out of sight of the sharp-eyed Apaches by secreting myself by day in caves and under the thick branches of the trees. Finally I managed to get to the Comanches, who were bitter enemies of the Apaches. They were glad to adopt me into their tribe and to use me as a scout. By this time I could speak not only the Apache tongue but knew some Spanish and also what English I had not entirely forgotten.

"For four years more I lived with the Comanches. My days with them ended when the tribe was finally conquered and taken to the reservation in Oklahoma. I was the last of the tribe to give up, and did so then only because of the pleadings of Quanah Parker. It took a great deal of work to make me over again into a white man. I had a hard struggle to forsake my Indian life and ways; but Quanah helped me to make the start towards a renewal of my old life.

"The mother of this remarkable Comanche chieftain went through the same kind of experience as I did, only hers was a far more sorrowful story. She was a white woman who as a little girl, Cynthia Ann Parker, had been captured by the Indians. When she was fourteen years of age a trader found her with the Comanches. She could not or would not speak a word of English. He offered to buy her, but no money could induce the Indians to part with her. A few years later she became the wife of Pete Nacona, one of the leading spirits of the tribe, and through her life was devoted to him and their children. In 1858 the Texans led by a young man named Ross, who afterwards became governor of the Lone Star State, attacked the Comanches and Pete Nacona fell fighting. His two sons, Quanah and another, escaped with the Comanches. Their white mother and her little daughter, Prairie Flower, were captured by the rangers. The eyes of the captives were blue. Cynthia Ann tried to escape, but she could not. The white men sent her with her child to live with relatives. There little Prairie Flower sickened and died, and the broken-hearted mother pined away with longing for her sons and the wild free life.

"Quanah Parker became the chief of the Comanches. He was a very intelligent and fair-minded leader, working always to keep an honorable peace between the Indians and the white men. His descendants still live in Oklahoma. The town of Quanah, Texas, bears his name.

"Chief Quanah Parker induced me to return to my people in Mason County. When I arrived home, my own mother could not recognize me, but my sister did at once. Mother would not believe that this wild looking creature who had forgotten his English tongue was her own son until searching my right arm she found a peculiar scar which identified me.

"Everything was done to make her long lost boy contented and happy, but I had a serious time readjusting myself. I was like a coyote in a cage, restless and mean. One night I broke through the window in an effort to escape. I had to be guarded to be kept from running back to the Indians. At last, however, I went to school and by hard work succeeded in becoming a decent citizen. When I had become a white person in my ideas and manners, I went back to Oklahoma where the Comanches were being helped as I had been to live a more civilized life.

"As a member of the tribe I received my allotment of land. Now I live part of the time among my old friends, the Indians, and part of it with my own people. The Indians in Oklahoma have become some of the solid citizens of our country. They are not only the first Americans, but also loyal Americans. They have played a real part in America's making. Some of the outstanding heroes in the World War had Indian blood in their veins. Americans owe much to the friendship, the intelligence and the constructive help of the redmen; and the descendants of these first Americans are still carrying forward with the spirit and courage of their fathers."

CHAPTER XXI

A ROUNDUP OF TEXAS STORIES

TALES that might be told of Texas and its picturesque people are legion. Only a few of these intriguing stories could be brought together in this limited volume. The wealth of other rare tales that may be found in old legends and in the lives of the men and women who have played their parts in the epic of the Lone Star Land can be only glanced at as we bring our part of the great story to its close.

Much of this additional treasure is being gathered by those who appreciate its vital value in helping to keep the story of America's making. There are myths and legends and songs of the Indians that bring us closer to the inner spirit of these children of nature. Charming tales of fancy like those that tell of the Texas bluebonnet, the lilies of Rio San Marcos, the waters of Waco, and the San Pedro Springs, add a touch of romance to the realm of Tejas. Legends of hidden treasure and of lost mines of silver and gold recall the days of the Conquistadores, or the later times of the bold buccaneers. *The Woman in Blue, The Padre's Beacon,* and *The Holy Spring of Father Margil at Nacogdoches,* with other like stories, help to keep the old mission bells chiming their message of peace and good will. Everywhere throughout Texas may be found precious stories to link us with the days of long ago.

That historic borderland abounds too in "story spots" around which legends linger. The "Enchanted Rock" of the Llano, the "Indian Bluff" on the Canadian River, the "Lovers' Leap," "The Cave of Montezuma," the "Medicine Mounds," and the treasured old Alamo, are but a few of these spots. Clinging to the old missions and to soldier posts of pioneer days is also a wealth of story stuff in which fact and fancy are intermingled.

Another source of rare stories is to be found in the lives of interesting characters who have played dramatic rôles in the history of the Lone Star Land. From the wandering miracle man, Cabeza de Vaca, down through the years, they have come to add color and romance to the epic tale. Gold-seekers and fur-hunters, courageous priests, filibusters and privateers, frontiersmen and pioneers, rangers and cowboys, soldiers and citizens—all have their picturesque parts in the historical pageantry of the vast Southwest. The life story of many a man who has risen to national fame is linked in some interesting way with Texas.

Sam Maverick, one of the signers of the Declaration of Independence for Texas, bequeathed his name in a strange way to our language. Sam, as a successful rancher, had cattle by the thousands. While he could attend to his growing herds, all went prosperously. The Civil War came, however, and played havoc with the regular order of life. Sam, enlisting on the side of the South, left his unbranded stock scattered far and wide over plains and hills. They soon became the prize of wandering folk who would promptly lasso and put their own brands on the "mavericks," as they came to call them. And unbranded cattle on the open range still are called "mavericks."

Gail Borden is another man whose interesting life story is woven into that of the Lone Star Land. A native of New England, Gail with his brother had joined the Austin colony. Of enterprising spirit, these two Bordens started the first newspaper in that realm, *The Telegraph and Texas Register.* This little publication not only gave the stirring news of the days when Texans were fighting for their freedom, but it also became a clarion voice of the struggling folk during those dark days. When the people were forced to flee before Santa Anna, the *Telegraph and Register,* said to have been carried on the backs of mules, still kept pouring out its fiery denunciations of the tyrant, Santa Anna. Its equipment was finally seized by the pursuing enemy and pitched into the river; but after the victory at San Jacinto, the Bordens speedily resumed the publication and carried on for the rest of the upbuilding of Texas.

One vital thing had happened to Gail Borden during that so called "runaway scrape." He heard the babies crying for food. It is said that he saw how one mother had managed to save milk for her baby by putting sugar into it. Here was the inception of the idea of preserving and condensing milk. Out of that simple beginning, born of stern necessity, has grown a great American industry. One of the counties in Texas is called *Borden,* and *Gail* is its county seat.

How another famous American reached a friendly hand to the people of Texas during the difficult days of the young Republic is revealed by the following letter:

Pokeepsie, August 9" 1860

May it please your Excellency:

In the year 1838 I made an offer of gift of my invention of the Electro magnetic Telegraph to Texas, Texas being then an independent Republic. Although the offer was made, more than twenty years ago, Texas, neither while an independent State, nor since it has become one of the United States, has ever directly or impliedly accepted the offer. I am induced, therefore, to believe that in its condition as a gift it was of no value to the State, but on the contrary has rather been an embarrassment. In connection, however, with my other patent it has become for the public interest as well as my own that I should be able to make complete title to the whole invention in the United States.

I, therefore, now respectfully withdraw the offer then made in 1838, the better to be in a position to benefit Texas, as well as the other States of the Union.

To His Excellency
Sam'l Houston
Governor of the State of Texas.

I am with respect and Sincere personal esteem
Y'r Ob't serv't
Sam'l F. B. Morse

Just what might have been the financial benefit to the Lone Star State had this generous offer been accepted, one cannot say. That it was made, however, shows something of the sympathetic interest Morse felt for the courageous Texans. That the offer received seemingly scant attention evidences the lack of appreciation not only of the leaders of that young nation but of our own United States for the wonderful invention contrived in leisure hours by this Professor of Art of the old New York University. The mighty import of the "Electro Magnetic Telegraph" was only beginning to receive recognition when the letter of withdrawal was penned. The name of Samuel F. B. Morse, through his friendly gesture to the struggling Republic of Texas, links forever with its history.

In the early part of April 1862, the pioneer telegraph brought a stirring story to some soldiers out on the old Overland Trail in Western Wyoming. A detachment of Captain Robert Burton's company of Utah troops had pitched camp for the night when an operator with them connected his portable instrument with the wires singing in the wind over their heads. His intention was to send a report of the detachment on to the Sweetwater Station, but striking a "busy wire" he caught some war news of tragic import. The boys of the troop gathered round the listening operator, eager for any word he might pass on to them. Finally, in broken sentences these words came:

"Big battle at Shiloh, Tennessee—Confederate

army defeated—General Albert Sidney Johnston, leading southern forces, killed—"

A hush fell over the group, broken only by the staccato clicking of the instrument as the further details of the story were being flashed across the continent. A brave and skillful commander had gone down fighting for a cause in which he sincerely believed. The South had suffered deeply in the loss of a leader who had proved his high merit as a gentleman and a soldier. It was a blow that fell hard upon the people of Texas.

The life of Albert Sidney Johnston had been woven into the vibrant story of the Lone Star State. He was born in Kentucky in 1803, and in 1826 was graduated from West Point. In 1834 he resigned his commission and in 1836 cast his lot with the fighters for freedom in Texas, serving first as a private in the Texan army. He rose rapidly from that humble place, becoming about a year later Commander-in-Chief of the Texan forces, and later Secretary of War of the New Republic. In 1839 he led a successful expedition against the Cherokees; and shortly after this he retired to the quieter life of the farm.

Annexation of Texas to the United States brought the Mexican War, and with it Albert Sidney Johnston was again on the firing line. He led a regiment of Texas volunteers into that conflict. At Monterey, while in the thick of the fighting, he had three horses shot from under him. The war over, he returned to his farm, but in 1849 he re-entered the service, this time as a major in the regular army of the United States. In 1855, he was Colonel of the Second United States Cavalry (later of the fifth) with Robert E. Lee as Lieutenant Colonel. In 1857 Colonel Johnston was assigned to the command of the forces sent to Utah to help straighten out some difficulties that had arisen there between the people and certain appointed officials. For about four years Colonel Johnston conducted the military affairs in that far frontier with such courage and skill as to win the respect of all.

At the outbreak of the Civil War he was still at Camp Floyd, an army post he had established southwest of Salt Lake on the Pony Express and Overland Stage Trail. When the choice had to be made, he threw his fortunes with the South, taking the southwestern trail to California, and returning by way of the Isthmus of Panama to join the forces of the Confederacy. It was only a few months after this that, leading his men as he had done at Monterey, the courageous leader was struck in the leg by a bullet. Despite the wound he carried on in the fray until he was stayed by the loss of blood, and then he died on the field of battle. His body now lies in the cemetery at Austin, the capital of Texas.

With this background sketch it is easier to catch something of the feelings of that band of Utah boys who listened to the story of the Battle of Shiloh out in the lonely spaces of Wyoming. One can more readily understand what Robert E. Lee must have felt at the word that his commander of a few years before had gone down in the storm of battle. As for the Texas folk, it was a tragic loss that came close to their hearts. The tomb of Albert Sidney Johnston will ever be a shrine for them.

There was a tie of blood between him and the Lone Star Land. His brother had died there when Lieutenant Magee and Gutierrez had led their little international army into the fight for the freedom of Texas. To young Albert Sidney Johnston, then living in Alexandria, Louisiana, this brother was a knight and warrior. His death must not go un-avenged. This was an impelling thought with the youth when he joined the Texas army under Sam Houston. It doubtless inspired him in the fight at Monterey. Jefferson Davis, who had seen him in action said, "Johnston was superb in battle."

It was tender consideration for his wife that caused Johnston in 1834 to resign from the army. Her health was such as to require a change. They moved to a farm in Missouri, but since she was not restored to strength there, they returned to Kentucky where, in 1835, she passed away. Their children were left with the grandmother, Mrs. Preston, in old Louisville. The saddened father, listening to an appeal from Stephen Austin for volunteers for Texas, threw his fortune into that cause.

As commanding general of the Texas army Johnston had his serious difficulties. It was difficult to keep his men during the intervals of peace satisfied on half rations of beans and meat. Somehow they managed, however; and with the fine help of such rangers as Jack Hays, Deaf Smith, Red-headed Karnes, Captain Seguin and "Big Foot" Wallace, the frontier was pretty well protected. There was constantly recurring trouble with the Indians during these times, the Mexicans helping to keep the Cherokees and the Comanches stirred up. The Cherokees were finally brought to terms and the Comanches stopped in much of their deviltry. Then General Johnston, in ill health because of his hard work in helping to settle these troubles, offered his resignation. What he received was only a furlough.

In 1843 he returned to Kentucky. While there, he married a cousin of his first wife and brought her back with him to his ranch in Brazoria County, Texas. Ranching proved not a paying investment for him. The life for which Albert Sidney Johnston seemed best fitted by nature was that of a soldier. He looked the part, being six feet one in height, with keen gray eyes, clear skin and firm mouth. He could command with firmness; he had tact; and withal he was of a kindly nature. He loved little children and would talk to them by the hour. It was for all these qualities and for his unswerving loyalty that the people of Texas hold this heroic man close to their hearts.

Another soldier hero whose life has been linked with Texas is Robert E. Lee. Both he and Ulysses S. Grant as young lieutenants were given some of their practical training on the Texas frontier. They also gained their initial experiences in actual warfare during our fight with Mexico.

After that conflict their military paths separated. Grant spent some time in California, while Lee was made Superintendent at the military academy at West Point. After filling this position with outstanding efficiency for some three years, he was made Lieutenant Colonel of a Cavalry Regiment stationed in Texas. In this position he served for three years, helping settle the Indian trouble in that untamed borderland. Transferred back to his home state in Virginia, Colonel Lee was brought face to face with the waxing conflict on the slavery question, he being in command of the forces that captured John Brown at Harper's Ferry. Following that raid into the state of Virginia and its tragic aftermath, Colonel Lee, in 1861, was transferred again to Texas.

It is said that while stationed at San Antonio, Robert E. Lee made his momentous decision. Jesse Bell, a friend of Lee in that city, sat up all one night with the great leader talking over with him the political situation. For days Lee struggled and prayed that he might make the right decision. President Lincoln offered to Colonel Lee command of the United States Army, but Lee said he could take no part against the South though he was opposed to secession and war. Finally, he resigned his commission in the United States Army. Lee had reverence for the government that his splendid father, Light Horse Harry Lee, had helped to found, but he could not raise his sword against his native state.

Because of his early soldier services in Texas, and because it was there he made his great decision to join the Confederacy, Texans feel they may lay some claim to Robert E. Lee. Every story of the State carries something of the story of this fine American hero. He was well known and loved by the Texas boys who fought in the Mexican War. It was while in Texas that he wrote many beautiful letters to his wife and sons. In one of these he said, "Duty is the sublimest word in our language.

You cannot do more. You should never wish to do less." When on the lonely frontier he wrote to his wife, "We are all in the hands of a kind God who will do for us what is best. . . . On Him I rely."

General Lee knew and valued the boys from Texas. They fought with courage and daring that challenged his admiration. "Get me more Texas boys," he is reported to have said, "and I'll win." It is recorded that of one regiment of rangers from the Lone Star State only one in five returned to their homeland. The rest had given their all for the cause this great leader had espoused.

When General Lee finally surrendered, the Confederates were out of food and ammunition. General Grant shared food with them. He permitted them to keep their horses, and in other ways showed consideration and respect for those who had fought so bravely against odds. The greatness of General Lee also shone forth in this hour. To his men he said: "Remember, we are one country. Do not bring up your children in hostility to the government of the United States. We are all Americans."

After the war, Lee left forever his military career. He refused attractive positions offered by wealthy northern friends. He also refused political honors from his native state, Virginia. He finally did accept a place of honor and service as president of the Washington and Lee University. The students and friends of that fine institution revere his memory.

The great General's horse, "Traveler," held a place of affection in the hearts of the Confederate soldiers. He was a handsome animal, some sixteen hands high. The General used to say that he was a Confederate Gray. This splendid steed carried his master in practically all the engagements and right up to Appomattox. Never was a horse more beloved.

The people of Texas are proud of the links that bind this great leader to their State. His priceless character has ever been a source of inspiration to them. He showed us all how to wrest victory out of defeat. Not only Texas but all America may well take pride in the life of Robert E. Lee.

It was the proved fighting qualities of Texans that led Theodore Roosevelt at the outset of the Spanish-American War to organize his "Rough Riders" in that State. His call brought together a force of cowboys and rangers and others trained in the wide open spaces of the whole West, but in a large measure they were boys from Texas. Colonel Roosevelt knew the mettle of these volunteers; for he had found his own rugged strength when, as a young man just out of college, he sought renewed health by turning to ranching in Montana. In later years he spent some of his vacations hunting in Texas.

A year or so before he enlisted his regiment of "Rough Riders," Roosevelt happened to be on a quest for peccaries, or wild hogs. Western Texas used the Mexican name "javelina"—pronounced "havelina"— for the little beasts. Out in Uvalde county the hunter from down East, finding a cowboy, asked, "Have you seen any peccaries?"

"Any what?" quizzed the Texan.

"Peccaries—these little wild hogs."

"Oh, you mean 'haveliners.' "

"Webster calls them 'peccaries,' " came the defensive reply.

"Wal, I don't know Webster," said the cowboy, "but I do know haveliners, and you can't fool me by callin' 'em 'peckerys!' You'll find a good many of them in the woods about here."

A few months after this, a cowboy walked into Colonel Roosevelt's tent at the rendezvous that had been set up in San Antonio for the enlistment of Rough Riders.

"Where is Teddy Roosevelt?" he asked.

"At your service," replied an officer.

"Wal, I'll be darned," came the response. "You're the 'pecky' feller I met out in Uvalde. Hope you know a 'haveliner' by this time. If you do, I'll join your regiment."

"I still stick to 'peccaries,'" said Roosevelt.

"You're hard sot in your notion, Colonel," returned the cowboy. "Anyway I'm ready to join. I want to fight something besides 'peckerys.'"

"Come along," said the Colonel. "It won't make any difference what we call the little wild hogs down in Cuba. What we need is some fighters."

This cowboy became one of Roosevelt's best friends. Later, when the Colonel had been elected President, the Texan was invited to visit the Roosevelts in the White House. There was a warm spot in the great American's heart for these boys who had charged with him up San Juan Hill. It was another fight to help wipe out the last vestige of the old tyrannical régime of the Spaniards in America. The spirit of the Alamo and San Jacinto was in that charge.

Another President of the United States was given a sample of the good humor and the fighting character of the Texans some years later in the White House. The incident, vouched for by one of the guests on the occasion, occurred just after Woodrow Wilson had been elected. Trouble with Villa and his raiders shortly before President Taft went out of office, left a problem for the incoming executive. To get some trustworthy information and advice from an authority on the situation, President

Wilson called Captain Bill McDonald of the Texas Rangers to a conference.

The splendid old frontiersman was invited to take dinner with the President and a few close friends at the White House. When the repast had been enjoyed, attention was turned to the Mexican question. After asking some pertinent questions and receiving helpful answers from his noted guest, the President remarked, "Captain McDonald, some one has told me you have said that if you had a thousand men, you felt you could clear up the border trouble for us."

"Well, Mr. President," came the reply. "Maybe I did make some such rash remark. But really I don't think I could do it with a thousand. I might with five hundred. You see I never had experience commanding so many men."

"It has also been reported," the President continued, "that you have expressed a doubt about the ability of our troops to settle the trouble."

"Perhaps I did make some such discouraging remark," admitted the Ranger.

"Now tell me, Captain," persisted the President, "just why you seem to hold the ordinary trooper in so light esteem."

"Well, Mr. President," replied the old Ranger with a twinkle in his keen eye, "I never did have much confidence in a fellow that blows his bugle before he shoots."

The Texas Ranger, from Jack Hays down through a long list of outstanding men of the frontier, embodies a tradition of individuality in fighting for law and peace. Out of the long years of training in the borderland, they developed a tone of character, not of the reckless, swashbuckling type, but one of quiet courage and determination,

and all through their other fine qualities was a saving sense of rugged humor.

Another outstanding American character that the Lone Star Land had a great part in developing is the cowboy. To the pioneer Spaniards is due, of course, the main credit for bringing ranch life into America. This is indicated by the name *ranch* itself, and by the many other terms like *lasso, corral, rodeo, broncho,* that have been added to our vocabulary from the cattle industry introduced by the

Spanish in long ago days. It remained, however, for Texans and others to bring this great industry up to the crest of its development in these later years.

It was the great cattle drives after the Civil War that brought Texas back to its feet. The romance of the old Chisholm Trail along which hundreds of thousands of long-horns were driven to the shipping points on the pioneer railroads, or trailed to fresh pastures in Colorado and Wyoming and Montana, is a part of the American epic. The vast ranches afterwards developed by men like Captain Richard King—from whom the term "Cattle King" is said to have come—and Colonel Goodnight, the "Father of the Panhandle," have played a major rôle in the drama of the great Southwest. Even courageous women had their parts in this challenging story. "Aunt Amanda" Burke, after her husband's death, carried on the work—managing their great ranch, and even making the journey from Texas to Abilene, Kansas, with her herd. Indian raids, prairie fires, and stampedes could not check this brave American woman. She was one of the thousands of pioneer wives and mothers who helped to make Texas.

These were the days when the Texas cowboy came to his own. The task of handling those Spanish bred cattle whose horns spanned six, seven, eight, or even in rare cases a generous nine feet, required courage and endurance and skill of high order. To trail them through dangerous Indian country was a call for daring men who knew the art of frontier fighting. Out of such training was developed the hard-riding, broncho-busting, straight-shooting, all-American cowboy that has taken his place in the hearts of young and old.

Some of the popular notions about the cowboy, however, need correcting. He was not, as too many folk like to believe, just a reckless hombre, clad in chaps and wearing a "ten-gallon hat"— quick on the trigger, and always ready "to shoot up a town" with little regard as to where his bullets struck. It is true that some cowboys, after spending days and days "on the lone prairie" or after driving their refractory long-horns for weeks along the old Chisholm or other trails, would give relief to the tension with a wild spree, and invite over-emphasized "two-gun" men of the "Wild Bill" type to start shooting. Such occurrences were a rarity, not the rule, in cowboy life. The Texas cowboy, in common with all other cowboys, was an upstanding American—earnest, honest, hard-working, generous to a fault, and always ready to lend a helping hand to a fellow in trouble.

The writer carries a precious memory of the first Texas cowboy he ever met. It was out in the "Badlands" of Wyoming, near old Fort Bridger. As a lone lad, hunting for a team of horses that had strayed away, he came upon this cowboy—one who had followed the old Chisholm Trail and the Oregon-Mormon trail into that region, and settled down to ranching. Well, this cowboy proffered his services to help find the lost horses, and trailed through the wilds with the boy until they were found. It took two days of searching; but the Texan would not take a cent of pay. Instead, for good measure, he guided the boy back over a shorter trail to the camp from which the animals had strayed.

The spirit of the old ranch days and the cattle trails still is echoed for us in the cowboy songs. "Bury Me Not on the Lone Prairie," "Get Along Little Dogies," "Old Paint," and "The Old Chisholm Trail" are but a few of the ballads that radiate these times. There was more than courage and endurance or even reckless daring in the cowboys. Many of them—like Charles Russell—were real artists; and not a few were poets and musicians.

Texas, we must remember, was not the "wild and woolly" region it has been too often pictured. It was an all-American realm peopled by upstanding men and women. Romance was there and courage and love of liberty. Yet with it all there was love, too, of education and the fine arts. Out of the

Lone Star Land have come many who have made contributions to America and the world in the realm of the artistic and the spiritual; and many born in other states have found their inspiration in Texas.

Sidney Lanier, the southern poet, lived for a time in old San Antonio. He had come there for his health; and he seems not only to have regained that but something more. At this time Sidney had not won fame through his poetry, but he was becoming rather well known as a musician. In San Antonio he met many who were kindred spirits with him in appreciation of the great art.

A group of music-loving Germans there had organized the *Maennerchor*. These sons of the *Vaterland*, to escape the troubles of the Revolution of 1848, had come to Texas bringing the artistry and the traditions of their homeland. They sought an outlet through music. A letter from Lanier reveals something of the enjoyment and the inspiration he gained through association with this group. Some excerpts from the letter follow:

"San Antonio, Jan. 30, 1873.
"Last night at 8 o'clock came Mr. Schiedemantal, a genuine lover of music and a fine pianist, to take me to the Maennerchor, which meets every Wednesday night for practice. Quickly we came

to a hall, one end of which was occupied by a minute stage with appurtenances, and a piano, and in
the middle thereof a long table at which each singer
sat down as he came in.

"Presently seventeen Germans were seated at the
singing table. Great pipes were all afire. The leader,
Herr Thielepape, an old man with white beard
and mustache, formerly mayor of the city, rapped
his tuning fork vigorously, gave the chords by
arpeggios of his voice (a wonderful high tenor
such as thou wouldst dream the old Welsh harpers
had wherewith to sing songs that would cut against
the fierce sea blasts) and off they all swung into
such a noble, noble old full-voiced *lied* that impe-
rious tears rushed to my eyes. . . .

"After a second song I was called upon to play
and lifted my poor old flute in air with tumultuous-
beating heart, for I had no confidence in that or
in myself. But *du Himmel!* Thou shouldst have
heard mine old love warble forth. To my utter
astonishment I was a perfect master of the instrument. Is not this strange? . . . Thou re-
memberest what a poor muddle I made at Marietts
in playing difficult passages; and I certainly have
not practiced; and yet there I commanded, and the
blessed notes obeyed me, and when I had finished
amid a storm of applause, Herr Thielepape arose
and ran to me and grasped my hand and declared

he had 'nefer heert der flute accompany itself perfore.'

"My heart which was hurt when I came into the music room, came forth from the holy bath of concords greatly strengthened and quieted and so remained today. I also feel better than in a long time."

The poetic muse would seem to have come to Lanier while he was in Tejas land, for he later wrote from San Antonio to his wife:

"All day my soul hath been cutting swiftly into the subtle, unspeakable deep, driven by wind after wind of heavenly melody. The very inner spirit and essence of all wind-songs, passion-songs, folk-songs, country-songs, sex-songs, soul-songs, and body-songs hath blown upon me in quick gusts like the breath of passion and sailed me into a sea of vast dreams, whereof each wave is at once a vision and a melody."

Georgia, the native state of Sidney Lanier, rightly claims first honor for this gifted poet, yet Texas takes pride too in the thought that some of his inspiration came from the Lone Star Land. Lanier's life story might be repeated in part by the stories of other great artists who have found inspiration in this same land of romance.

CHAPTER XXII

TEXAS TRAILS OF TODAY

ON Saturday, June 6, 1936, the writer, driving his automobile through the canyon-like streets of New York City, turned on the car radio. An international broadcast originating at the Texas Centennial Exposition in Dallas was just beginning. This message came through with ringing clearness:

"The State of Texas sends greetings to all the peoples of the world on the occasion of the celebration of her one hundredth birthday, and invites you to join us here at the exposition in 1936."

A clicking key of the Postal Telegraph system started the message round the world. In a few seconds the sentence had reached New York. Then it was flashed on to London. From there it sped to Leningrad. Thence to Tokio. It leaped across the Pacific to San Francisco, and then, after encircling the globe in just two minutes and five seconds, it flashed back to Dallas, where the electric instrument released silver shears on the table in the middle of the Auditorium gate. A white ribbon was cut in twain, and as the ends fluttered to the ground, the Texas Centennial Exposition was formally opened to the world.

All this magic story came out of the ether into an automobile moving under the shadows of great skyscrapers, in the heart of the metropolis of the world. Instinctively the first message sent by the inventor of the electric telegraph flashed through the mind of the listener: "What hath God wrought!"

Nor was the mysterious story yet complete. Very soon the stirring pageantry of the Six Flags was being flashed to the world by means of the radio. Out in the great "Cotton Bowl" before a mighty concourse of people, four centuries of Texas history was sketched in thrilling drama. Millions more listened to the vivid portrayal of the historical pageant.

First came horsemen in gorgeous array suggestive of the days of Coronado and De Soto, bearing the banner of Castile. They set this flag of old Spain flying once more over the land of Tejas. Then from far-off Madrid, Spain's minister of Foreign Affairs, Señor Barcia, gave greetings of his nation and recounted briefly the story of pioneering Spaniards in that vast borderland.

As this pageant passed, a blare of trumpets announced the coming of another nation into this realm. The princely La Salle with his followers, bearing the *fleur de lis*, came again to set this historic flag of France by that of Spain. Then from overseas in Normandy where La Salle was born, came the voice of one of his countrymen, the gifted author, André Maurois, expressing the good wishes of France, and paying tribute to the splendid French leader whose brilliant life's work had ended in old Texas.

The panorama passed on to the days when Texas was part of Mexico, and the flag of that nation was added to those of the two older nations. Again came a voice over the radio—that of Frank Chapa of San Antonio, a descendant of Lorenzo de Zavala. This speaker, too, brought something of the story of Mexico and Texas, and expressed the congratulations and good will of the sister nation south of the Rio Grande.

Next came pageantry depicting the story of the newborn Republic of Texas. The flag of the Lone Star Land was set proudly in its place. Then Andrew Jackson Houston, grandson of General Sam Houston, speaking from the city of Houston, voiced the spirit of the founders of the young nation, telling of their splendid fight for freedom and their building of a great American state.

Another cavalcade of horsemen in uniforms of gray came next with the banner of the Confederacy. As this flag, filled with treasured memories, was set flying, another voice was heard from Richmond, Virginia. It was that of Dr. George Bolling Lee, grandson of General Robert E. Lee, bringing words of greeting from the Old Dominion and a message of peace and good will for all America.

The inspiring panorama of history was rounded to a dramatic close by the placing of our own Stars and Stripes in the galaxy of colorful banners. With patriotic fervor the great audience in the "Cotton Bowl," and thousands of others "listening in," sang the national anthem. Then Governor Allred of Texas introduced Daniel C. Roper, Secretary of Commerce, who brought greetings and good wishes from the President of the United States, and voiced for our nation appreciation of the spirit and the progress of the Lone Star State, so impressively portrayed in its Centennial Commemoration.

This splendid pageantry marking the opening of the Texas Centennial Exposition was but one of hundreds of celebrations commemorating the hundredth anniversary of the birth of the Lone Star State. In every part of the land of Tejas, and in many other states and countries where Texans and friends of Texas live, this historic year has been remembered with rejoicing and gratitude. Through historical drama, fiestas, pioneer reunions, musicales and operettas, home-comings, water and other carnivals, rodeos, founders' days, fairs, mission plays, flower, fruit, honey, and watermelon festivals, old trail pageants, jamborees and jubilees, commemorative programs in schools and churches, banquets, balls, barbecues and picnics—all of Texas has recalled with gladness and appreciation the story of the making of a great all-American state.

Many of these stirring celebrations commemorated particular events of import in the history of Texas. Even in November of 1935, Gonzales, often called "the Lexington of the Texas Revolution," celebrated the opening battle of the war that brought another republic into being. The Texan victory over Cos at San Antonio in December, 1835, was not forgotten. The hundredth anniversary of the signing of the Texas Declaration of Independence at Washington on the Brazos, was impressively commemorated on March 2, 1936. San Antonio, on historic April 21, remembered the Alamo most beautifully with a "Battle of Flowers." On April 21, the victory at San Jacinto was celebrated not only in Texas but elsewhere throughout our land. Americans in all our states and peoples in other lands, were brought by the magic of the radio closer to this epic story of the rise of the Lone Star.

What a strikingly different picture Texas presents today in contrast with that of years of long ago. In the onsweep of the centuries the old landmarks have largely disappeared, the old trails have been all but obliterated. One finds it difficult, almost impossible at times, to locate the old story spots, or to retrace the historic highways. The former are generally hidden within the towns and cities that have sprung up everywhere over the state; the latter are largely buried beneath paved highways and railroads that bind the various parts of the vast region together with bands of cement and steel. Over these, millions are speeding daily, too often oblivious of the history that has made their progress possible.

The old Spanish Trail, stretching from the Louisiana border to the Rio Grande, is not the dusty, rutty road of the bygone years, but a paved highway. Along the route that the dashing Frenchman, St. Denis, and his band of men in 1714 led their pack train laden with goods with which he hoped to open up trade with Mexico, there now are scores of towns that throb with commercial activities. Thousands upon thousands of laden freight cars and trucks are carrying the commodities and luxuries of life, where in the long ago Cabeza de Vaca with a peddler's pack upon his back carried on his simple bartering among the tribes of redmen.

Vessels flying the flags of many different nations are constantly entering and leaving the harbors all along the Texas coast. How many of the thousands who sail these waterways in the comfort of luxurious steamships remember Narvaez with his men striving vainly to navigate these waters in their horsehide boats, or think of the crestfallen followers of the proud De Soto battling through these same waves in their crude ships back to Mexico? How many of them pause to recall the tragic experiences of La Salle with his vessels wrecked on these shores, leaving him and his handful of soldiers and settlers stranded there?

Not far from these scenes of disaster of the days long past is Galveston Island, which Lafitte and his privateering band made a luxurious rendezvous with wealth seized from Spanish ships. It is now the site of one of the busiest marts in the world. A great city which after tragic experiences with gulf storms has protected itself from treacherous winds and waves by building huge sea walls, sends forth its laden vessels to every other port on the seven seas. Perhaps a few of the older sailors that ship with these vessels may at times spin their yarns of the rovers that plied these waters in earlier days, for stories of the pirates and privateers still cling to these shores.

Another great city, Houston, named for the hero

of San Jacinto, has been built close to another historic spot dear to the heart of Texas. Along the old Buffalo Bayou, once the haunt of alligators, but now deepened and widened into a waterway for ocean liners, the decisive battle of San Jacinto was fought. The battleground, preserved as a beautiful state park, still vibrates with memories of the courageous Sam Houston and his heroic men yelling, "Remember the Alamo! Remember Goliad!" and charging on Santa Anna and his host to win a glorious victory for the cause of freedom. This will ever be sacred ground for not only Texas but for liberty-loving people everywhere.

In the heart of historic San Antonio is another shrine that also radiates patriotism and heroism to all the world—the treasured old Alamo. Though great modern buildings encompass it, and the hum of a busy city beats ceaselessly like waves against its walls, yet within the quiet of its ancient rooms and court one may dream back the days of long ago and feel something of the dauntless spirit of those who there died that Texas might be free.

Round about San Antonio and at old Goliad and Refugio, San Saba, and other places are other missions, or ruins of them. Their bells for the most part are silent; and except at one—the Mission Concepcion—no sounds of worship may now be heard. Yet the spirit of devotion that builded these outposts of civilization in the long ago still echoes in the hundreds of church bells that chime throughout the cities on the Sabbath Day; and thousands upon thousands of worshipers still find spiritual strength and comfort in the story of the Master and His messages of truth and light. It was this story and message that the saintly Mary Coronel de Agreda, Father Massanet, Father Margil and the humble friars who caught the inspiration of these leaders, strove with sacrificial patience to plant in the hearts of the Indians of Tejas land.

Comparatively few redmen live in that realm today. In the warfare that was waged through the years over that borderland, many of these first Americans were killed. The remnants of once powerful tribes were removed in the after years to the Indian Territory. Over the region once dominated by the Tejas Indians vast plantations have been spread with cotton as the main crop. Along the coastal plain where the root-digging Indians among whom Cabeza de Vaca and his companions fell, have been turned into bountiful gardens and truck farms. The plains of the farther west, over which the fierce Comanches, Lipans and other nomadic tribes followed the buffalo, have been turned into ranches which now produce much of the beef, mutton, and other choice meats that help to feed the world.

It was during the days that followed the Civil War that the cattle industry began to rise to national proportions in Texas. To regain their fallen fortunes, the ranchmen would gather their scattered longhorns and make great drives into the northern states. Thus was developed the historic old Chisholm trail which led from the Lone Star Land on northward where it linked with the Union Pacific Railroad—the pioneer of our transcontinental lines. At Abilene, Dodge City, Kansas, or other frontier stations along the route, the cattle would be shipped on to Kansas City, Chicago and other centers. Thus the great meat-packing industry began to develop; and also the practice of holding the cattle in the corn-growing areas until they had become corn-fed beef.

As the pioneer ranchmen began to venture farther and farther into the western regions of Texas, it was natural that conflict with the Indians should rise. This had been their happy hunting ground. Great herds of buffalo, antelope, deer and other game still roamed through that untamed region. The Comanches and other tribes would often raid the little settlements, and even attack the pioneer forts the settlers had raised for their own protection. It was during 1836 that the Parker Fort on the Navasota River was thus attacked and the little girl, Cynthia Ann Parker, with other children and some mothers, was carried into captivity. This fort, in replica, has been restored and its site of about one thousand acres has been dedicated as a state historical park.

After Texas had joined the union, a number of other forts were established at strategic points along the old trails to the West. The Gold Rush of 1849 brought Fort Worth, named after General Worth, a frontier leader. This old army post is now one of the leading cities of Texas—a great grain and packing and distributing center of the vast Southwest. More than a score of beautiful parks with miles and miles of pleasant drives, with hundreds of beautiful homes have helped to transform the old military post of frontier days into a thriving, forward-looking town of today.

Waco, where a log fort was built as early as 1837, by the Texas rangers, was another historic place that felt the boom of the Gold Rush days. This town on the Brazos saw many of the covered wagon trains going westward. The great cattle drives in the later years brought other history-making activities close to this place which in earlier times was a spot round which the Indians, after whom it was named, loved to linger. Today it is a center for the thousands of rich farms that have sprung up on the fertile black land over which the buffalo used to roam.

On March 28, 1846, General Zachary Taylor raised the American flag and mounted cannon over Fort Brown at the very southernmost point in Texas. The act touched off the war between Mexico and the United States; but the result of that conflict was to fix the Rio Grande as part of the boundary line between the two countries. And Fort Brown, now Brownsville, at the "toe of Texas," where the Rio Grande empties into the Gulf of Mexico, is the southernmost city in the United States. It is the great port of entry into the vast valley of the Rio Grande.

How much frontier history links with that stream which winds for nearly a thousand miles from its headwaters in the Sierra Madre Mountains between Texas and Mexico all the way to the sea! It would take volumes to tell half the stories of the Indians and Spanish and Mexicans and Texans who were connected with that borderland. The trails of the first Spanish adventurers and of the Mission Fathers, crossed the stream. The captives of the Santa Fe Expedition were taken over the river into the dungeons of Mexico. The ill-fated battle of the Mier was close to its banks. Many a famous ranger, in pursuit of red raiders or of white outlaws, has trailed into the valley of the Rio Grande.

Today that valley is not the wild and dangerous place it was in those earlier days. Auto highways and railroads and airways make it easy of access. Towns and cities that have sprung up all along the old river take away the loneliness. Vast orchards of citrus fruits that spread over the valley add to the riches of Texas and to the markets of the world. The lower part of the great valley is a vast garden and orchard spot. Farther up the river are the great ranches, stocked no longer with longhorns and mustangs, but with pure-bred cattle and horses. Round El Paso, the historic gateway city of two nations, are also smelters which refine the ore brought out of the mountains around that city. The valley of the Rio Grande is yielding undreamed wealth, but its treasures of tradition are as yet among its practically untouched riches. These remain for the artist and the author to bring forth.

Austin, the beautiful capital of Texas, is also rich in these materials that might make intriguing stories and inspire real art. The memory of a great statesman and scholar clings round its name. To look upon its beautiful residences, its stately buildings, its attractive parks and its other beauties, makes it difficult to believe that this city less than a century ago was located in the region of the buffalo, and that it was subjected to almost constant Indian warfare. One finds it hard also to bring back the days when it was the capital of a young nation; yet the old French Embassy still stands on the hill—a museum now in which are kept relics that help those days to live again. A great deal of the history of Texas centers in the city that bears the name of the far-seeing Moses Austin and his son who won the name of "The Father of Texas."

Even to hint of the wealth of present day progress in other places in the great state where choice stories of America's making can be found, would take added volumes. A roll call of the names of the counties, cities, towns, and villages in the Lone Star Land is almost a roster of Texas heroes. It is not lack of appreciation, but lack of space that prevents telling the stories of these centers of history and industry, and of the courageous men and women whose very lives have been woven into their making. The years to come must bring forth more and more of the splendid story.

It is good to feel in this Centennial year that with all its progress and prosperity the sons and daughters of Texas are treasuring their rare heritage of history. It is gratifying also that the all-American aspect of the challenging story is coming to be appreciated. The luster of the Lone Star is but the brighter because it truly radiates the light of all the other stars in our flag. It was born out of the spirit of our own America, and built by the sons and daughters of the American Revolution, working with other lovers of freedom from other lands.

TEXAS TRAILS OF TODAY

All America and all the world respond with full heart to the message of invitation flashed round the globe to join with Texas in the commemoration of her Centennial Year. It is a celebration that radiates the courage and initiative and the inner spirit of our America.

BIBLIOGRAPHY

BOLTON, HERBERT EUGENE, *The Spanish Border-lands*, Chronicles of America Series. Yale Press.

BRANCH, E. DOUGLAS, *Westward*. Appleton.

CROCKETT, DAVID, *Life of David Crockett—An Autobiography*. A. L. Burt Company.

DOBIE, J. FRANK, *Coronado's Children*. Southwest Press.

GILLETT, JAMES, *The Texas Ranger*. World Book Company.

JAMES, MARQUIS, *The Raven*. Bobbs Merrill Company.

KENDALL, GEORGE WILKINS, *Texas Santa Fe Expedition*. Lakeside Press.

LOCKRIDGE, ROSS FRANKLIN, *La Salle*. World Book Company.

PENNYPACKER, MRS. ANNA J. HARDWICKE, *History of Texas*. Published by Author.

PIKE, ZEBULON M., *Southwestern Expedition*. Lakeside Press.

ROOSEVELT, THEODORE, *Winning of the West*. Putnam.